COLONEL PATRICK TONYN

GOVERNOR OF EAST FLORIDA, 1774-1784

Loyalists in East Florida

1774 to 1785

THE MOST IMPORTANT DOCUMENTS PERTAINING THERETO

EDITED WITH AN ACCOMPANYING NARRATIVE

By Wilbur Henry Siebert, F.R.H.S.

RESEARCH PROFESSOR IN THE OHIO STATE UNIVERSITY

VOLUME I

The Narrative

Southern Historical Press, Inc.
Greenville, South Carolina

This volume was reproduced from
An 1972 edition located in the
Publisher's private library,
Greenville, South Carolina

All rights reserved. No part of this publication may be reproduced,
stored in a retrieval system, transmitted in any form, posted
on to the web in any form or by any means without the
prior written permission of the publisher.

Please direct all correspondence and orders to:

www.southernhistoricalpress.com
or
**SOUTHERN HISTORICAL PRESS, Inc.
PO BOX 1267
375 West Broad Street
Greenville, SC   29601
southernhistoricalpress@gmail.com**

Originally published: DeLand, FL. 1929
Reprinted by:
Southern Historical Press, Inc.
Greenville, SC
ISBN #0-89308-979-6
All rights Reserved.
Printed in the United States of America

INSCRIBED TO

The Honorable John Batterson Stetson, Jr.

FORMERLY A PILOT AND CAPTAIN IN THE AIR SERVICE
OF THE UNITED STATES
AN ORGANIZER OF THE FLORIDA STATE HISTORICAL SOCIETY
AND
ENVOY EXTRAORDINARY AND MINISTER PLENIPOTENTIARY
TO POLAND
IN APPRECIATION OF HIS STIMULATING INTEREST
IN A NEGLECTED FIELD OF AMERICAN HISTORY
HIS VALUED FRIENDSHIP
AND HIS EMINENT PUBLIC SERVICES

Foreword

WHILE The Florida State Historical Society was still in its infancy, Mr. Victor H. Paltsits of the New York Public Library, with his well-known generosity which has led him to aid scholarly enterprises in many parts of the world, suggested that it might be appropriate for the Society to publish a series of documents existing in manuscript form in the New York Public Library. These materials—a volume of transcripts from the originals existing in the British Record Office—consisted of the petitions presented to the British Commissioners to inquire into claims for losses of property suffered by British loyalists of the period of the American Revolution in consequence of the recession of the province of East Florida to Spain in accordance with the terms of the treaty of 1783 between England and Spain. Mr. Paltsits's suggestion was favorably received.

Mr. Paltsits also suggested that the one scholar to undertake the editing of the claims was Professor Wilbur H. Siebert of the Ohio State University, whose many years of work on documents of this nature admirably fitted him for the task. Happily, Professor Siebert was willing, nay, enthusiastic, to edit the volume of transcripts. The present publication—Number Nine of those issued by The Florida State Historical Society—is the result.

The work, as prepared, consists of two parts, and is being published in two volumes. Part One—issued as Volume One—has been written entirely by Professor Siebert. This consists of a connected narrative in which are detailed the events of the American Revolution involving the participation of British loyalists of East Florida, or those loyalists who went to East Florida from other neighboring provinces, either during or at the close of the Revolution. The Committee on Publications believes that Professor Siebert's account, with its copious annotations showing sources and clarifying obscure points, is a real contribution to the history of the American Revolution, and, as such, the Committee offers it to the members of The Florida State Historical Society. This volume contains also a carefully compiled bibliographical list of manuscripts, books, and other materials used by Professor Siebert during the course of his writing.

Part Two, which corresponds to Volume Two of the work, will appear shortly. It consists of the claims of the loyalists as above mentioned. These petitions and schedules have been most carefully edited by Professor Siebert, who has spared no pains to present the manuscript in as strict conformity to the original as possible. The claims are the natural concomitant of the first volume, and, like it, a contribution to our knowledge of the American Revolution.

The Committee on Publications believes that special attention should be directed to Professor Siebert's "Additional Notes," which appear in Volume Two. They are mainly—not entirely—biographical in character, and bring together from many sources information concerning persons mentioned either in the Narrative or in the Claims of the loyalists. They add greatly to the value of the work. The Committee takes this opportunity to express to Professor Siebert its appreciation of his careful and conscientious work on these volumes, which form not only a work of high scholarship but a much needed clarification of certain phases of American history.

The Committee also desires to thank Mr. Carl Purington Rollins of the Yale University Press for his care in their design, and Mr. G. T. Bailey and his assistants of the same Press for their unflagging interest and zeal in seeing them "through press."

JOHN B. STETSON, *Chairman*,
J. FRANKLIN JAMESON,
CHARLES B. REYNOLDS,
GEORGE PARKER WINSHIP,
   Committee on Publications.

Preface

IN writing of loyalism in East Florida, I have found it necessary to give the history of Governor Tonyn's administration, and the experience of the British subjects under the régime of Governor Zespedes; and, since a large proportion of them removed to the Bahamas, Jamaica, and Dominica during the time of much correspondence on the subject, the conditions they found there and their influence on those conditions constitute the necessary sequel to my story.

I have already dealt with these matters in a very incomplete way in an earlier publication. In the present volume I have used much new material, as the subjoined Bibliography (in which reasonably full titles are given) will attest. For the opportunity to prepare this new work I am indebted to Mr. John B. Stetson, Jr., who is himself an enthusiastic student of the earlier phases of American history, including those of Florida, and indirectly to Mr. Victor H. Paltsits of the New York Public Library, who, without my knowledge, put me in the way of a valued introduction. To Dr. James A. Robertson, the executive secretary of The Florida State Historical Society and the general editor of its publications, are due my thanks for his continued interest in my labors, his patience during unavoidable delay, and his reading of the proof sheets of these volumes. To the Publications Committee of The Florida State Historical Society I am indebted for the generous foreword. I am also indebted to Mr. Julien C. Yonge of Pensacola, Florida, for the loan of copies of a number of contemporary documents; to the Division of Manuscripts of the Library of Congress and its *director, Dr. J. Franklin Jameson, for the use of transcripts; to the St. Augustine Historical Society for photographs of old plans of that town; to Mr. Worthington C. Ford of the Massachusetts Historical Society for a photograph of the front page of one issue of* The East Florida Gazette; *and especially to the Public Record Office in London for the use of a large body of East Florida material.*

WILBUR H. SIEBERT

March, 1929.

Contents

I. The First Fifteen Months of Governor Tonyn's Administration, March, 1774-August, 1775	3
II. Early Effects of the Revolution in East Florida, August-December, 1775	21
III. Measures for the Defense of East Florida, February-July, 1776	33
IV. Campaigns against East Florida, July, 1776-September, 1778	41
V. The Expeditions from St. Augustine to Sunbury, Savannah, and Charleston, November, 1778-April, 1780	71
VI. Later Operations of the Loyalist Regiments from East Florida, March, 1780-April, 1781	83
VII. The First General Assembly of East Florida, March-November, 1781	91
VIII. The Exodus of Refugees from Savannah to East Florida, May-August, 1782	101
IX. The Influx of Refugees from Charleston to East Florida, August-December, 1782	113
X. The Evacuation of East Florida, February, 1783-June, 1784	137
XI. The Completion of the Evacuation under the Governorship of Zespedes, June, 1784-November, 1785	161
XII. The Refugees from East Florida in the Bahama Islands and in Jamaica and Dominica, 1783-1810	181
Bibliography	211
Index	229

Illustrations

Governor Patrick Tonyn — *Frontispiece*
    From an engraving in the Department of Prints and Engravings of the British Museum

Map of East Florida (1776) — 44
    By Bernard Romans. From a photographic copy made by the Harvard College Library

Plan of St. Augustine (1782) — 102
    From an old engraving in the Map Division of the Library of Congress

Manuscript plat of St. Augustine (*circa* 1784) — 120
    From the original in the collection of the St. Augustine Historical Society

First page of *The East Florida Gazette*, Vol. I., No. 5 — 134
    From a photographic copy made by the Library of the Massachusetts Historical Society

Lieutenant John Wilson — 152
    By courtesy of Miss Emily L. Wilson of St. Augustine, a granddaughter of Lieutenant Wilson

The Narrative

PART I
LOYALISTS IN EAST FLORIDA
1774-1785

Loyalists in East Florida
1774-1785

Chapter I.

The first fifteen months of Governor Tonyn's administration, March, 1774-August, 1775.—The period of Tonyn's governorship.—The agencies and powers of the provincial government.—The first meeting of the council with Tonyn.—William Bartram concerning the towns of the Seminole Indians and the trading posts of Spalding & Co.—Coöperation between the commissioners of trade and plantations and the Society for the Propagation of the Gospel in providing missionaries for East Florida.—The Rev. John Forbes, M.A., rector of St. Peter's church at St. Augustine.—The Rev. John Leadbeater, absentee from St. Marks.—Indian alarms.—The oaths of allegiance and supremacy.—Dilatory claimants for grants of land.—Trade relations with the Creek Indians.—Jonathan Bryan's attempt to lease the Apalachee Old Fields.—The admission of Arthur Gordon to the council and his immediate suspension.—Chief Justice William Drayton and Dr. Andrew Turnbull involved in Bryan's affair.—Indications of the Revolution.

THE British administration had been in existence for nearly a decade in East Florida when Governor Patrick Tonyn[1] arrived on March 1, 1774. He was forty-nine years of age at the time, had been commissioned a captain of the 6th Dragoons in 1751, and served with that regiment in Germany in 1758 as a part of the Hanoverian contingent in support of Frederick the Great, whom William Pitt apostrophized as the prince who stood, "the unshaken bulwark of Europe, against the most powerful and malignant confederacy that has ever yet threatened the independence of mankind." Three years later, Tonyn was promoted as lieutenant colonel of the 104th Regiment,[2] and was finally sent to East Florida as governor, at the head of which he continued until in June, 1784, when Governor Zespedes, with a Spanish garrison and

---
[1] See Additional Notes, II. pp. 310-313.
[2] T. 77/20, No. 6; *Hist. MSS. Comm., Dartmouth MSS.*, p. 348; Appleton, *Cyclopaedia of Am. Biog.*; E. F. Henderson, *Hist. of Germany*, II. 166.

a few military and civil officers, came to assume control. The last fleet of British transports left the province on November 19, 1785, with Governor Tonyn, several other officials, and those British subjects who had remained to the final day. Thus the period of Tonyn's governorship included the era of the Revolution, during which East Florida continued loyal to the king, hatched plots, and took part in military expeditions, welcomed thousands of loyalists from Georgia and the Carolinas, sought to remain under British protection even after evacuation was ordered, and spent nearly two and a half bitter years in passing through the evacuating process.

According to the letters patent issued in October, 1763, by which the government of East Florida was erected, a council was provided for the colony. This board was to consist of twelve men, of whom two were to be the chief justice of the province and the surveyor general of customs for the southern district. When the circumstances of the colony should admit, a general assembly was to be called by the governor, with the advice and consent of the council. Legislation in keeping with the laws of England was to be enacted by the governor and council, and in due time by the general assembly, and courts for the trial of civil and criminal causes were to be established by the governor and his council. Grants of land were also to be made by the governor to certain classes of persons under specified conditions, including grants of town lots. For their convenience and their security against the Indians or other enemies, the planters were to be settled in townships, and the governor was to lay out these areas so as to comprise about twenty thousand acres each. Such districts were to be granted to persons who would undertake to settle them within a limited time at their own expense with a proper number of useful inhabitants.[3]

Of the twelve members of the council those present at Governor Tonyn's first meeting with the board on March 9, 1774, were Lieutenant Governor John Moultrie, Chief Justice William Drayton, Provost Marshal General William Owen, Dr. Robert Catherwood, the Rev. John Forbes,[3a] and Messrs. Witter Cuming and John Holmes. These gentlemen heard the

---

[3] Shortt and Doughty (eds.), *Documents relating to Const. Hist. of Canada*, pt. I. 120, 127, 132, 133, 137-147, 152, 157-165; C. W. Alvord, *The Mississippi Valley in British Politics*, I. 200, 207, 213; Carter in *Mississippi Valley Hist. Review*, IV. 324-325; *Annual Register*, 1763, p. 111.

[3a] See Additional Notes, in Volume II. of this work, p. 360.

reading of certain articles of the governor's instructions. He then gave to the clerk of the market the scales, weights, and measures he had brought from England as standards. After Tonyn had urged the need of procuring a parsonage for the rector of the parish of St. Augustine and the Rev. John Leadbeater had presented a mandamus from the king appointing him rector of the parish of St. Marks, the state oath was administered to the latter.

In opening East Florida to settlement by the English, the lords commissioners of trade and plantations made "comfortable provision" for "able and worthy missionaries to go and reside there." They also requested the Society for the Propagation of the Gospel in Foreign Parts to select proper persons for that service. The society sent bibles and prayer books for the churches and a supply of these, together with a quantity of pious tracts, to be distributed among the poor by the missionaries and schoolmasters. It also asked the commissioners to provide comfortable houses for the missionaries to live in.

In April, 1764, the society recommended the Rev. John Forbes, M.A., to be minister at St. Augustine, and he was duly assigned. In the following June he was in London and joined with two other missionaries, who were going to West Florida, in petitioning the commissioners to see that decent places of worship and suitable furniture for the same, as well as houses for their reception, should be provided. A month later the commissioners approved a list of the necessary furniture for the churches, including the communion plate, two surplices, one large folio Bible for the desk, and two large folio prayer-books. The cost of the entire list of items was not to exceed twenty guineas for each church.

Mr. Forbes soon arrived at St. Augustine and began his ministrations in a building that occupied the site of the Spanish bishop's house. This property had been given to the Church of England at the transfer of the province in 1764, although it had been bought by John Gordon, an English Catholic. It was not until the winter of 1773-1774 that a substantial edifice with a tower and steeple, called St. Peter's church, was erected, and Mr. Forbes took possession as its rector. A glebe, extending from the gates of the town to the outer lines, had been presented to the parish by Governor James Grant.

Late in March, 1769, the Rev. John Frazer was appointed as the second missionary to East Florida. He was at first assigned to St. Marks. Less than two years before this appointment Dr. Andrew Turnbull had arrived from the Mediterranean with fourteen hundred Italians, Minorcans, and Greeks for his colony of New Smyrna on Mosquito [now Ponce de Leon] Inlet. By mid-August, 1768, these people were all settled on plantations under the supervision of overseers. They had with them two Roman Catholic clerics, Father Pedro Camps, a priest, and Father Casanovas, a friar. As the Greek Catholics were outside the Roman communion and were favorably regarded by the Anglican Church, Mr. Frazer was transferred to New Smyrna. At his death in 1772, Lieutenant Governor John Moultrie arranged with Mr. Forbes to visit the colony at intervals. On these occasions he was a guest in the mansion of Dr. Turnbull, which stood four miles back from the settlement. At the end of three years, the term for which the Roman Catholic clerics had been appointed, they sought an extension of their time and the aid of two assistant priests. To this end Father Camps carried on secret correspondence with the bishop of Cuba. In 1774, a vessel was seized in Mosquito [now Ponce de Leon] Inlet by Turnbull's order, and letters were found in the possession that revealed the unlawful correspondence. The immediate result was the conviction and execution at St. Augustine of the priest and several Minorcans on the charge of high treason.

Meantime, Mr. Forbes had risen to a place in the provincial council, and the Rev. John Leadbeater had appeared at St. Augustine with a mandamus appointing him to the parish of St. Marks. He had been designated for this mission early in November, 1773. In the following summer, having suffered with an affliction of boils, Mr. Leadbeater decided to return to England for the benefit of his health and obtained leave of absence from Governor Tonyn, but did not take advantage of it. Tonyn offered him the appointment as schoolmaster in addition to his clerical position and an advance of salary to £100 a year, a quarter of which the governor would pay himself. This sum, together with the fees paid by the boys, would have totaled £150 *per annum*. But Mr. Leadbeater declined this "very handsome proposal," as Tonyn called it, and said that he would not live or raise his family in East Florida for five times the amount. These matters were contained in a letter written by Tonyn to the earl of Dartmouth on May 15, 1775, in reply to one transmitting the king's command that Mr. Leadbeater be given leave of absence. The clergyman was informed of this order and of Dartmouth's expectation that he would return within a reasonable length of time, the limit being set by Tonyn at March 1, 1776. However, it was not until late in October, 1775, that Mr. Leadbeater left the province.

The governor explained to Dartmouth that his absence would impose heavy burdens on Mr. Forbes, who was "indefatigable, very exact and scrupulous in doing his good offices," that the plantations must be visited and the Mosquito settlements not be left without a clergyman, that unavoidably much would remain undone as Mr. Forbes would be the only minister in East Florida until Mr. Leadbeater returned, or another in his place. If a proper successor could be found who would undertake "the careful education of youth" Tonyn would make his salary equal to that designed for Mr. Leadbeater. The governor hoped that meanwhile Dartmouth would consent to allowing Mr. Forbes at least half of the salary assigned for St. Marks. However, the Rev. John Kennedy was appointed on December 24, 1776, as vicar of that parish and received a part of the absent incumbent's salary from him. Later Mr. Kennedy was granted leave of absence by Tonyn and returned to Scotland. Thence he wrote to Mr. Leadbeater late in January, 1783, that he could not engage to serve at St. Marks after its expiration in June of that year. Mr. Leadbeater, who was then at Thornton and still an absentee, accepted his vicar's resignation in February, 1783, and wrote that if he could not find a proper successor he would have been almost tempted to cross the Atlantic once more, but that such a plan was now at an end. As late as April 27, 1785, Mr. Leadbeater, who was still at Thornton, wrote for his salary of £100 covering the biennium from June 24, 1782, to June 24, 1784, as minister at St. Marks.

In his letter of mid-May, 1775, to Dartmouth, Tonyn had ventured to object to office-holders in East Florida applying to his lordship for leave of absence and thus establishing a sort of independence of the governor. They seemed to imagine that they could thus continue absent, even to the great inconvenience of the province, and receive their salaries in defiance of the governor. He therefore humbly suggested that in case of future applications for leave the gentlemen concerned would be referred to him. Mr. Leadbeater's case of absenteeism could scarcely have been a better illustration of what the governor anticipated.

The rector's justification of his return to England and protracted absence from East Florida appears in his petition for amends for the loss of his benefice and about four hundred acres of land by reason of the cession of the province to Spain. Permission to return was granted, he states, on account of his infirm state of health and on the conditions of providing a curate to serve his parish and take care of the school at St. Augustine. Soon after his arrival in England his numerous children were "deprived of the Assistance of their Mother," and he might have added that he had previously made up his mind to rear them in that country. Any credit to the Society for the Propagation of the Gospel for helping to maintain missionaries in East Florida is confined to the early part of the Revolution. The last order for the allowance to a clergyman who had gone thither was issued by the society in 1779.[4]

The Indians of East Florida were the lower Creeks or Seminoles, who had nine towns at this time, according to the botanist, William Bartram. Several of these towns lay along the old Spanish road, west of Picolata Fort and St. Johns River, namely, Suolanocha (Jolta-noga on the map), Cuscowilla or Alachua, and St. Marks at the head of Apalachee Bay. The other Seminole towns named by Bartram were Talahasochte, Caloosahatche, and those of which he knew only the designations used by the traders: Great Island, Great Hammock, Capon, and Forks. Besides these nine towns, which contained on the average about two hundred inhabitants, there were some small Seminole villages. Villages and towns together gave a total of scarcely two thousand people. After much contact with these Indians in

[4] C. O. 5/540, pp. 51, 59, 129, 141, 143; C. O. 5/571, Minutes of the Council, March 9, 1774; A. O. Class 1, Roll 149, Bundle 1261; Florida Historical Society, *Quarterly*, V., No. 4 (April, 1927), p. 196, and VII., No. 3 (January, 1929); Carita Doggett, *Dr. Andrew Turnbull and the New Smyrna Colony*, pp. 29-47, 85, 97-99; C. O. 5/555, pp. 147-150, 463-466; C. O. 5/560; *Sermon preached before the Inc. Soc. for the Propagation of the Gospel in Foreign Parts*, London, February 18, 1780, p. 67; Andrews, *Guide to the Materials for Am. Hist., to 1783, in Public Record Office of Gt. Brit.*, II. 107, 233. See also Volume II. of this work, p. 297.

1774, Bartram characterized them as contented, joyous, and friendly and thought that they did not lose from their countenances the look of "youthful, joyous simplicity," even in their extreme old age. The captives among the Seminoles were so well treated that they were no worse off than their masters, and when they married they were given their freedom. The Seminoles took a childish delight in extravagant stories and were fond of games and gambling.

However, they were much given to hunting deer, bear, wolves, and other wild animals, and they traded the skins of these creatures, besides honey, wax, and other products for the clothing, utensils, and superfluities which they could obtain from their white neighbors. This trade was in the hands of Spalding & Co. or Spalding and Kelsall, who in 1774 had not less than five trading posts in East Florida. Several of these were in Indian towns. The senior member of the company was James Spalding, who lived at Frederica on St. Simon Island, off the coast of Georgia. Here Bartram visited him early in the spring of 1774, on his way to East Florida to gather seeds, roots, and curious specimens for Dr. Fothergill of London, England. Already in the previous year, Bartram had stopped at the company's stores on a bend of St. Marys River, about sixty miles from the coast. The approximate location of this post is marked on certain maps by the place-name "Traders' Hill." Not long after this, some young braves, considering themselves ill treated by the traders, plundered the upper post on St. Johns River, about thirty miles south of Lake George. The storekeepers fled to a small island, carrying with them some of their goods, and left the Indians in possession of the post. The company discontinued trading relations with the Seminoles at this and other stations for a few weeks, when a council was held in St. Augustine between Governor Tonyn and the chiefs, which decided that the storekeepers should be indemnified for the loss of their goods by the chiefs of the plundering bands. The revival of trade with the Seminoles was effected during the spring and summer of 1774, missions being sent out for the purpose from the company's principal station, which was situated on the west bank of St. Johns River a few miles north of Lake George. The agent in charge of the storehouses here, which were enclosed by a palisade, was Charles McLatchie. In the middle of May he sent a party of traders with a stock of goods in a large boat to take charge of the upper station, about sixty miles farther up the river. It was promptly surrendered to them by a white man and his Seminole wife.

Mr. McLatchie next delegated an old trader and a few other men to go and reëstablish trade with the Alachua tribe of lower Creeks at their town of Cuscowilla or Alachua, nearly sixty miles to the northwest of his post. Here they met the chiefs and other tribesmen in the council house and ratified the agreement recently made at St. Augustine, together with some commercial provisions of local import. By this action, trade was resumed at Cuscowilla, the event being celebrated by a feast that Chief Cowdriver gave in the banqueting hall, some of his best steers being killed and roasted for the occasion.

Cuscowilla, the capital of the Alachua tribe, may be regarded as a good example of a Seminole settlement. It was admirably located on a ridge of sand hills several hundred yards from a large lake, the intermediate slope being occupied by an open grove of tall pine trees. The lake abounded with various kinds of fish and wild fowl. Of the latter, great numbers arrived from the north as cold weather came on. The town comprised about thirty habitations, each consisting of a dwelling house of two rooms and twenty yards behind it a second structure. This house in the rear was open in front for use as a summer pavilion, while the other part was enclosed and kept for the storage of provisions. Each dwelling stood in its clean square yard surrounded by a low bank of earth and had its small garden, in which beans, Indian corn, melons, tobacco, etc., were grown. In the public square were the council house and banqueting hall. About two miles distant was an enclosed plantation belonging to the community and cultivated by the labor of all its members, although each family had a definite plot from which it gathered its own share of grain and other produce. Of this it contributed a small part to the public granary, which stood in the center of the plantation. Bartram notes that both the Alachua Indians and most of the other Seminoles had imbibed something of the Spanish civilization, that some among them were professed Christians, and that many more wore little silver crucifixes.

After the completion of the mission to Cuscowilla, McLatchie sent out a party on a similar errand to Talahasochte on Little St. Johns River, near Apalachee Bay. On the arrival of this party Chief White King gave a feast of roast bear meat, hot bread, and honeyed water in the banqueting house and then repaired with his guests and warriors and the other chiefs to the council-house. There they smoked the calumet, drank coffee, and puffed their own pipes. The request from the Indians, that their trading house be opened again, met with the chief trader's promise that he would collect his pack horses and bring goods to them.

Like Cuscowilla, this town contained nearly thirty habitations of the kind already described, but it had a more spacious council house. The town was situated on the elevated east bank of the river. Its inhabitants shaped their large canoes from the trunks of cypress trees, making some that could carry twenty or thirty persons. In these boats they made their hunting and trading expeditions down the west coast and even to the Bahamas and Cuba, bringing back sugar, coffee, spirituous liquors, and tobacco in exchange for furs, deerskins, bear's oil, dried fish, honey, beeswax, and other articles. In small sloops, the Spaniards made journeys from Cuba to Talahasochte or St. Marks to trade, or to the bay of Calos to fish. On the shore of the bay, not far from a considerable town of the Seminoles, they salted and cured quantities of fish and bartered them with the Indians and traders for skins, furs, etc., which they carried back to Cuba. The trader at Talahasochte could usually get from the Spanish vessels goods requisite for his trade at better terms than he could buy for from the Indian stores in Georgia or St. Augustine.

Although generally friendly and peaceful with their white neighbors and the Indian tribes to the northward, the Seminoles did not regard with favor the Choctaw nation in West Florida. In the autumn of 1774, about forty Seminoles came from St. Augustine to Spalding & Co.'s lower trading post on St. Johns River, between Rollstown and Lake George. They were going to hunt on the borders of their enemies, the Choctaw Indians, and expected to fight with them. Long Warrior, the leader of the Seminole party, wanted blankets, shirts, and other articles for some of his companions, but was evidently unable to pay in full for the intended purchases. Under the circumstances Charles McLatchie, the agent, was certainly generous. After a conference with Long Warrior in the council house in the presence of both white men and Indians, McLatchie proposed the immediate payment of half the price of the goods and the payment of the remainder on the return of the party.[4a] Governor Tonyn and other officials at St. Augustine had sought the aid of the Seminoles and other tribes, distributed presents among them, and entertained large parties of Indians at the provincial capital for days or weeks at frequent intervals, but never succeeded in doing more than sending out small bands on the warpath, usually in company with a party of rangers. The employment of the Indians, even on the limited scale attainable, was costly to the British government in money, in retaliation on the part of the Georgia settlements, and in the small residuum of military results.

Early in 1774, there had been Indian alarms on the northern frontier of East Florida, and a party of men had been sent to St. Marys River to see what the situation there was. On May 30, Governor Tonyn reported to the council that the frontier was again quiet and that the planters who had fled from their farms had gone back and were engaged in their usual occupations. The council was also informed of a letter from Governor Sir James Wright[4b] of Georgia, stating that he had issued a proclamation against all trade and intercourse with the upper and lower Creek towns for the purpose of inducing the Indians to "do common justice" and abstain from further hostilities. As Governor Wright requested Tonyn's coöperation, the council recalled the fact that Lieutenant Governor Moultrie's proclamation of February 2, 1774, was still in force, forbidding all persons within East Florida from supplying the Creeks with arms, ammunition, or other necessaries until they had given satisfaction for certain murders they had committed in Georgia. At this meeting of the council royal instructions were read in regard to the mode of granting land in the future, and also an extract of a letter from the earl of Dartmouth declaring that it was not intended to preclude those persons, who had hitherto obtained orders in council for lands in America but had not located them, from carrying such

---

[4a] Bartram, *Travels through North and South Carolina, Georgia, East and West Florida* (etc.), 1792, pp. 22, 55, 60, 61, 76, 77, 94, 95, 109, 154, *passim*. See also Volume II. of this work, p. 366.

[4b] See Additional Notes, in Volume II. of this work, p. 346.

orders into execution, nor to preclude any claim to a grant of land founded on any antecedent step that could give title to such a grant.[5]

At the next meeting of the council, June 14, 1774, a proclamation was ordered to be published, requiring the chief justice and the other justices to administer the oaths of allegiance and supremacy to those persons in East Florida who were over eighteen years of age, but were not natural-born subjects of the king and had not been naturalized, or made free denizens by any act of parliament, or taken the oaths as required by law. This action was taken at the instance of the governor. A week later Captain Frederick George Mulcaster, a brother of George III., who was the engineer at St. Augustine, was admitted a member of the council, and Francis Levett, Jr., was appointed provost marshal general in place of William Owen, who had resigned and left the province. At the council meeting of July 19, it was ordered that all persons who had hitherto obtained warrants of survey for lands in East Florida but had not carried them into execution, or persons who had a claim to a grant of land founded on any antecedent step that could in equity give a title to such grant, should apply immediately in order that grants might be passed and the officers might execute the warrants. All persons were required to carry their grants through the several offices within the next six months. As these regulations deprived the messenger of the council of fees, Governor Tonyn, with the advice of the board, ordered a salary of £25 a year to be paid to the messenger.[6]

Early in October, Arthur Gordon was appointed advocate general of the court of vice-admiralty, and, in compliance with the royal command that all traffic with the Creek Indians be prohibited until tranquillity be restored, a proclamation was issued. Parties of the troops on horseback and a body of rangers under command of Angus Clark, were active during the disturbance, while lodging and food were still supplied to visiting chiefs and braves. On December 20, Tonyn laid before the council a copy of the peace concluded with the upper and lower Creeks by Governor Wright and John Stuart, the superintendent of Indian affairs, two months before at Savannah. Hence a new proclamation was issued for the renewal of

---

[5] C. O. 5/571, Minutes of the Council, May 30, 1774.

[6] *Ibid.*, June 14, 21, July 19, 1774. Concerning Captain Mulcaster, see Volume II. of this work, p. 327.

trade with the Indians under certain regulations, and the measures of Governor Wright in Georgia for carrying on the trade were followed in the main.

At this time also the council learned through a letter of Governor Wright, dated October 21, 1774, that a week before a "kind of lease" had been signed by fifteen Indians with Jonathan Bryan, granting to the latter a large tract of land in East Florida, and that Wright, who sent a copy of the document, had canceled it at the request of the Indians. Governor Tonyn informed the board that he had already ordered legal steps to be taken to bring Bryan to justice, including the issuing of a writ for contempt of the royal prerogative and claiming damages in the sum of £10,000 from Bryan as a trespasser on the crown lands. The council then authorized a proclamation against Bryan, in which the people were cautioned not to enter into such illegal transactions. In another letter from Governor Wright, dated November 16, it was intimated that certain gentlemen of high station in East Florida were involved with Bryan.[7] As this affair contributed its share to serious consequences in the province, it should be explained more fully. The lease taken by Bryan was for ninety-nine years on the Apalachee Old Fields, lying in northwestern Florida and extending westward to the Apalachicola River and Apalachee Bay. This tract was said by Superintendent Stuart to contain not less than five million acres of land. For it Bryan was to pay the Creek nation annually a hundred bushels of Indian corn. He intended to go into cattle raising on a large scale, attract settlers, and build a town, and promote the commerce of the region. When the interpreters at Governor Wright's behest told the Indians what the conveyance contained, a number of them became wrathful, and some of the signers tore their marks and seals from the deed. Late in January, 1775, the council of East Florida learned from a letter of Governor Wright that Chief Justice William Drayton and Dr. Andrew Turnbull, of their own number, were mentioned in Georgia as being concerned in Bryan's enterprise, and that a letter from one of them had stated that they were willing to expend £500 in securing the royal approval of the lease or a grant of the land. Attempts were made to apprehend Bryan, but he was warned by a

[7] A. O. 1, 1261/148; C. O. 5/571, Minutes of the Council, December 20, 1774.

friend while on his way into Florida and returned in haste to Georgia. He would certainly have found himself in toils if he had fallen into the hands of Governor Tonyn, but he let the matter of the lease drop and was not prosecuted. Governor Wright was already engaged in his struggle with the whig party in Georgia, and Bryan, who was a leading citizen of that province, was to become a prominent leader of the "Liberty Boys."[8]

On July 13, 1775, Tonyn informed his council that he had received an intercepted and opened letter from the earl of Dartmouth in an extraordinary manner, as it was enclosed in one from Chief Justice Drayton explaining that he had received it from a near relative in South Carolina. Dartmouth's letter related to Bryan's "fraudulent purchase" of land from the Indians and declared it to be "big with the greatest mischiefs" and one that could not be "too strenuously opposed." The letter further said that the king approved of every step Tonyn had taken in the affair, and characterized Drayton's connection with it as "diametrically opposite" to his duty to the king, but expressed the hope that he had already repented. Otherwise he would "meet with the severest marks of His Majesty's displeasure."[9] This whole episode created bad feeling between Tonyn and his friends on the one hand and Drayton, Turnbull, and their friends on the other, as will later appear.

Drayton was commanded to appear before the council on July 18 to explain matters connected with the intercepted letter from Dartmouth. Nothing in the minutes of this meeting indicate that he was then questioned. However, Arthur Gordon presented a mandamus from the king appointing him to serve as a member of the board. After he had taken the oaths Tonyn suspended him until the royal pleasure should be further known, for reasons which he said would be transmitted to the ministry. We have two accounts of this affair which differ widely in certain significant respects, one by Tonyn written to the earl of Dartmouth the day after this council meeting and the other by Gordon written to the same gentleman a week later. Gordon says that he received a letter on July 16 from Robert

[8] C. C. Jones, Jr., *Hist. of Georgia*, II. 144-146; C. O. 5/571, Minutes of the Council, January 21, 1775.

[9] C. O. 5/571, Minutes of the Council (East Florida), July 13, 1775.

Knox "covering" his mandamus and waited on Tonyn two days later before the council meeting and asked if notice of his appointment to the council had been received. The governor replied that it had not been mentioned in his instructions and that Gordon had not been recommended to him. Gordon said that he had been appointed at the same time with Captain Frederick George Mulcaster, who had been summoned to the board by Tonyn's order, but the latter remarked that he wished to learn the king's pleasure before taking any further step and that he would speak to Gordon later after matters then pending had been disposed of. Meantime, Gordon might keep the mandamus, which had not been obtained with his permission. Gordon explained that he had been recommended by Lieutenant Governor John Moultrie and the council to Governor James Grant, who had applied to the earl of Hillsborough, and presented his mandamus which had been passed on August 11, 1772, before Tonyn himself had been appointed governor, that consequently the latter's permission could not have been requested, that the arrival of the commission had been delayed by one cause or another though he had written for it at the time, that it was a positive order from the king and might be presented to Tonyn with as much propriety as to a former governor, and that he was uneasy at being pointed out as a man obnoxious to Tonyn and begged to be informed what had placed him at such a disadvantage. Thereupon, the governor acknowledged his respectful conduct toward him.

When the council met later in the day Gordon delivered a letter to its messenger signifying the receipt of his mandamus and, after waiting two hours, was admitted, given the usual oaths, directed by Tonyn to take his seat, and immediately suspended until the royal pleasure should be known, without explanation. The council then adjourned.

According to Tonyn's account Gordon opened the conversation by expressing the hope that nobody had imparted a bad impression of him and that the governor would have no objection to his applying for a mandamus appointing him to the council. He stated that he had been recommended by Lieutenant Governor Moultrie at the same time with Captain Mulcaster, who had been called to the council while he had not. Tonyn answered that he had summoned the captain to fill the vacancy left by Mr. Owen's departure from the province. At this juncture, Gordon produced his mandamus and showed it. Tonyn, noting its early date, thought a mistake had been made, since the appointee had not been mentioned in his instructions of 1773, and said that he would talk later with him after a detachment had been sent to Lord Dunmore in Virginia and that in case anything was wrong he could then write to Lord Dartmouth. Nevertheless, Gordon's letter giving notice of his appointment was delivered and read by Tonyn to the council, which thought the applicant's procedure unfair and favored his suspension. Tonyn regarded it as an offense "personal to" his office, but was not willing to show the least disrespect to Gordon's royal commission. Gordon should therefore be admitted to the board and then suspended for the indignity of first seeking the governor's approval of his application for a mandamus and then producing it from his pocket, like a highwayman his pistol, in Tonyn's own words, after the latter had "reserved his consent." The governor also objected to Gordon's pressing his claim after seeming satisfied to postpone it. But in the last paragraph of his letter Tonyn lets the cat escape by characterizing Gordon as "the image in wax of Drayton and his creature as is also Mr. Penman, a shopkeeper who gives himself many airs, and some few others." He continues that Penman "was an underling Clerk of Mr. Peter Taylor, when paymaster to the Army in Germany last War." His final reason for suspending Gordon from the council was that he (the governor) had formed a resolution some time before to investigate the practices of the attorneys in the courts as people in general had been loudly complaining of their extortions.[9a]

On July 19, Drayton attended the meeting of the council and answered questions put by the governor. In the course of the examination Drayton freely admitted that Dartmouth's letter had been sent to him by William Henry Drayton, a member of the council of South Carolina; declared that he had declined to discuss the political differences between the colonies and Great Britain with his relative, and denied that he had ever received "any intelligence of the operations of groups of men in the Carolinas," or that they had ever sought information from him as to the "strength or state of East Florida." A letter from William Henry Drayton was then produced

[9a] C. O. 5/555, pp. 167-174, 209-213, 217, 225. See also Volume II. of this work, pp. 319, 320.

and copied into the journal, which showed that he was on the side of the colonies and that Chief Justice Drayton shared with him "knowledge of some proposed schemes" to bring about their success.[10]

During the year 1775 various indications of the Revolution reached East Florida. On January 21, the provincial council was informed of the order in council of October 19 of the previous year, prohibiting the exportation of gunpowder, or other ammunition, or arms of any kind from Great Britain, or carrying such supplies coastwise, and a proclamation was published to that effect. On June 9, 1775, a circular letter from the earl of Dartmouth, dated early in March, was read to the board. In this letter Dartmouth stated that the king hoped a resolution of the house of commons, which accompanied it, would "further the cause of peace." The resolution provided that when the governor, council, and assembly, or general court of a province should engage to make provision for the support of its own civil government and administration of justice, it would be proper, in case the proposal should be approved by the king and houses of parliament, and during the time that such provision was made, to forbear to levy any duty, tax, or assessment on the province, except only duties for the regulation of commerce, the net income of these duties being carried to the account of the province. On July 17, the council learned from another circular letter from Dartmouth that the orders of the commander-in-chief of the royal forces in North America were supreme in all cases relating to the operation of those troops. Several acts of parliament dealing with American affairs were also read, together with a proclamation of the States General of the United Provinces prohibiting the exportation of military stores to America for six months. Governor Tonyn then informed the board that he had received letters from General Gage at Boston and Governor Dunmore of Virginia calling for the immediate embarkation of a detachment of sixty men of the 14th Regiment and the company at New Providence for Virginia to aid Dunmore, who had been insolently threatened by the people of that province.[11]

The 14th Regiment occupied the barracks, which were some distance to the southward from the settled part of St. Augustine.

[10] C. O. 5/571, Minutes of the Council, July 19, 1775. See also Volume II. of this work, p. 316.

[11] C. O. 5/571, Minutes of the Council, January 21, June 9, July 17, 1775.

First Months of Governor Tonyn's Administration 19

Bernard Romans, who was an assistant to Surveyor General William Gerard de Brahm and drew the map of East Florida in 1776 reproduced in this volume, described these barracks as "stupendous piles of buildings . . . large enough for five regiments when it was a matter of great doubt whether there will ever be necessity to keep one whole regiment here. . . . Most men would think the money spent would have been better laid out in roads and fences throughout the province." He adds that the convent with the church had been "taken into the body of the Barracks." This last reference is to the Franciscan convent and the church "Nuestra Senora de la Leche," both of which had been conveyed to John Gordon when the Spaniards had left East Florida in 1763 and 1764. The convent is said to have had the best well water in the town and was taken possession of because it supplied the most commodious quarters for the British troops. It was found to be poorly adapted to its new use, and more extensive surrounding buildings of wood were later erected.[11a]

During the winter of 1774-1775, the road from the Cowford on St. Johns River to St. Marys was under construction by Charles Wright, Esq. In St. Augustine, the state house seems to have been carried to completion by the latter part of October, 1775. Those who had it in charge during these months were John and William Hewitt and Ralph Laidler. Another important piece of construction executed in part, at least, during this year was the stone wall along the bay to protect St. Augustine against the encroachment of the sea. This work was done by Alexander Gray, Esq.

[11a] For De Brahm, see Additional Notes, in Volume II. of this work, p. 331; for Romans, *ibid.*, p. 342; see also Florida Hist. Soc. *Quarterly*, VII. No. 3 (January, 1929), pp. 224-225; A. O. 1, 1261/148.

Chapter II.

Early effects of the Revolution in East Florida, August-December, 1775.—The first act of hostility against the province.—The arrival of a schoolmaster.—Military assistance for Lord Dunmore.—East Florida becomes a retreat of safety for loyalists.—Inducements for them to come and settle authorized by the king.—Prominent refugees at St. Augustine.—Captain Moses Kirkland goes as their messenger to General Gage.—The reduced garrison in East Florida.—The question of the security of property in the province.—The council meetings in November and December.

ON August 7, 1775, Governor Tonyn reported the first act of hostility against East Florida, namely, that a South Carolina sloop had come alongside of Captain Lofthouse's brigantine *Betsy*, a vessel just arrived from London with a large quantity of gunpowder for the garrison and merchants of St. Augustine, had boarded it off the bar, carried off its supply of powder, and sailed to the northward. The government vessel was sent in pursuit, with an officer and thirty men of the royal troops and a few pieces of ordnance on board. At the next session of the council, on August 19, after the usual oaths had been administered to Captain Frederick George Mulcaster as a member of the board and to Benjamin Dodd as provost marshal general, Captain Alvara Lofthouse, commander of the *Betsy*, and others entered complaint against Henry Laurens, Captain Clement Lemprière, and certain other men of South Carolina for the confiscation of the powder. They submitted fragments of a letter signed by Laurens, which Lemprière had dropped with a draft for £1,000. The letter contained directions as to where the *Betsy* might be found, and ordered the seizure of Captain Lofthouse if he would not sell the powder. Soldiers of the 14th Regiment, who had been on board the *Betsy*, were heard on August 21. One of these asserted that Lemprière had offered him £100 to go with him and £50 for every man he would bring. His statement was supported by the testimony of the others. The council then ordered the announcement of a reward of £200 for the apprehension of Lemprière or any of the other persons named therein, for piracy.[12] Captain Lemprière's sloop was the *Commerce*, which had sailed from Beaufort with a force of twenty-one whites and five blacks. The *Betsy* had a crew of twelve men, supplemented by twelve soldiers from shore and two pieces of cannon. After boarding the brigantine, Lemprière had placed Captain Lofthouse under guard, spiked his guns, removed one hundred and eleven barrels and thirty-seven kegs of powder to the *Commerce*, and sailed away with his prize.[13]

Late in August it was reported to the council that a schoolmaster had arrived from England, and was being employed on trial. The quarterly charges that he was authorized to levy for each scholar were: two milled dollars for entry money, two milled dollars for teaching English and writing, and three milled dollars for teaching English, Latin, Greek, arithmetic, and writing. The estimate for the civil establishment of East Florida from June, 1774, had already provided a salary of £25 each for a schoolmaster at St. Augustine and another at St. Marks.[14]

On September 12, Governor Tonyn and his council decided that it would be improper to send to Lord Dunmore in Virginia more than the detachment of sixty men, in view of the fact that three companies of the 16th Regiment promised as a reinforcement of the garrison by transfer from Pensacola had not yet arrived at St. Augustine. They also resolved to send the necessary arms, ammunition, provisions, and bedding for the immediate use of the detachment. Under date of August 29, Dunmore had asked for the entire 14th Regiment, provided the three companies of the 16th had arrived. On September 14, Tonyn wrote to General Gage at Boston concerning the detachment for Dunmore, the seizure of the gunpowder by Captain Lemprière, and other matters. In the course of his letter he said that East Florida had hitherto depended for a constant supply of provisions on the northern provinces, being engaged in cultivating more valuable products, by which he doubtless meant indigo, turpentine, pitch, tar, and lumber. Now, however, that his province was cut off from all communication with those to the northward, the inhabitants were in a state of anxiety

---

[12] C. O. 5/571, Minutes of the Council, August 7, 19, 21, 1775.

[13] Force, *Am. Archives*, 4th ser., III. 703, 704, 705; McCrady, *South Carolina in the Rev., 1775-1780*, pp. 21-22.

[14] C. O. 5/571, Minutes of the Council, January 21, August 21, 1775.

about provisions for the year's consumption. Referring to Dunmore's request for the 14th Regiment, Tonyn regretted the need for its removal, and remarked that the three companies of the 16th, perhaps far from complete, might be enough to check the disaffected in East Florida, but not sufficient if the province should be attacked by an external enemy. He had been assured that a plan to attack East Florida had been under consideration in Carolina, and he felt sure that the fort and ordnance stores at St. Augustine were "a great object to the rebels of Carolina and Georgia." He had been told that Carolina had four thousand troops in arms. If that province were invaded East Florida would be in a state of perfect security, and it might be of importance to preserve communication with the Creek Indians. Already some people had come to East Florida, Tonyn writes, from the other provinces "as a retreat of safety" and more were coming, but the withdrawal of their means of safety rendered them unhappy, and they probably would not settle. That was unfortunate, he intimates, for the province was "becoming an asylum to the friends of the Constitution."[15]

The reason why loyalists from Georgia were resorting to St. Augustine, Tonyn gives in referring to the disaffection of that province, the government of which had been "entirely wrested" from Sir James Wright by the "rebel committees." Should General Gage think it necessary to secure a firm post in the south, Tonyn knew of no better place than St. Augustine, which could not be snatched away while the 14th Regiment remained. He added that he was sending privately to the southern parts of Georgia to obtain by open boats a supply of rice and corn, and, if he succeeded, the command in Virginia could be furnished with provisions sometime thereafter.[16]

On November 1, 1775, a communication from the earl of Dartmouth, dated four months earlier, was laid before the council of East Florida, stating that the king wished to afford protection to such of his subjects in the rebellious colonies as were "too weak to resist the violence of the times" and too loyal to concur in the measures of those supporting the rebellion, that it was hoped that East Florida might prove to be "a secure Asylum for

---

[15] C. O. 5/571, Minutes of the Council, September 12, 1775; Force, *Am. Archives*, 4th ser., III. 703, 704. See also Additional Notes, Volume II. of this work, p. 346.

[16] Force, *Am. Archives*, 4th ser., III. 704-705.

many such" and also furnish those supplies to the West India islands which they could not then procure from other provinces, that all instructions and restrictions respecting the sale of lands be suspended for the present and gratuitous grants, exempt from quit-rent for ten years, be made to those persons seeking refuge from the other colonies in East Florida, that the exportation of lumber to the West Indies be encouraged by licensing persons to cut it on the crown lands and giving security for landing it on some island belonging to the king, and that the exportation of all other produce be confined by law to places also belonging to the crown.[17] It was therefore ordered that the customs officers should not clear ships, or other vessels, to any other places than those belonging to the English crown. In accordance with these instructions, Governor Tonyn issued a proclamation inviting loyalists to leave the provinces then in revolt and find a welcome and a refuge in East Florida, where they would receive free grants of land and enjoy many other advantages. Copies of this proclamation were sent into Georgia and South Carolina, and were to be seen posted in public places in Charleston and Savannah, if not in other towns. The invitation thus widely circulated, not only with the approval but also at the instance of the British government, had a marked effect in encouraging the immigration of loyalists into East Florida, as shown in some of the documents.[18]

Among the refugees who arrived at St. Augustine during the latter half of the year 1775 were Colonel John Stuart, the superintendent of Indian affairs for the southern district, who took his seat in the council on July 17 and attended its meetings to February 13, 1776; Thomas Browne, who had not been long from England and was intensely British in his antagonism to the council of safety in Georgia; Daniel McGirth, who was cruelly treated by American officers in Georgia and took vengeance for it throughout the Revolution; Allan Cameron and Captain Moses Kirkland, who at the end of August, 1775, was frustrated in his plans for an attack on Fort Charlotte and Augusta by William Henry Drayton. The presence of these men in St. Augustine made that place the center of far-reaching schemes to put down the Revolution in the south as soon as possible by appealing for the early dispatch of a British force to operate in that region, to secure the

---

[17] C. O. 5/571, Minutes of the Council, November 1, 2, 1775.
[18] See these in Volume II. of this work.

friendship and active coöperation of the Indian tribes against the American partisans, to organize regiments of refugees to act with the Indians and the royal troops or to perform scout duty, destroy the enemy's crops, or bring in cattle, provisions, and negroes from beyond St. Marys River. In other words, these plotters took the initiative in formulating a program of aggression in the south, which, if it had been promptly adopted and adequately supported by the British military and naval commanders, might have turned the tide in that section.

Early in June, 1775, the provincial congress of South Carolina had received information that Superintendent Stuart[19] was exercising his powerful influence over the Indians in favor of the British cause. It ordered his arrest, but he had received a warning from Governor Wright of Georgia. He at once went on board the armed schooner *St. John* at Cockspur and retired to St. Augustine. From there he replied to letters from the committee of intelligence at Charleston, asking him to answer for his conduct and making his property a pledge for the good behavior of the Indians. He said that he considered himself as discharging his duty to the king, that the tranquillity on the frontier of South Carolina during his long superintendency could not induce a belief that he could use his influence to make the Indians fall upon innocent people, and that if his estate was to be a security for the good behavior of the red men its tenure would be precarious for him, depending largely on the conduct of the inhabitants of the provinces. False accusations had been circulated about him, he alleged, namely, that he had called down the Indians and that he had been supplied with quantities of arms and ammunition with which to arm the Indians and negroes. During the next six months, at least, Superintendent Stuart lived at St. Augustine, on intimate terms with the other prominent refugees and with Governor Tonyn, while carrying on negotiations with the Indian nations.[20]

Thomas Browne, a young planter on the east side of the Savannah River above Augusta, had made himself obnoxious to the Liberty Boys of that

---

[19] See Additional Notes, in Volume II. of this work, p. 321.

[20] Force, *Am. Archives*, 4th ser., III. 1775, 1681-1682; Sabine, *Loyalists of the Am. Rev.*, II. 341; McCrady, *South Carolina in the Rev.*, 1775-1780, p. 18.

town, and at the beginning of August, 1775, in a coat of tar, had been given an ignominious ride in a cart. Before being provided with the means of conveyance home, he had been forced to promise allegiance to the American cause and to discountenance the loyalists in Ninety-Six District. Nevertheless, he at once concerted the capture of Augusta with General Robert Cunningham. Men were raised, but Cunningham lost interest in the plan. After Browne had been published, early in August, in the *Georgia Gazette*, as a person inimical to the liberties of America, he retired to Charleston and thence to St. Augustine. There he was commissioned nearly a year later by Governor Tonyn to raise a corps of loyalist rangers. Thenceforth he was active in garrisoning outposts, sending out scouting parties, conducting raids into the enemy's territory, and taking part in military expeditions.[21]

In the early days of the Revolution, Daniel McGirth was in the scouting service on the American side in Georgia. He suffered unjust punishments by the action of a court-martial on a fictitious charge brought by a whig officer, who coveted his favorite mare, Gray Goose. McGirth soon escaped from prison and rode away on his mare. He and his brother James then joined Captain John Baker's party of seventy mounted men and went to attack Jermyn Wright's fort on St. Marys River, about a hundred miles west of St. Augustine. The attack was clearly unsuccessful even before the schooner *St. John*, lying two miles below the fortification, sent three armed boats to reinforce the garrison. After a detachment from Baker's force had fired on the leading boat and killed or wounded several of the crew, the whole party retreated and went into camp about eight miles distant. During the night the McGirths deserted to the enemy, taking with them most of the horses belonging to the command. Later they were given commissions in Browne's corps of rangers.[22] The McGirths probably took refuge in East Florida in 1775. More than a decade afterward, Jermyn Wright testified in London that late in that year his plantations on St. Marys were already destroyed and his people routed by the rebels, and that he never occupied those lands afterward.[23]

---

[21] See Additional Notes, in Volume II. of this work, pp. 323-325.
[22] *Ibid.*, pp. 328-330.   [23] See Volume II. of this work, pp. 171-172.

Captain Moses Kirkland, who was a prosperous planter of Ninety-Six District, South Carolina, was at first regarded as a friend of the American cause. Indeed he took part in the seizure of Fort Charlotte and its stores of ammunition in July, 1775, by order of the council of safety. This was the first overt act of the Revolution in South Carolina. Very soon after this, however, he had definitely changed sides, and was procuring signers to a resolution in support of the royal government. At the end of August, persons assembling in arms at Kirkland's instigation were warned by William Henry Drayton, a member of the council of safety, that they would be dealt with as enemies. His followers now deserted or held aloof. At St. Augustine it was reported that a reward of £2,000 had been offered for his arrest, that he had escaped with his young son from a party in pursuit, and after a journey of two hundred miles had reached Charleston and taken refuge on board the sloop-of-war *Tamar*. Kirkland had then visited Lord Dunmore, himself a refugee on board the ship *William* in Norfolk Harbor. From him he had received a letter to General Howe, telling of the bearer's influence among the people of the back country and of his persecutions as a loyalist. About September 25, 1775, Kirkland arrived at St. Augustine, where he was given additional letters. One of these, from Lieutenant Governor Moultrie to General James Grant, said, among other things, that the adjacent colonies had "done everything to starve" the inhabitants of East Florida, that the rebels were trying to win over the southern Indians, and that Kirkland would be a powerful agent if a British expedition should be sent into the south. Three letters of different dates were from Superintendent Stuart to General Gage. The first spoke of messages he had sent to the Indian nations on his arrival at St. Augustine. The second communicated a talk held between the Cherokees and Allan Cameron, deputy Indian agent to that nation, which was so favorable that Stuart intended to send his brother, Henry Stuart, among them and the Creeks. The talk indicated that the Cherokee chiefs were ready to lead their warriors against the back settlements. The third doubted the advisability of an indiscriminate attack on those settlements since the "great majority of the frontier and back inhabitants of Carolina" were attached to the British government. Hence Stuart proposed a concerted movement between the red men and their well-disposed neighbors. He added that the Allatchaway Indians were then in St. Augustine and that he was expecting answers to dispatches he had sent to other nations. Besides the above letters Kirkland was supplied with the latest survey of Georgia, a plan of Charleston, a drawing of the harbor, and other plans prepared for him by Captain Mulcaster, the engineer. He also had a copy of the returns setting forth the strength of the garrison at St. Augustine for August, September, and October, 1775, and letters from Governor Tonyn, Major Jonathan Furlong, and others.[24]

Another refugee who was in St. Augustine at this time was the above-named Allan Cameron, who was also entrusted with letters to be carried to Boston. He had been "ill-used in Charleston" and "obliged to leave his country on account of an affair of honor," and was going north to offer his services to General Gage in the hope of "getting in time an Ensigncy." In Norfolk Harbor he visited Lord Dunmore on board the ship *William*. There he met Dr. John Connolly, who had just returned from Boston after laying his plans before the commander-in-chief. These plans, which were approved by Gage, provided that Connolly should go to Detroit and collect a force from the nearest posts for transportation in the spring by *bateaux* down to Fort Pitt, which was to be seized and made headquarters for further operations. The disaffected on the upper Ohio were to be crushed, and the loyalists collected into disciplined regiments. A sufficient garrison being left at the fort, the remainder of the force was to advance across the Allegheny Mountains, "establish a strong post at Fort Cumberland, descend the Potomac and seize Alexandria," which was to be well fortified. Here Connolly's command would be met by Lord Dunmore with his fleet and "all the force of the lower part of Virginia." Thus the northern colonies would be severed from the southern. Dunmore had appointed Connolly lieutenant colonel commandant of a corps to be called the Queen's Royal Rangers, and Allan Cameron was commissioned a lieutenant in this corps. On November 13, they, together with another adventurer, started in a flat-bottomed schooner for Norfolk to go up the Chesapeake and the Potomac

---

[24] E. A. Jones (ed.), *Journal of Alexander Chesney*, Ohio State University *Bulletin*, October 30, 1921, pp. 67, 105-106; Force, *Am. Archives*, 4th ser., III. 836; IV. 316, 317, 336. Concerning General James Grant, see Volume II. of this work, p. 309.

and thence overland on horseback to Detroit. A week later they were apprehended in an inn near Hager's Town, Maryland. On December 29, Cameron and Connolly were sent to Philadelphia and incarcerated in the jail.[25] This practically terminated Connolly's great plot, which was evidently intended to be executed in connection with the schemes of Superintendent Stuart and his fellow-loyalists at St. Augustine.

That Captain Kirkland accompanied Cameron on the journey to Norfolk is shown by a letter of Governor Tonyn, in which he wrote that he was sending Kirkland to Virginia and that he desired Lord Dunmore to dispatch him without a moment's loss to General Gage at Boston. About the time that Connolly and his companions set out for Chesapeake Bay, Kirkland sailed for Boston. The mission of the former was to isolate the south and save Virginia to the crown; the mission of the latter was to induce the British military and naval commanders at Boston to send an expedition to Charleston and, in coöperation with the bodies of southern loyalists and Indians, save the lower south for the king. These were great projects, emanating from the brains of American loyalists, but they were doomed to failure. The catastrophe that had overtaken Connolly, Cameron, and Smyth, was also to overtake Kirkland, and only a little more than two weeks later. On December 5, 1775, the vessel on which Kirkland was making his voyage, was captured by a continental schooner when nearing its destination. The unfortunate messenger from St. Augustine was sent to Washington's headquarters at Cambridge, Massachusetts, and later transferred to the custody of the Continental Congress at Philadelphia.[26] The South Carolina delegates received his papers and forwarded them by special messenger to Charleston, where they were laid before the provincial congress. The disclosures thus made were also communicated to the

[25] Force, *Am. Archives*, 4th ser., III. 788, IV. 318, 342; McCrady, *South Carolina in the Rev., 1775-1780*, pp. 38, 46, 47, 187-188; Drayton, *Memoirs of the Rev.*, II. 296-297; *Biennial Report*, Department of Archives and History, West Virginia, 1911-1912, 1913-1914, pp. 39-41; *Pennsylvania Magazine of History and Biography*, January, 1889, pp. 411-417; *Proceedings of Am. Antiquarian Soc.*, October, 1909, pp. 19-21; J. F. D. Smyth, *Tour in United States of America*, I. 232.

[26] E. A. Jones (ed.), *Journal of Alexander Chesney*, pp. 105-106; Force, *Am. Archives*, 4th ser., IV. 615, 616, 617, 618; V. 533.

whig authorities in Georgia. On December 23, only eighteen days after Kirkland was taken, Lord George Germain wrote to Deputy Governor William Eden of Maryland that "an armament of seven regiments, with a fleet of frigates and small ships," was then in readiness to proceed to the southern colonies to attempt the restoration of legal government, adding that they were to go first to North Carolina and thence either to South Carolina or Virginia, as circumstances might require.[27]

Before the weakening of the garrison at St. Augustine, the full strength of the 14th Regiment was three hundred and twenty-two, including both officers and men. Of the Royal Artillery there were only ten officers and men. After the departure of the two detachments for Williamsburg, Virginia, that is, by October 1, 1775, only a little more than half of the regiment was left, of which about ninety were on duty at St. Augustine and small detachments at New Smyrna, Matanzas, the Cowford, the Lookout tower, and on St. Johns River. The removal of the detachments to Virginia caused such dissatisfaction that the refugees and merchants thought of removing with their families and effects to the West Indies. In a letter to Vice Admiral Graves, Governor Tonyn complained that the sloop *Savage*, stationed on the Florida coast, and the schooner *St. John*, stationed at New Providence, both harbored at the island "out of the way of action" instead of protecting merchant vessels coming to St. Augustine with ordnance supplies and ammunition. The arrival of the armed schooner *St. Lawrence* on October 2, with twenty-three recruits and a quantity of ammunition, gave widespread pleasure, because it was to be an addition to the naval defense of the province. To afford further protection to St. Augustine, Superintendent Stuart decided to keep about fifty Indians encamped near the town during the winter. Captain Mulcaster remarked that the reduced garrison consisted of only the colors, Major Furlong and five other officers, and about eighty men. He could not refrain from giving Brigadier General Grant a little gossip, namely, that a copy of severe verses had appeared at Payne's corner in criticism of Governor Tonyn and his lady for flogging their negroes, and he added that there was much truth in the verses. Spencer Man had more serious things to say to the same correspondent; he wrote that East Florida

---

[27] Force, *Am. Archives*, 4th ser., IV. 440-441. On Lookout tower, see Volume II. of this work, p. 379.

was "going back every day" and that he believed Tonyn had neither the ability to point out nor the "interest to procure any good" for the colony.[28]

Refugees continued to arrive at St. Augustine singly and in parties. Among them were Captain James Phillips of Jackson's Creek, South Carolina, and his company, who had taken part in the siege of Ninety-Six Court House late in November, 1775. The force of nearly two thousand besiegers broke up for lack of unified command, and Phillips's company retired to Jackson's Creek and thence to Pacolet River. Here they remained for a fortnight, after which they were conducted in two divisions to Colonel Ambrose Mills's plantation on Green River in North Carolina. Mills furnished the guides who led them through the Cherokee and Creek nations on their way to St. Augustine.[29]

On November 1, 1775, the governor and the council of East Florida considered a presentment of a grievance made by the grand jury at the previous June sessions. The presentment complained "with some degree of vehemence and dissatisfaction" that property was insecure in the province, and the jury desired the judge, Chief Justice William Drayton, to order the publication of the presentment in the neighboring provinces, which he did. The governor and the council objected to these measures on the grounds that property was equally secure by law in East Florida as elsewhere in the British dominions; that the publication of the complaint might be construed as indirect approbation of rebellion and would tend to discourage loyalists, who were "cruelly oppressed" in other provinces, from taking shelter in East Florida, and that the judge, if unable to remove the defect, supposing that it existed, should have softened it and given proper support to the provincial administration, as required by his duty to the king and country. The governor and his board called attention to the assurance previously given by Chief Justice Drayton to two gentlemen who contemplated settling in East Florida, but thought that its government was a military one and that their property would not be secure. Drayton had told them that they were mistaken, that no other than English law—the standard of the provincial government—existed in the peninsula.[30]

[28] Force, *Am. Archives*, 4th ser., III. 706, 788, 834, 835; IV. 316, 319, 329, 332, 335.
[29] E. A. Jones (ed.), *Journal of Alexander Chesney*, pp. 6, 100, 101, 130.
[30] C. O. 5/571, Minutes of the Council, November 1, 1775.

On November 3, the council gave orders to Major Furlong to post a detachment at Picolata Fort and assign another to barracks at St. Marks Fort, and to Captain Greaves of the *St. Lawrence* to receive on board a supply of gunpowder as a present for the Indians and attend during the approaching congress of the head men of the Creek nation with Governor Tonyn and Superintendent Stuart.[81]

At the council meeting of December 21, Martin Jollie presented a royal mandamus appointing him a member of the board and took the oaths. He had come from Grenada, one of the British West Indies, several months before, to settle in Georgia with some thirty negroes, but, finding that province in rebellion, he went to his tract of a thousand acres on St. Marys River, formed a settlement, and was soon shipping products to the West India market. At the same session of the council, James Tims was appointed customs officer for St. Marys. A request from Major Furlong to be permitted to leave with the remainder of the 14th Regiment for Virginia on board the *St. Lawrence* and another vessel, was refused on the grounds that the three companies of the 16th Regiment, recently arrived, were in a weak state and incomplete, a detachment having not yet come from Pensacola, and that the departure of the *St. Lawrence* would partly deprive East Florida of needed protection.[82]

[81] C. O. 5/571, Minutes of the Council, November 3, 1775.
[82] *Ibid.*, November 2, 3, December 21, 1775; Force, *Am. Archives*, 4th ser., III. 837.

Chapter III.

Measures for the defense of East Florida, February-July, 1776.—The defensive measures proposed by Tonyn.—Correspondence with rebels forbidden.—The suspension of Chief Justice Drayton from office.—The address of loyalty to the king. —The contest between Governor Tonyn on the one hand, and Chief Justice Drayton and Dr. Andrew Turnbull on the other.—Turnbull's colony at New Smyrna broken up.—Raids on frontier plantations.—The formation of the East Florida Rangers.—Defensive measures on St. Marys River.—The help of the Indians sought and the formation of a militia proclaimed.

ON February 2, 1776, Governor Tonyn, with the council's approval, gave instructions to Major Furlong to employ as many soldiers as possible on the defensive works, to require all vessels coming into port at St. Augustine, except those of the royal navy, to anchor at the ballast bank to be searched for arms and armed men, to have the batteries fire at any vessel approaching nearer than the place designated, and to employ certain signals to show that vessels might come in. The governor also proposed the establishment of a volunteer company, to consist of a captain, other officers, and twenty-five privates, a troop of light horse, and a militia to repel attack or invasion. He further urged that the inhabitants be required to report to the commanding officer the number of their male slaves who could be trusted with firearms in an emergency, and that the Indians within the province be invited to hunt in localities not too remote for them to render aid, if wanted. It was agreed that the publication of a proclamation announcing the establishment of the militia, the troop of horse, and the company of volunteers be postponed until Governor Tonyn could find out the number of men able to bear arms. At the end of March, he was able to report that there were forty-two on St. Marys and Nassau rivers, fifty-three on St. Johns, and two hundred at New Smyrna.[33]

Meantime, on February 6, a proclamation was ordered to be issued forbidding correspondence with rebels in the neighboring colonies and requiring all inhabitants of East Florida to bring to justice any persons concerned therein. At this meeting also the governor submitted the following charges

[33] C. O. 5/571, Minutes of the Council, February 2, 6, 13, 1776.

against Chief Justice Drayton: 1. that Mr. Drayton had been associated with Jonathan Bryan in the fraudulent purchase of the unappropriated lands in the province from the Indians; 2. that he had not only failed to give his opinion in writing as to the proper procedure against Bryan, but had also delayed the provost marshal's departure until Bryan had gone; 3. that Mr. Drayton's letter from William Henry Drayton was "full of matters of great political consequence"; and 4. that Mr. Drayton had acted with great impropriety and with mischievous intentions toward the government by handing to the grand jury the resolutions of the council and receiving from it observations thereon, as well as an address, thus erecting a kind of tribunal to take cognizance of the proceedings of the council and governor. A copy of these charges was sent to Chief Justice Drayton, who was heard in his own defense at the meeting on February 13. The board then decided unanimously that Mr. Drayton be suspended, and he was notified to that effect.[34]

At the council meeting of March 30, the Rev. John Forbes was appointed chief justice in Drayton's place until the royal pleasure should be known, after which the board discussed the conduct of its clerk, Dr. Andrew Turnbull, who was also secretary of the province. Three days earlier Dr. Turnbull had presided over a meeting of citizens at Wood's tavern, which adopted an address of loyalty to the king in contravention of Tonyn's rash assertion that he did not believe there were six loyal subjects in the province. It was a representative gathering, including such men as Spencer Man, Captain Robert Bisset, James Penman, George Middleton Powell, Frederick Rolfes, Jacobus Kip, and Colonel James Moncrief. Turnbull said that many of the signers owned more property singly than the governor and council collectively, with the single exception of Lieutenant Governor Moultrie. A committee of "the oldest and principal inhabitants" was appointed to present a copy of the address to the governor, and Turnbull was himself to carry the original to England. The governor manifested his displeasure to the committee, and soon forwarded another address to the mother country signed by his own friends and accompanied by a letter saying that the government could rely on these men and their negroes for aid

[34] C. O. 5/571, Minutes of the Council, February 2, 1776; Carita Doggett, *Dr. Andrew Turnbull and New Smyrna Colony*, pp. 110-115.

Measures for Defense

in case of invasion. As Turnbull had received warning by word and by letter that Tonyn intended to throw him and others into the dungeon at the fort, he departed without leave of absence for England with his friend Drayton.[35]

Tonyn reported the facts above mentioned, and all the members, except Martin Jollie, favored Turnbull's suspension, and the governor so wrote him. Mr. Jollie maintained that he could not believe, after several years' acquaintance with Dr. Turnbull, that he intended to bring the provincial administration into contempt, or that his conduct had that tendency. At the next meeting (April 8) Mr. Jollie resigned from the board and gave up his office as assistant judge. Captain Benjamin Dodd was now appointed a member of the council, and David Yeats was named secretary of the province and clerk of the council in place of Dr. Turnbull. Governor Tonyn wrote to Lord George Germain alleging that the two absentees had "become Patriots for the cause of America," that they had reprobated the measures of the ministry, and that Turnbull in particular had declared in company that America was right, the ministry wrong, and that Lord North would answer for its measures with his head. He strongly intimated that from this Turnbull-Drayton faction intelligence was being sent to the revolutionists concerning the state of the garrison at St. Augustine and all measures being taken in the province.[36]

After a conference between Turnbull and Germain in Westminster, the latter wrote a letter reproving Tonyn for his treatment of Drayton and telling him that it was the recommendation of the lords of trade and the pleasure of the king that the suspension be removed and that no part of Drayton's salary be withheld. Tonyn was also advised to prevent any injury to the colony of Turnbull and his co-proprietors at New Smyrna, and to use his best endeavors to promote its growth and the advantage of the owners. When the news that the Declaration of Independence had been adopted by congress reached St. Augustine, Samuel Adams and John Han-

---

[35] C. O. 5/571, Minutes of the Council, March 30, 1775; Carita Doggett, *Dr. Andrew Turnbull and New Smyrna Colony*, pp. 116-120, 130-133. On Colonel Moncrieff, see Volume II. of this work, p. 341.

[36] C. O. 5/571, Minutes of the Council, April 8, 1775; Carita Doggett, *Dr. Andrew Turnbull and New Smyrna Colony*, pp. 136-137.

cock were burnt in effigy on the plaza. On July 19, Tonyn reported that a band of Indians had broken into the homes of some of the colonists and committed other depredations at New Smyrna. Apart from warning the Indians, he took no other action. Turnbull charged that he prevented the colonists from being supplied with staple provisions, and that for this reason they would not enlist in the militia then being raised. Colonel Bisset, who lived near New Smyrna, thought that not more than one company could be raised there, but he feared, as did Andrew Turnbull, Jr., Dr. Turnbull's nephew, when an American privateer appeared in the offing, that a number of the white colonists would join the crew. Accordingly, steps were immediately taken to defend New Smyrna by arming those of its men who could be trusted and disarming the others. The arrival of Germain's letter of reproof in September evoked a complaint from Tonyn that he had been obliged to reinforce the guard, always kept at New Smyrna, to prevent disorder, just when troops were needed to protect the northern frontier of the province against the depredations of the enemy. The permanent guard, to which Tonyn referred, was a little detail of eight men to police the district.[87]

Lord Germain persuaded Turnbull to withdraw the charges he had filed with the lords of trade against Tonyn, on condition that the lords would ignore the latter's charges against Turnbull. Furthermore, Germain promised to recommend Turnbull's reinstatement in the council of East Florida if he would apologize for departing to England without leave of absence and give assurance of respectful behavior in the future. To Tonyn he wrote that offenses arising from mistakes and infirmities should be passed over among men engaged in supporting the crown and promoting the prosperity of their province.[88]

Dr. Turnbull landed in New York in November, 1777. When he reached St. Augustine early in December he found many of his colonists there, especially the women and children, who were begging for bread around Tonyn's residence. The able-bodied men were already in service on board

[87] Carita Doggett, *Dr. Andrew Turnbull and New Smyrna Colony*, pp. 137-143; Fairbanks, *Hist. of Florida*, p. 223; Dewhurst, *Hist. of St. Augustine*, p. 123.

[88] Carita Doggett, *Dr. Andrew Turnbull and New Smyrna Colony*, pp. 151-152, 154-156. Concerning Lord George Germain, see Additional Notes, in Volume II. of this work, p. 317.

of the cruisers, or had enlisted in the militia or the corps of East Florida Rangers, while the others were building hovels for the women and children on small lots given them north of the town, or were fishing along the shore of the inlet. Several scores of the colonists had died in St. Augustine from exposure during the heavy rains of August and September. The court of sessions had declared many of Turnbull's indentured people to be still bound by their contracts, but Tonyn had disregarded its decision, and most of them with his encouragement had removed from New Smyrna to the capital. James Penman, who was Dr. Turnbull's attorney, Chief Justice Drayton, and Captain Robert Bisset all affirmed that Tonyn had broken up the colony to get recruits for his provincial commands. The governor wrote to Germain that the discharge of the colonists would be no real loss to the proprietors of New Smyrna, as the cost of their maintenance would always equal the value of their labor.[39]

Raids on the scattered plantations along St. Marys River began late in 1775. Two settlements belonging to Jermyn Wright of Georgia, one about twelve miles from the river's mouth and the other some eighty miles farther up the stream, were visited by raiding parties from across the border at the close of the year. These parties burned the buildings, cut the dams, and committed many other depredations. Mr. Wright removed his negroes back to Georgia and abandoned these plantations a few months later. In the latter part of May, 1776, a similar raid was made on a tract of twelve thousand acres owned by William Chapman, and being developed in part as a rice plantation. Mr. Chapman, with the aid of his agent and his own two sons, was able to remove some of his slaves and effects to Amelia Island at night after the first visit of the rebels. A few days later, the Chapmans found their rice destroyed, their tar kiln and other structures burned, and the negroes they had left on the place dispersed. Even on Amelia Island they were harassed by the ravages of crews brought there by armed galleys. They therefore retired to a small tract of land which they bought near Picolata Fort on St. Johns River, where they engaged in producing naval stores and cutting lumber.[40]

Under stress of these recurring attacks on the northern frontier of East

---

[39] Carita Doggett, *Dr. Andrew Turnbull and New Smyrna Colony*, pp. 165, 169-170; C. O. 5/557, pp. 420-422.

[40] See Volume II. of this work, pp. 215-216.

Florida, Governor Tonyn turned to Thomas Browne and Daniel McGirth[41] to embody a corps of rangers, commissioning the former as lieutenant colonel on June 1, 1776. These two loyalists found recruits among their fellow refugees and the colonists from New Smyrna. Henry Manin, formerly of North Carolina, who probably retired to St. Augustine with Superintendent Stuart, was appointed a captain, and Robert Phillips, a brother of Captain James Phillips, a lieutenant in the East Florida Rangers. Daniel and James McGirth were also given officers' commissions. It was a matter of complaint by Colonel Augustine Prevost,[41a] who had arrived in East Florida with six companies of the fourth battalion and several of the third battalion of the 60th Regiment, about September 1, 1776, that the rangers were not placed under his orders. Lieutenant Colonel Browne had not been in command of his partly embodied corps more than a few weeks when fresh depredations aroused excitement and fear among the planters of St. Marys River. In the spring of 1776, Captain Benjamin Dodd had come to the province and had purchased two plantations, one on the south side of St. Marys and the other on Trout Creek. Late in the summer the buildings on the former were left in ruins by a band of rebels, and the outpost in that neighborhood, lately reinforced to one hundred men, had been driven to the south side of St. Johns River after six of their number had been captured. To keep the settlers from abandoning their plantations and harvests and bringing their negroes to St. Augustine, Colonel Prevost and Governor Tonyn joined in filling an armed shallop and the tender *Otter* with a force of regulars, rangers, and Indians to go to the support of the outpost and the armed schooner already there. Writing to General Howe on September 9, 1776, Prevost explained that he had come to St. Augustine with orders to discipline the troops, but that he found it necessary to employ the recruits in repairing the neglected fortifications.[42]

On St. Marys River was a fort commonly known as Wright's which, if it was built by Jermyn Wright, was not under his command after 1775. It was not until September of the following year that he left Georgia, going to St. Augustine where he remained nearly three years. He then returned

---

[41] See Additional Notes, in Volume II. of this work, pp. 323, 328.

[41a] *Ibid.*, p. 353.

[42] *Hist. MSS. Comm., Am. MSS. in R. Inst.*, I. 58.

into Georgia and stayed until April, 1782. Thence he sailed for England.[43] However, the fort called by his name early became a station from which armed parties of loyalists made sallies into Georgia. It also helped to emphasize the fact that St. Augustine was a center of militant loyalism. Such parties were often accompanied by a band of Indians. This practice was in accordance with Governor Tonyn's proposal to his council early in February, 1776. Later Tonyn had written to General Howe suggesting that the Indians be employed in warfare, and Howe had replied under date of August 25 that he concurred fully. In fact, he recommended that Tonyn use every means to employ them in the defense of East Florida, or against the invaders of the province in their own country. This letter to the governor was accompanied by one to Superintendent Stuart, enjoining him to be very active in seconding Tonyn's endeavors.[44]

Already in May, Tonyn had received intelligence that some of the Georgians were planning to prevent cattle belonging to persons residing in East Florida from being driven across St. Marys, and to commit further depredations on the plantations along that river and St. Johns. Lieutenant Grant was therefore sent with the armed schooner *St. John*, having a detachment on board, and other vessels to guard the passes of St. Marys. The settlers of that district were ordered to drive their cattle across St. Johns River. The attempt was made to keep persons from entering the province without examination by the commanding officer, to apprehend rebels, and to intercept letters to and from Georgia. Several refugees from this province had an unusual complaint to make, namely, that certain officers of the royal navy had seized property belonging to them. The council sent this complaint to Lord Germain with a representation of the detriment inflicted by such acts upon the good name of East Florida.[45]

Early in July, 1776, the board found it necessary to offer a reward of £100 for the arrest of George Mills and Bryan Docherty, two inhabitants, who had joined the enemy and recently threatened the Russel plantation. A month later a force of between two hundred and forty and three hundred

---

[43] See Volume II. of this work, p. 171; Egerton (ed.), *R. Comm. on Loyalist Claims, 1783-1785*, p. 115, n. 1; Sabine, *Loyalists of the Am. Rev.*, II. 460.

[44] *Hist. MSS. Comm., Am. MSS. in R. Inst.*, I. 56, 84.

[45] C. O. 5/571, Minutes of the Council, May 20, 1776.

men was sent from Georgia on board a schooner, a large flat, and another vessel to capture the *St. John* in St. Marys River, destroy the settlement there, and do other mischief. The *St. John* and the detachment under the command of Captain Graham were obliged to retire before this force, and people living on Amelia Island carried their negroes to the mainland and sent a call for help to St. Augustine. This led the governor and council to seek assistance from the Seminoles and Creeks. The Seminoles promised their aid and dispatched a band of braves to St. Augustine a few days later. It took longer to hear from the Creeks, since the messages to them were transmitted through Mr. Tait, the agent in that nation, and Superintendent Stuart, who was at Pensacola. Meanwhile, a proclamation was issued requiring all loyal subjects to meet and embody themselves under proper officers to assist the royal troops, prohibiting persons from keeping boats and canoes on the west side of St. Johns River and St. Sebastians Creek after sunset, and forbidding anyone to pass St. Johns without the written permit of the governor.[46]

[46] C. O. 5/571, Minutes of the Council, July 4, August 6, 1776.

Chapter IV.

Campaigns against East Florida, July, 1776-September, 1778.—The Lee-Moultrie expedition.—Lieutenant Colonel Fuser's retaliatory movement and the destruction of Fort Barrington.—Colonel Samuel Elbert's expedition.—The humble petition and address of forty-nine refugees from Georgia and its results.—The appointment of Captain Kirkland as deputy Indian agent.—Raids into Georgia.—Mutual fear of invasions entertained by the Georgians and Floridians.—Brigadier General Robert Howe's expedition.—The arrival of three hundred and fifty refugees from South Carolina and the formation of the South Carolina Royalists.—The arrival of the Scopholites.—The formation of a troop of horse by Colonel Prevost.—The retirement of Colonel Murphey and four hundred insurgents to East Florida.—John Hamilton and associates leave North Carolina and join Governor Martin in New York.—The embodiment of the Royal North Carolina Regiment at St. Augustine and its operations to the northward.—The advance of Howe's expedition.—The affair at Alligator Creek bridge.—The tribulations of Howe's army.—Prevost's defensive measures.—Legislation against the loyalists in Georgia and the Carolinas.—The situation of the refugees in East Florida.—The charges against Governor Tonyn in Dr. Turnbull's memorial.—The renewal of hostilities between Drayton and Tonyn.—The trial and second suspension of Drayton.—The address to the governor from inhabitants and refugees.—Chief Justice Drayton removes to South Carolina.—Tonyn's severe treatment of Turnbull.—Raids of "Tonyn's banditti" into Georgia.—The prospect of an invasion from East Florida.—Expenditures for refugees and prisoners of war.—Exports from East Florida in 1776, 1777, and 1778.

IN the summer of 1776, a committee of leading Georgians was sent by the colony to confer with Major General Charles Lee at Charleston about the unprotected condition of that province. In the course of the conference the committee referred to the necessity impelling the inhabitants and soldiers of East Florida to make inroads into Georgia for provisions. It reported that according to accounts there were more than a thousand British troops then at St. Augustine, while on its western frontier Georgia had as neighbors at least fifteen thousand Indian warriors of the Creek, Cherokee, and Choctaw nations, who had been much tampered with by the enemy and might easily be supplied with ammunition from the Floridas. General Lee was asked to state the case to the general congress, and obtain the money to pay enough men to defend Georgia and to build fortifications and supply guard-boats for the purpose of cutting off communication between the Florida provinces and the Indians. In a letter to the continental congress, Lee stated that Georgia was of the last importance to the common cause, that the mode of protecting it recommended by the committee was wise, and that with the permission of the congress he would attempt to reduce East Florida had he a sufficient force.[47]

Along in July, Colonel McIntosh of Georgia, with a part of his regiment, marched south within two miles of St. Marys River, which separated Georgia from East Florida, to reconnoiter the fort maintained there by the two brothers of Governor Sir James Wright, Jermyn and Charles. The place was garrisoned by a number of other loyalists, who had their negroes with them besides many others who had fled thither. McIntosh's party was fired on by an outpost, but returned the fire and killed one man and took nine prisoners.[48]

Lee moved to Savannah at the end of July to arrange for an expedition against East Florida, taking troops with him. On his arrival he propounded the following questions to the council of safety at Savannah: 1. What would be the advantages of an incursion into East Florida? 2. Would the advantages compensate for the trouble and expense, in view of the recent abandonment of the post on St. Marys, the spoliation of the country down to the St. Johns, and the impossibility of transporting cannon and other essentials and of collecting a sufficient force to reduce St. Augustine? 3. How could provisions be conveyed to the troops? The council replied to these questions that an invasion would drive the people from their plantations to the castle of St. Augustine and create such a scarcity of food that the garrison would be forced to surrender, but, even if it did not, the withdrawal of the enemy from the Georgia line would stop the loss of negroes, attach the Indians to the American cause, and enable a troop of horsemen to range on the west side of St. Johns River, thus preventing intercourse between the Creeks and the people of East Florida. The privateers of that province would cease their attacks on the Georgia coast. As for getting provisions to the troops, they could be conveyed by the inland passage to Pico-

---

[47] Force, *Am. Archives*, 5th ser., I. 6.
[48] *Ibid.*, 5th ser., I. 435-436, 685, 720, 1076. See also Volume II. of this work, p. 347.

Campaigns against East Florida

lata Creek, less than twenty miles from St. Augustine. Curiously enough, neither the council nor Lee mentioned the unhealthy season of the year as a vital objection to the incursion that was about to be undertaken.[49]

Lee had brought with him some Virginia and North Carolina troops and a contingent of two hundred and sixty South Carolina continentals. He placed Colonel William Moultrie, brother of Lieutenant Governor John Moultrie of East Florida, in command, and provided him with the necessaries required for the expedition. During the preparations for the march, Lee was summoned to Philadelphia by the continental congress, and left orders for the North Carolina and Virginia troops to follow him. Colonel Moultrie was thus under the necessity of marching with a greatly reduced force. The expedition got no farther than Sunbury, Georgia, on account of sickness among the officers and the high death rate among the men—fourteen or fifteen a day. The unhealthful season and the swamps of the Ogeechee had interposed insuperable difficulties between Moultrie's little expedition and its objective.[50]

On September 4, 1776, in the midst of alarm about the aggressions from Georgia, Governor Tonyn and his council had to drink the bitter cup of reinstating Mr. Drayton in the chief-justiceship. This was done in compliance with a letter from Lord Germain conveying the word that it was the king's pleasure that the suspension of that gentleman from his office should be removed. Accordingly, a letter was written to Mr. Drayton to that effect. The next day a petition was laid before the board asking for assistance in protecting Lady Egmont's plantation and the other settlements on St. Marys River, and letters of marque were granted to Lieutenant John Mowbray, commander of the sloop *Rebecca* of ten guns, as had been done nearly a month before in the case of Captain George Osborne, to help protect the province. At the same time Colonel Prevost was requested to place a detachment of an officer and thirty-five privates on board the *Rebecca* and another of a sergeant and twelve men on the royal schooner *St. John* of four guns, both of which were to proceed at once to St. Johns River and

---

[49] Force, *Am. Archives*, 5th ser., I. 6, 685, 720.

[50] Drayton, *Memoirs of Am. Rev.*, II. 335; Ramsay, *Hist. of the Rev. in South Carolina*, I. 152; McCall, *Hist. of Georgia*, II. 95; C. C. Jones, *Hist. of Georgia*, II. 247-250; McCrady, *South Carolina in the Rev.*, 1775-1780, pp. 202-203.

coöperate with the detachment already stationed there in assuring safety to the planters. As the colonists at New Smyrna were reported to be inclined to mutiny, Colonel Prevost was asked to augment the detachment there to eighteen or twenty men.[51]

Nine days later, word was brought of Lee's expedition against St. Augustine by Captain Stanhope of the king's ship *Raven*. Fearing a siege, the council authorized the dispatch of trusty persons for fuller intelligence and the collection of spare arms from the inhabitants and cannon from the shipping, while the governor agreed to send vessels to St. Johns River and Mosquito Inlet [now Ponce de Leon Inlet] to gather all available provisions on those waters and bring them to St. Augustine as soon as possible. In compliance with Tonyn's request, Captain Squires kept his ship, the *Otter*, lying off the bar for the time being and sent Lieutenant Wright with the sloop *Tuncastle* to join the *St. John* and the *Rebecca* in St. Johns River.[52]

A retaliatory expedition was organized in East Florida in the opening weeks of 1777. It comprised about one thousand men, of whom five hundred were regulars under the command of Lieutenant Colonel Lewis V. Fuser, one hundred East Florida Rangers led by Lieutenant Colonel Browne and Daniel McGirth, a body of Creek Indians, and a battery of fieldpieces. A detachment of this force on reaching St. Marys River placed a garrison in Fort McIntosh, and crossed into Georgia. Browne and his men gathered in some cattle and a store of rice, while the Indians, approaching nearer to Fort Barrington, took some fifty head of horses belonging to the garrison there. As soon as Fuser's force had again assembled, he advanced to the fort and demanded its surrender. Its commanding officer, Captain Richard Winn, signed a capitulation, and his men, seventy-five in number, laid down their arms, and were dismissed on parole. The British and loyalists kept the fort three days, until Fuser heard that troops were on the march to intercept him. Then he burned the post, and led his expedition back to St. Augustine. Nevertheless, the American planters as far as the Sapello River deserted their settlements, fearing the advance of Briga-

[51] C. O. 5/571, Minutes of the Council, September 4, 5, 1776.
[52] *Ibid.*, September 14, 1776.

Lower Towns
Antient Country of the Timookah's a Tribe of the Old Apalahches
Great Swamp
ST. ANDREWS
St. MATTHEWS
Port Royal Entrance
Savannah Sound
Sapello I.
Cumberland Sound
Cumberland I.
New Town
Great Talbot I.
St. Johns River
Apalache
Alachua
Picolata Fort
AUGUSTIN
Matanza Inlet and Fort
Rolls town
Cape St. Blas
Roebuck Pt.
Bottom of the Bay
BAY OF APALACHE
Cayo Anclote
Mosquito Inlet
New Smyrna Entrance
Cape Canaveral
Hillsboro Bay
BAY OF TAMPA
SPIRITU SANTO
Tortolas
Hillsboro Inlet
Jups Inlet
Grenville Inlet
Lake Mayacco
Rio Secco
Rio Nuevo
OLD TEGESTA
Cape Florida
Cape Roman or Punta Larga
CHATHAM BAY formerly Bay of Juan Ponce de Leon
THE PROMONTORY OF EAST FLORIDA
RICHMOND BAY
Martyrs Reefs and Shoals
GULF OF FLORIDA
E. FLORIDA
Carlos Harbour
Sanybel I.
Memory Rock
C O
A T

dier General Prevost and his entire army from East Florida. Browne and his rangers brought off nearly two thousand cattle. Of these about eighteen hundred were driven across St. Johns River, and were sold by Governor Tonyn to dealers at twenty-five shillings a head. After being butchered, the beef was retailed in the public market at three pence a pound. Fuser's expedition reached St. Augustine on March 5, 1777.[53]

In the early part of April a force proceeded from Savannah against East Florida. This movement was planned by Button Gwinett, recently elected president and commander-in-chief by the council of safety. Under the command of Colonel Samuel Elbert two battalions of continentals marched for Sunbury, whence they sailed on May 1 to go inland. At the mouth of the Altamaha they learned that a few of the inhabitants had lately sought protection south of St. Marys River, and that Hester's Bluff was being fortified with cannon in anticipation of the invasion.

This expedition, the weak state of the garrison at the time, the distrust in Tonyn's ability to coöperate with the military department in adequate defensive measures, and the antagonism to him on the part of certain leading men, led them to express themselves in regard to the situation. On the morning of May 8, 1777, Captain Robert Bisset, Robert Payne, Andrew Turnbull, Jr., Spencer Man, Alexander Gray, and a few other gentlemen gathered at James Penman's to confer about what was best to be done to protect the settlements on St. Marys River and the province at large. After some time, Chief Justice Drayton arrived and spoke freely against the measures and blunders of the administration, stating it was said that he would be the first to sign a petition for Tonyn's removal and agreeing to join with those present "to capitulate with the Rebels." He seems also to have suggested the propriety of waiting on the governor to propose the capitulation, that is, the purchase from the enemy of neutrality and freedom from molestation. It was agreed that Messrs. Bisset, Payne, and three others should call on Tonyn at once and urge such action.

This was done, and on the same date the governor wrote to Lord George

[53] *Collections* of Georgia Hist. Soc., V. pt. 2 (Order Book of Samuel Elbert), pp. 15-26; Capt. L. Butler, *Annals of the King's R. Rifle Corps*, app. II., "Memoir of Maj. P. Murray," p. 302; McCall, *Hist. of Georgia*, II. 98-103; C. C. Jones, *Hist. of Georgia*, II. 260-263.

Germain that the committee had waited on him and expressed great apprehension of danger in case Colonel Elbert and his troops should attack East Florida and had begged leave to offer terms and money provided they would not destroy their property. Tonyn says that he expostulated with the committee on the disgrace of the proposed capitulation and gave them great hopes that by a spirited coöperation with the king's troops a "very good account of the rebel invasion" could be rendered, that St. Johns River was a strong barrier, and that, since the adjacent territory was now well guarded by troops, rangers, and Indians, it would be difficult for the enemy to pass. With this the proposal was dropped, and no more was heard of it for a few months.

By May 19, Elbert and his men had landed on the north end of Amelia Island. Colonel Baker advanced with one hundred and nine volunteers, crossed St. Marys, and reached Sawpit Bluff, or Rolfe's sawmill, on May 12. He sent out a party to reconnoiter for Elbert, and on the 17th was routed at Thomas's Swamp, near Nassau River, by Lieutenant Colonel Browne and a force of three hundred men after being drawn into an ambush by some East Florida scouts and Indians led by Daniel McGirth. About forty of Baker's men surrendered and, with the exception of sixteen, were put to death by the Indians. On Amelia Island, Lieutenant Ward was killed while attempting to secure the inhabitants at the south end of the island. In retaliation a party of Elbert's men was landed with instructions to burn the houses and destroy the stock on Amelia Island.[54]

Colonel Elbert did not attempt to penetrate into East Florida. The inland passage between the mainland and the island was guarded by two armed vessels, Hester's Bluff was crowned by a battery and its cannon, and the mouth of St. Johns River was protected by two warships. Elbert's men were suffering from the increasing heat, their stock of provisions was getting low, and they were becoming discontented. The expedition pushed up St. Marys River, its commander believing that it was impossible to enter East Florida without the "rascals" there "having timely notice" of his approach from secret enemies among the Americans, who carried on a

---

[54] C. C. Jones, *Hist. of Georgia*, II. 265-269; Capt. L. Butler, *Annals of the King's R. Rifle Corps*, app. II. 303; C. O. 5/559.

regular correspondence, he said, with their Florida neighbors. At any rate, his operations would keep the Floridians out of Georgia, prevent their getting supplies, and plunge them into continual alarms. At Wright's place Lieutenant Colonel Harris landed with a detachment to go up the river to the fort and thence to the Satilla in search of small parties of the enemy supposed to be hunting for beef north of St. Marys. Late in May four men deserted from the expedition and went over to the enemy. Soon thereafter Colonel Elbert received a message from Major James Mark Prevost, then at Graham's Redoubt, saying among other things that in the future all small parties found in arms beyond the limits of Georgia would be regarded as robbers and murderers, in accordance with an order from General Sir William Howe, that only self-preservation had induced Governor Tonyn to permit some of the Indians to take the warpath, and that not until the intended invasion of East Florida by General Lee had parties of the Creeks made their appearance in Georgia. In this letter also Major Prevost applied for those Creek Indians and other prisoners of war who were then confined in Georgia. At the end of May Colonel Elbert began his homeward march. On June 1, he was joined at Old Town on the Satilla by Lieutenant Colonel Harris and his party. Thence by way of Fort Howe he returned to Savannah, while the fleet proceeded to Sunbury.[55]

Early in May, 1777, Colonel Augustine Prevost was promoted to the rank of a brigadier general, his command being extended to include West Florida. The advance of Colonel Elbert had induced Governor Tonyn to summon the Creek Indians and ask for the dispatch of the Cherokees into South Carolina or Georgia. Prevost wrote to General Howe six weeks after Tonyn's appeal that the rebels had been baffled and had returned into Georgia, that the Indians had been rendered unreliable by the work of American emissaries, and that in the space of a few days East Florida "could be invaded either by land or water by an army well supplied with artillery, provisions, &c." He asked permission to enroll a troop of mounted rangers and wanted Superintendent Stuart to find means of protecting the Cherokees, who had been recently defeated severely by the combined

---

[55] *Collections* of Georgia Hist. Soc., (Order Book of Samuel Elbert), V. pt. 2, pp. 27, 28, 31-33, 36-37; C. C. Jones, *Hist. of Georgia*, II. 264-269.

efforts of Virginians, Carolinians, and Georgians and were now threatened with destruction for their loyalty. That the Creeks were already inclined to the American side was shown, he thought, by the enforced flight of Stuart's agents from their nation after being robbed.[56]

The policy of the king in council, during Governor Grant's administration, of making numerous grants of land in East Florida of twenty, ten, and five thousand acres to noblemen and other speculators, had preëmpted most of the desirable land in the province and prevented numbers of the refugees from obtaining small tracts for settlement. This situation had been set forth in a humble address and petition presented by forty-nine loyalists from Georgia to Governor Tonyn on November 1, 1776. This group of planters, merchants, and others included Andrew and Lewis Johnston, sons of Dr. Lewis Johnston of Savannah, who had been president of the council in Georgia and treasurer of that province, James Christie, Peter Edwards, Charles William Mackinen, William Panton, Alexander Paterson, Henry Yonge, Jr., Jermyn and Charles Wright, and Alexander Wylly. The petitioners had acknowledged the many blessings they enjoyed under the "most auspicious" reign and mild government of George III, had told how from the beginning of the Revolution they had risked their lives and fortunes by opposing the pernicious measures of the ringleaders of the rebellion in Georgia, how they had tried to maintain peace until they were no longer able to bear the repeated insults and persecution from their old friends and neighbors, and had fled to East Florida for refuge and gratuitous grants of land as promised in Tonyn's proclamation of November 2, 1775, with such part of their property as they could bring.

After testifying to the governor's "unwearied zeal" in the royal service and the kind reception, assistance, and protection they had received from him, they had complained that the many grants of large tracts of land on the east coast of Florida and the claims of the Indians to the most valuable lands near Alachua prevented them and many other loyalists who were awaiting a safe opportunity to enter the province from reaping the benefit of the royal bounty for themselves and their families.

In another address presented at the same time the petitioners had made

[56] *Hist. MSS. Comm., Am. MSS. in R. Inst.,* I. 105, 107, 119, 190, 195, 197-199.

public and grateful acknowledgment of "the unexampled attention and tenderness" Tonyn had shown to their distresses by rendering them every assistance and had expressed their satisfaction at the permission he had given to some of the loyalists to remove their property and import provisions from colonies in rebellion. They had justified this on the ground that it was absolutely necessary for the subsistence of the garrison at St. Augustine and of the greatest advantage to the inhabitants in general, whose numbers had been greatly increased by the refugees from different rebellious provinces. They had deprecated the frustration of Tonyn's intentions by some of the officers of the British navy and had closed by praying the governor to recommend and forward their petition to the king.

Tonyn had promptly sent it to Lord George Germain together with a letter of transmission and a list of large grants of land in East Florida, showing that nearly one million and a half acres had been bestowed by orders in council and that only sixteen proprietors of the one hundred and eight who had received these extensive tracts had as yet complied with the condition of making settlements thereon, "that many industrious subjects of small fortune" had been prevented from settling in the province, and that the petitioners together with many other deserving refugees could not find land suitable for occupation.

These communications had been referred to a committee of the board of trade and plantations for consideration. On March 11, 1777, the committee reported to the king that as he might resume all grants where no settlement had been made at the expiration of three years from the date of the grant, it was advisable for him to direct the governor, with the advice of his council, to issue warrants of survey for tracts of five hundred acres or less to those refugees who intended to become inhabitants of the province, even if the lands to be surveyed fell within the boundaries of expired grants. It was recommended also that the governor be further instructed not to issue a patent superseding a subsisting grant until notice had been given the first grantee or his attorney to show cause before the governor and council within six months if the said grantee was in the province or, in case of his absence, twelve months, why such patent should not be issued to the applicant, the costs of any ensuing process to be defrayed by the latter. If at the expiration of the notice nothing appeared to the contrary, the governor should issue the grant containing the usual conditions. In due time these instructions were transmitted to Governor Tonyn, and he proceeded to break up some of the large grants of land for the benefit of the refugees.[56a]

On March 1, 1777, Captain Moses Kirkland reappeared at St. Augustine after an absence of nearly a year and seven months. He had escaped from the jail in Philadelphia on May 7, 1776, and came as the bearer of dispatches from General Howe to Superintendent Stuart and Governor Chester at Pensacola. At the end of three weeks, Stuart appointed him his deputy for the district of the Seminole Creeks, and late in July sent him with several of their chiefs to engage their warriors for action when summoned, and to distribute presents among them. Allan Cameron, Stuart's agent to the Cherokees, was sent among that nation to have its braves ready for service. The Choctaws and Chickasaws were reported to be well disposed. During the last three months of this year the loyalists in the back country of Georgia and Carolina were constantly conveying intelligence to the leaders in East Florida. Scouts and Indians from the latter province made frequent raids into Georgia, carrying off cattle without which the Floridians would have been in dire straits for meat. Colonel Samuel Elbert was collecting troops preparatory to establishing strong posts to the southward in an effort to overawe the enemy. In February, 1778, Lieutenant Colonel Browne, with his East Florida Rangers, of which four companies had been completed, and some Indians, was encamped at Fort Tonyn on St. Marys. He had "two trusty Palatines" out in the field to entice four hundred deserters and prisoners from service in the Georgia ranks into East Florida. He also sent his rangers and Indians across the Altamaha to collect cattle for the garrison at St. Augustine and for the province."[57]

On each side of St. Marys there was fear of a concerted invasion from the other. Brigadier General Prevost received intelligence in February, 1778, that the Americans were preparing for such a movement, and the Georgians were equally apprehensive, especially since the force in East Florida was being strengthened by a stream of refugees "from the great

---

[56a] C. O. 5/557, pp. 43-49; C. O. 5/563, pp. 492-512.

[57] *Hist. MSS. Comm., Am. MSS. in R. Inst.,* I. pp. 190, 193, 195; *Letters of Joseph Clay,* Savannah, Ga., 1776-1793, p. 50; Force, *Am. Archives,* 4th ser., V. 1235, VI. 434, 435.

Defection" in the back country of South Carolina. Many small parties of five or six men each, and one of twenty, were reported in Georgia as going from Carolina into Florida during "some months past." Late in February, Governor Tonyn was extending hospitality to a body of Creeks and expecting more daily. They seemed ready to take the warpath against Georgia, but the upper Creeks were irresolute, and a few of their towns had been lost to the royal service. The lower Creeks of the neighborhood had cooperated whenever he had sought their aid. Even Prevost admitted that their war bands kept parties of the revolutionists from distressing the plantations on St. Johns River. It was these friendly Indians and the East Florida Rangers commanded by Browne who made frequent sallies into Georgia, bringing back sometimes thousands of cattle for the supply of the garrison and the province.[58]

On March 1, Moses Kirkland returned to St. Augustine after an absence of more than a year and a half, having escaped from jail in Philadelphia. He proposed an expedition against Georgia and the western frontier of South Carolina, but Prevost and Tonyn withheld their approval until the commander-in-chief should consent. Prevost objected that the time for preparation was too short and that the expedition would reach the interior just when sickness abounded there. Under Tonyn's orders, Browne and his rangers, together with a few Indians, entered Georgia as a scouting party and took Fort Barrington, a small post on the Altamaha garrisoned by three officers and twenty men. In the early days of April, Browne, who was back again with his scouting party at Fort Tonyn on St. Marys, heard that a contingent of an American force under the command of Colonel Samuel Elbert, numbering about seven hundred men and seven field-pieces, was advancing, that two-thirds of his militia were on the Altamaha, and that his galleys and transports had reached the Sapello. Elbert's contingent was part of an expedition against East Florida that was being conducted by Brigadier General Robert Howe, in which eleven hundred continentals from South Carolina and Georgia and considerable bodies of militia from those provinces participated.[59]

[58] *Hist. MSS. Comm., Am. MSS. in R. Inst.*, I. 197-198.
[59] *Ibid.*, pp. 228, 259; Force, *Am. Archives*, 4th ser., V. 533, 1235, 1702.

Late in March, Captain Kirkland sailed from St. Augustine for Philadelphia to submit his plan of an expedition to the northward to General Howe, then retiring from command, and to his successor, Sir Henry Clinton. Although both these officers approved the project, Kirkland did not return to the south until five months later, when he accompanied Lieutenant Colonel Archibald Campbell's expedition from New York that captured Savannah.[60]

Since March 1, Captain John York of East Florida had been under orders to procure the coöperation of the loyal militia of Georgia and South Carolina with the troops at St. Augustine. A number of these militiamen wished York to conduct them to East Florida, but for some unknown reason he refused to undertake it. The explanation no doubt is to be found in Howe's campaign to the southward, which was then being organized. Late in April, three hundred and fifty loyalists from the Broad and Saluda rivers in South Carolina arrived at Fort Tonyn and were conducted to St. Augustine. They were survivors and descendants of the Palatines. They had started on their flight as a body of about five hundred men, but many of them had been driven back. Of those who pushed on to their destination one hundred and fifty had horses. They presented a memorial to Brigadier General Prevost saying they were willing to serve under him but wished to remain a part of the troops of their own province, choosing their own officers and receiving the same pay as their comrades at home. Prevost embodied two hundred and sixty of them as the South Carolina Royalists and placed them in charge of his brother, Major James Mark Prevost, for drill and discipline. They comprised four companies of infantry of forty-five men each and two troops of rifle dragoons of forty men each. They were assigned to duty on St. Johns River and were there joined by Joseph Robinson, a major of militia from Broad River, South Carolina, whence he had fled to Pensacola. Coming to St. Augustine, he was commissioned lieutenant colonel of the new corps, the titular command with the rank of colonel being given by General Clinton to Alexander Innes, former secretary to Governor Lord Campbell of South Carolina. Innes served as inspector

---

[60] E. A. Jones (ed.), *Journal of Alexander Chesney*, p. 106; *South Carolina Hist. and Genealogical Magazine*, XVIII. 69-71.

general of provincial forces, being on duty at New York. The other officers of the South Carolina Royalists were nominated by Robinson, including Major Evan McLaurin, who had come in 1777 from Spring Hill in the Dutch Fork, South Carolina. The corps was to consist of eight companies of fifty rank and file each, but it never had more than three hundred and eighty-six men. In December, 1779, McLaurin's name appeared on its muster-roll as lieutenant colonel, a rank which he shared thereafter with Robinson.[61]

By November 1, 1777, the East Florida Rangers numbered one hundred and thirty men, besides the commissioned officers. They were then receiving their clothing and provisions, one shilling a day, and any plunder that might fall into their hands; but Colonel Prevost complained that they were under "no kind of regulation or restriction." In the previous July, Prevost had secured permission from General Howe to organize a troop of fifty mounted rangers for purposes of pursuit. This troop was completed before Christmas, 1777. Early in February of the following year Governor Tonyn consented to having the East Florida Rangers serve under Prevost's command. By this time the corps had reached its full complement, namely, four companies.[62]

The arrival of the South Carolina Royalists and their fellows at Fort Tonyn was reported almost immediately at Savannah by the captain of a vessel which had been taken into the port of St. Augustine and then released. He told that they numbered between three and four hundred, and that they expected seven hundred more to follow them. This item is preserved in one of the letters of Joseph Clay, a revolutionist and merchant of wide business connections in Savannah, who feared that the coast and trade of Georgia would be harassed by a large sloop of fourteen guns commanded by Captain Adam Bachop.[63]

[61] Savary (ed.), *Col. David Fanning's Narrative*, p. 11; *Hist. MSS. Comm., Am. MSS. in R. Inst.*, I. 239, 240, 252, 258, 260, 261, 274; E. A. Jones (ed.), *Journal of Alexander Chesney*, Ohio State University *Bulletin*, October 30, 1921, p. 6, n. 39, p. 83; Capt. L. Butler, *Annals of the King's R. Rifle Corps*, I. app. II, "Memoir of Maj. P. Murray," p. 303; *Second Report*, Bureau of Archives, Ont., 1904, pt. II. 1132; H. E. Egerton (ed.), *R. Comm. on Loyalist Claims, 1783-1785*, pp. 61-62.

[62] *Hist. MSS. Comm., Am. MSS. in R. Inst.*, I. 124, 148, 166, 193.

[63] *Letters of Joseph Clay*, Savannah, Ga., 1776-1793, pp. 70-71.

Shortly after the arrival of the band of South Carolinians came an even larger company of loyalists, known as the Scopholites from one of their leaders, Colonel Scophol of the South Carolina militia. They had assembled near Ninety-Six early in April, 1778, coming from the interior of the province. After crossing the Savannah River, some forty miles below Augusta, they were joined by a party from Georgia under the command of Colonel Thomas. The number of the combined force was between four and five hundred men. Passing through scattered settlements, they plundered and destroyed on their way to East Florida. In June they were in camp on St. Marys River and were later sent to convey their booty beyond the St. Johns. At the end of May, Joseph Clay had written that parties from East Florida were still committing depredations by land and water. By that time, or earlier, the revolutionists had found it dangerous to attempt to bring rice from Broughton Island. Already by mid-April, Colonel Elbert had received intelligence of about four hundred insurgents under the leadership of a Colonel Murphey, so styled, who were evidently on their way to St. Marys. Two prisoners, who had escaped from these insurgents, came to Elbert's headquarters at Fort Howe on the Altamaha and reported them, giving the additional information that at least fifteen hundred more men from the back parts of South Carolina intended to join them. Elbert mentioned that seven men from Colonel Marbury's regiment, which was stationed beyond the Ogeechee, had deserted to the enemy on the march, and that he himself hoped when the insurgents little expected it to "give them a brush at St. Marys."[64]

Political refugees from North Carolina also arrived in East Florida during this time. Colonel David Fanning arranged with Colonel Ambrose Mills of Green River in the former province to embody five hundred loyalists for the purpose of joining the British at St. Augustine. This plan was betrayed, and Colonel Mills and sixteen others were lodged in Salisbury jail. Doubtless some of Mills's men succeeded in crossing St. Marys River. Lieutenant Colonel John Hamilton, a merchant of Halifax, North Carolina, was imprisoned in the summer of 1777 for refusing to take the oath

[64] C. C. Jones, *Hist. of Georgia*, II. 287; Sabine, *Loyalists of the Am. Rev.*, II. 267; *Letters of Joseph Clay*, Savannah, Ga., 1776-1793, p. 76; *Collections* of Georgia Hist. Soc., V. pt. 2 (Order Book of Samuel Elbert), pp. 125-126.

to the state and renounce allegiance to the king, with the option of quitting the country in sixty days. A considerable number of his fellow loyalists found themselves in the same predicament. On August 27, Hamilton wrote from Hillsboro to Governor Richard Caswell, enclosing a petition on behalf of his brother Archibald, himself, and others to be permitted by the council to leave the state. He said that the party would be ready by September 25 at Halifax or Edenton, as might be decided, for escort under guard. He also promised to transmit a list of his associates in due time. This party of loyalists, like others from North Carolina, proceeded to New York, where Governor Josiah Martin then was. On January 23, 1778, Governor Martin wrote to Lord Germain that not less than one hundred and fifty of these refugees had arrived since the preceding August, including Messrs. Hamilton and Macleod, the latter being a Presbyterian clergyman. These two, he added, "had formed a well concerted plan by drawing out of that province, for His Majesty's service the loyal Highlanders, of whom they have two hundred and seventy odd men actually under the most solemn engagements to join them on a summons." Doubtless Mr. Hamilton was commissioned lieutenant colonel by Governor Martin.

Some months later he and his comrades proceeded to St. Augustine, where he formed his corps, the Royal North Carolina Regiment, partly of refugees from the other southern provinces. In his subsequent operations to the northward, he gained many recruits. In the early summer of 1780, two of his officers, John Moore and Nicholas Welsh, enlisted thirteen hundred men in Tryon and the adjoining counties of North Carolina and in the latter part of June met disaster at Ramsour's mill at the hands of a much smaller force dispatched against them by General Griffith Rutherford. In a letter to Sir Henry Clinton, written at the end of the same month, Lord Cornwallis asserted that these loyalists had been "excited by the sanguine emissaries of the very sanguine and imprudent Lieutenant Colonel Hamilton." By mid-August, 1780, the Royal North Carolina Regiment comprised eight companies and numbered four hundred and sixty men.

A few days later, in the battle near Camden, South Carolina, Hamilton was wounded, but his regiment accompanied Cornwallis and his army on his advance into North Carolina, where the officers for twenty-two companies of royalist militia were appointed by Hamilton's orders, these companies being apportioned among Anson, Chatham, Cumberland, Orange, and Randolph counties. By laws enacted in 1777 and 1779 by the general assembly of North Carolina, the property of John and Archibald Hamilton and several scores of their fellow loyalists was confiscated. John also lost his possessions in Virginia by the law of forfeiture passed there in the spring of 1779. It is generally conceded that Lieutenant Colonel Hamilton was a gentleman of culture and refinement, both brave and honorable as a soldier, and that he did not tolerate plunder and murder by his troops.[65]

In the spring of 1778, the expedition against East Florida, conducted by Brigadier General Robert Howe, moved to the southward. With the expedition marched a group of thirty South Carolina loyalists with the double purpose of avoiding the necessity of taking the state oath and of getting within the British lines in East Florida. As one of their number, who was sent ahead to find a path of escape, did not return, they continued with Howe's force.[66] At Frederica, Colonel Elbert, with three hundred men and two fieldpieces on board three galleys, surprised the armed ship *Hinchenbrook*, the sloop *Rebecca*, and a brigantine, and effected their capture without the loss of a man. This loss was reported by General Prevost in a letter of April 27, which erroneously stated that the vessels had been destroyed by the enemy.[67] Meantime, the *Perseus*, *Daphne*, and *Galatea*, which were in the service of East Florida, cruised off the coast, and brought several prizes to St. Augustine, including merchant ships from France with the chevalier de Bretigny, sixteen of his officers, and two hundred of his men, who had come over to join the Americans. They were kept as prisoners of war in the state house.

[65] J. W. Moore, *Hist. of North Carolina*, I. 249-251; Egerton (ed.), *R. Comm. on Loyalist Claims, 1783-1785*, p. 221; Savary (ed.), *Col. David Fanning's Narrative*, p. 12; *State Records of North Carolina*, XI. 596-597, XIII. 367, XIV. xiii, 866-869, XV. 261, XXIV. 9, 12, 123, 209-214, 263; D. Schenck, *North Carolina, 1780-1781*, pp. 273-274; Ashe, *Hist. of North Carolina*, I. 547, 579, 598, 680; E. A. Jones (ed.), *Journal of Alexander Chesney*, pp. 72, 102; *Clinton-Cornwallis Controversy*, I. 235; Sabine, *Loyalists of the Am. Rev.*, I. 511-512, II. 100-103. See also Additional Notes, in Volume II. of this work, pp. 333-335.

[66] *Hist. MSS. Comm., Am. MSS. in R. Inst.*, I. 197-198; Egerton (ed.), *R. Comm. on Loyalist Claims, 1783-1785*, p. 49.

[67] Butler, *Annals of the King's R. Rifle Corps*, app. II. 303.

Campaigns against East Florida

The approach of Howe's force aroused Prevost to active measures of defense and stirred Governor Tonyn's fears, especially as Superintendent Stuart's agents had told the lower Creeks and the Seminoles that their services would not be needed. The governor tried to undo this mischief by sending an express urging the warriors of the nearest Creek towns to come to St. Marys at once. Another aggravation was Prevost's objection to Lieutenant Colonel Browne's exercising command over British officers of lesser rank in the regular service. Fearing the worst, Tonyn issued a proclamation in May, 1778, calling on all inhabitants not already in military organization to take up arms. He had already collected a hundred recruits to man his galleys and floating batteries.[68]

On May 26, the Americans were at Fort Howe, and were receiving intelligence of the disposition of the troops in East Florida. According to their information three hundred men were on St. Marys, sixty with two 24-pounders on St. Johns River, three hundred and fifty Scopholites at the head of Trout Creek, three hundred and twenty men in garrison at St. Augustine, and eighty below that place. They heard also that Tonyn's militia numbered only a hundred fighting men and the Indians only a hundred and fifty renegades. They had even heard rumors of the dispute over Browne's military authority to the effect that the East Florida Rangers threatened to desert in a body on account of it. The officers beyond the St. Marys were equally well informed concerning the strength and movements of Howe's troops. Prevost's plan was not to oppose them until they reached the provincial boundary, where Browne and his rangers would resist their passage of St. Marys River with the support of Major Prevost and the South Carolina Royalists. In case the latter force was obliged to retreat, it would be protected by a small fortification on the north side of St. Johns River and an armed vessel stationed there. Batteries and two detachments of regulars would hold the south side. Ten miles behind these Prevost and the garrison would have their position, except a number of men left at St. Augustine to protect Fort George.[69]

On June 23, the Americans crossed the Satilla and encamped not far

---

[68] *Hist. MSS. Comm., Am. MSS. in R. Inst.*, I. 243-244, 247, 252.
[69] *Ibid.*, I. 253, 259, 261, 266.

from Fort McIntosh on St. Marys River. On the following day, about one thousand of them landed at Amelia Narrows, and began to cut a passage through. On account of the wrangling between the East Florida officers and their men at this juncture, Lieutenant Colonel Fuser could not muster a force sufficient to oppose the invaders and had to retire and fortify St. Johns Bluff. On June 26, the expedition arrived at Armstrong on St. Marys. Thence a reconnoitering party advanced to the north side of that river to a swamp opposite Fort Tonyn.

The people of St. Augustine were so alarmed by the approach of Howe's men that many of them carried their valuables on shipboard. The intelligence received by the Americans was that the two lines of defense of the town were weak and in bad repair, that press gangs of negroes were working on the fortifications, that the garrison of the castle had plenty of provisions but not the population of the town, and that the harbor of St. Augustine was without a war vessel.

Brigadier General Prevost advanced with a force to St. Johns River and Colonel Browne with the rangers and Indians to St. Marys, where he took post at Fort McIntosh. Browne and his party quickly found themselves hemmed in by General James Screven and Colonel White with their detachments. Nevertheless, they managed to escape into the Cabbage Swamp. Major Prevost with a body of regulars and the South Carolina Royalists, numbering together about four hundred and fifty men, moved forward and took post at Alligator Creek bridge. Thence he sent Major Graham with two hundred men, including some of McGirth's rangers, toward the swamp to afford relief to Browne and his marooned party. Issuing from the interior of the morass, where many of them had lost their guns, Browne's men proceeded a few miles farther to reconnoiter, while Major Prevost dispatched a detachment under Captains Murray and York to disperse a party of Americans encamped at Nassau Bluff. The British detachment soon fell back to Alligator Creek, and Browne and his rangers followed a little later. As the latter were crossing the bridge into camp, a pursuing party of the enemy attacked, shouting, "Down with the Tories!" The rangers under Captains Smith and Johnston stood to the defense until the British regulars caught up their arms and relieved them. A few of the rangers were wounded, including Captains Johnston and Smith, and General Screven was also wounded, after which the Americans fled. On the following morning, Major Prevost and part of his men retired to Six Mile Creek, leaving a few Indians to observe the enemy. On June 30, Lieutenant Colonel Browne sent word to Governor Tonyn from Alligator Creek bridge that he had met and driven back the rebels with the aid of Major Prevost's regulars. Retiring at once to Fort Tonyn, the East Florida troops evacuated and burned it on July 2. A day later Howe's men took possession, and found stores and baggage buried under the barracks. Advices were received here, and soon confirmed, that a detachment of the East Florida Rangers under Captain Moore had been attacked near Augusta, Georgia, and the officer killed and twenty of his men taken.[70]

In this account of Howe's "campaign to the southward," which is based chiefly on John Faucheraud Grimké's chronicle and Major Patrick Murray's memoir, nothing has been said of the tribulations through which the American army passed, but the hospital returns show that half of the men were on the sick list, that before the retreat was ordered more than three hundred of the South Carolina Continentals had died, and that the total loss of the expedition exceeded five hundred men. Under such conditions, and with the command torn by factions, it is no wonder that a council of war, convened at Fort Tonyn on July 11, decided in favor of abandoning the expedition. If the expedition had had competent leadership and been conducted at the proper season it might have subjugated St. Augustine.

Brigadier General Prevost had begun to place his troops in the posture of defense in different locations as early as May 1. The intelligence brought to St. Augustine about a month later was that the enemy had a camp of two thousand men near the former site of Fort Barrington and another of eighteen hundred on the Ohoopee River, besides six galleys at Darien in the Altamaha. After the Americans had advanced to the south side of St. Marys River, General Prevost had repaired to the Cowford on the St. Johns; and from there, on July 11, he wrote to General Clinton that he

[70] Capt. L. Butler, *Annals of the King's R. Rifle Corps*, app. II. 304-305; *Hist. MSS. Comm., Am. MSS. in R. Inst.*, I. 251, 269; *Collections* of Georgia Hist. Soc., V. 2 (Order Book of Samuel Elbert), p. 176; McCall, *Hist. of Georgia*, II. 137 ff.; Moultrie, *Memoirs of Am. Rev.*, I. 212-236; C. C. Jones, *Hist. of Georgia*, II. 293-303.

had left the garrison in charge of Lieutenant Colonel Fuser, that orders had been sent to Major Prevost and his corps of South Carolina Royalists, reinforced by one hundred and seventy regulars, to approach St. Marys as near as prudence would permit in order to favor the retreat of Lieutenant Colonel Browne and the East Florida Rangers, to protect the planters on the branches of the Nassau in bringing off their effects, and to intercept any advance parties of the enemy. The rangers had declined in number to fifty or sixty men from desertion and other causes, and fell back under orders on Major Prevost's force just in time to escape from a forward detachment of one hundred and twenty mounted Americans. This detachment was checked by the light company posted north of the St. Johns. In turn Major Prevost and his men fell back to a strong position six miles north of the Cowford. The East Florida parties took at different times some prisoners and about ninety horses, besides disabling many others. General Prevost reported that Howe's land force numbered scarcely more than twenty-five hundred men, while his naval force near the mouth of St. Marys consisted of five galleys, two flats, and other craft carrying three hundred and fifty men, thirty cannon ranging from four- to eighteen-pounders, and some swivels.[71]

On August 30, a privateer entered Mosquito Inlet [now Ponce de Leon Inlet], committed depredations, and carried off thirty negroes from New Smyrna. The *Otter*, which was sent to intercept it, was stranded and lost in a gale on Cape Canaveral. As St. Marys Harbor served as a roadstead for British warships and the armed vessels of the province, Captain Keith Elphinstone urged the erection of a post for their protection, while Prevost besought General Clinton to send arms, ammunition, fieldpieces, and men-of-war for coast defense. Late in September, a party of Creeks visited St. Augustine, evidently bringing news of Indian raids into the neighboring provinces.[72]

The increasing bitterness of the struggle in the Carolinas and in Georgia and the enactment of laws by their assemblies late in 1777 and early in 1778 that weighed heavily upon the loyalists, were reflected in numerous

[71] *Hist. MSS. Comm., Am. MSS. in R. Inst.,* I. 259, 271-272.
[72] *Ibid.,* pp. 293, 302, 304.

accessions of refugees to the population of East Florida. In September, 1777, an act was passed in Georgia for the expulsion of the internal enemies of the state, and less than five months later two other measures were adopted by the assembly at Savannah: one to prevent the dangerous consequences that might arise from the practices of disaffected persons under its jurisdiction, and the other for attainting of high treason those named in the act and for confiscating their estates. In November, a law was enacted in North Carolina for confiscating the property of all persons inimical to the United States, of those who should fail to apply for citizenship within a specified time, and of those who, though applying, should be denied citizenship. This law was supplemented by a drastic enforcement act early in the following year. Section XXXVI of the constitution adopted by South Carolina in March, 1778, provided that all officers, civil and military, must take an oath to the state, abjure allegiance to the crown, and swear to defend the state against the king, his assistants, and adherents. In the same month the assembly of South Carolina passed an act obliging every free male inhabitant to give assurance of fidelity and allegiance to the state. This test act was supplemented by two ordinances adopted in October, one exacting the oath of allegiance to the state or immediate sale of one's property and departure within a month thereafter, and the other empowering the president or commander-in-chief, with the advice of the privy council, to confine all persons whose going at large might endanger the safety of the state. These drastic laws stimulated flight to East Florida to such a degree that nearly seven thousand loyalists from Carolina and Georgia are said to have entered the province during the year 1778.[78]

[78] C. H. Van Tyne, *The Loyalists of the Am. Rev.*, pp. 325, 333, 339, 340; *Statutes of South Carolina*, I. 144, 147; *State Records of North Carolina*, XXIV. 9-12, 123, 209-214; Nevins, *The Am. States during and after the Rev., 1775-1789*, pp. 97, 365, 372. G. R. Fairbanks, *Hist. of Florida*, p. 226; S. Lanier, *Florida*, pp. 194-195; *Collections* of Georgia Hist. Soc., V. pt. 2, pp. 62-63. Among the loyalists who came in from South Carolina in 1778 were George Schobert and Christian Sing, both from Ninety-Six District, who joined the South Carolina Royalists; Robert Phillips, a brother of Colonel John Phillips of Camden District, who became a lieutenant in the East Florida Rangers; Robert Robinson and his family of Charleston, who were permitted to leave in the sloop *Vulture* for St. Augustine and arrived in July; John Imrie, also of Charleston, and Benjamin Lord and his family, who likewise came in July. In the following September Governor Tonyn appointed Mr. Lord acting surveyor

At the end of April of the year above mentioned, Brigadier General Prevost wrote from St. Augustine that "the great increase of public expenses arising from the support of the unfortunate refugees from the neighboring colonies" would require a sum additional to that sent in the previous July. Obviously, many of the exiles were dependent on public funds supplied through the commandant until they could find remunerative employment, or enter a provincial corps or the militia. Not a few came with means enough to buy, or build, houses in St. Augustine, and to acquire and clear land, erect buildings, and make other improvements on plantations which they developed and worked in many instances with the labor of the slaves they had brought with them. Numerous instances will be found in the documents printed in the second volume of this work of grants of land, large and small, made to refugees as well as to the older inhabitants by Governor Tonyn.[74]

The governor had been accused in England in one of Dr. Turnbull's memorials of granting lands to some persons not entitled to them and refusing grants to others who had no claim or right thereto. This charge did not refer to grants made to the refugees. Turnbull also alleged that Tonyn had decided causes cognizable in the courts of justice only; that he had borrowed money from many of the inhabitants, giving them bills payable in London that came back protested; that he had obtained receipts for public work done and then refused to pay the workmen; that he had bought up staple provisions and tried to sell them at a double price; and that he inflicted cruel punishments on his servants and negroes, often with his own hands. James Penman had received some of the protested bills, and the officers of the garrison undoubtedly knew that a master builder had refused to repair the platform for the guns in Fort George on account of

general of East Florida. Among the Georgians arriving in the same year was James Robertson, acting attorney general of his province, who was banished for refusing to take the oath of abjuration. After spending three months in the island of New Providence, he went to St. Augustine but returned to Savannah on its surrender to the British (*Second Report*, Bureau of Archives, Ont., 1904, pt. I. 674, 676, II. 1132; E. A. Jones (ed.), *Journal of Alexander Chesney*, pp. 60, 61. See Volume II. of this work, pp. 18, 20, 195, 196; Egerton (ed.), *R. Comm. on Loyalist Claims, 1783-1785*, pp. 61, 62).

[74] *Hist. MSS. Comm., Am. MSS. in R. Inst.*, I. 242.

Tonyn's failure to pay workmen. Chief Justice Drayton, who had accompanied Turnbull to England, had refused after their return to try the cases of the colonists from New Smyrna who claimed release from their indentures.

Drayton's return from England with his friend, in November, 1777, was the occasion for a renewal of hostilities not only between Turnbull and Tonyn but also between Drayton and the governor. In fact, late in the preceding September, a deposition had been made by James Coats at the instance of Tonyn in regard to the "capitulation" proposed by a group of gentlemen, including Drayton, early in May of that year at the time of Colonel Elbert's expedition to St. Marys River. On his return and reinstatement in the office of chief justice, Drayton failed to call on the governor, giving as an explanation—according to Tonyn—that to do so would have the appearance of triumph and insult and that matters had gone too far to permit cordial relations between them, although the governor claimed that he had intended to behave toward Drayton "with freedom and candor and seek a general reconciliation." Instead of so doing, however, he made a charge against the chief justice of having been deficient in giving the aid to government that might have been expected from one in his position as a zealous servant of the crown. Drayton conveyed this information to Lieutenant Colonel Fuser in a letter of November 28, reminding him that in the previous spring he had offered twenty-two of his negroes to work on the fortifications and had enlisted as a volunteer in Fuser's battalion of the 60th Regiment. He also asked him to declare these and other instances of his readiness to aid the king's officers and state whether Fuser had any reason to think him deficient in his duty either as an official or a loyal subject.

Colonel Fuser replied on December 3 that he was afflicted to hear that differences still existed between his majesty's subjects in St. Augustine, that all animosity should be laid aside in view of the rebellion, that it was to be expected that the enemy was "flushed with their late success," and that the Indians had been unfavorable to the Floridians for some time. He enclosed the desired evidence of Drayton's zeal in behalf of the crown and stated that James Penman, Spencer Man, and others had been accepted as volunteers in his battalion. He also enclosed a letter signed by the officers of the third and fourth battalions of the 60th Regiment at his request that they had read both Drayton's letter and Fuser's reply and believed that the latter was founded on fact.

Tonyn spent the next twelve days in procuring letters and affidavits from Lieutenant Colonel Thomas Browne, Captain James Moore, Alexander Gray, Robert Payne, Captain Robert Bisset, James Penman, Jermyn Wright, and Captain George Osborne concerning Drayton's promotion of the proposed capitulation in the preceding May and his criticisms of the provincial administration and in preparing a "replication to Drayton's defense." These documents he laid before his council.

On December 11, the governor's charges against the chief justice were read to the board by its clerk, after which Drayton presented his defense and left a copy. Two days later Tonyn brought several gentlemen to give evidence in support of the charges, but the absence of other witnesses caused delay. Part of the evidence was heard on December 15, although Drayton was not yet ready with his witnesses. The trial was completed on the next day. In his replication Tonyn insisted that Drayton's public conduct was far from what he represented it to have been, that he treated "with asperity" an anonymous publication, which was a brief list of satirical queries and answers reflecting on those who had recommended the capitulation, that Drayton was then prosecuting Mr. Mackie, the surgeon of the East Florida Rangers, for defamation and reporting a hearsay story about himself, that the officers of government were in the first instance accountable to him for their conduct, that Drayton had joined the 60th Regiment instead of the militia, thus avoiding submission, he might have added, to the governor's military command, and that the officers of the regiment had little opportunity to know Drayton's character, since some of them had arrived but lately and most were foreigners "unacquainted with the Civil Constitution" of the province. The hearing of the evidence on both sides having been finished on December 16, including Drayton's defense and Tonyn's replication, the council voted to suspend the chief justice until the king's pleasure should be known.

A phase of the struggle between these two officials, which appears to have been omitted from the replication but was referred to in an address to

Campaigns against East Florida 65

the governor at this time "from the Inhabitants of East Florida and Refugees from neighboring Provinces," was a petition to the throne in the name of the grand jurors, inhabitants, and refugees prepared by the grand jury under the influence of Drayton and the anti-Tonyn faction. This petition expressed the conviction that the present provincial régime left much to be desired as regards security, intimating that a general assembly to legislate for the improvement of local conditions and the common defense was highly desirable. The establishment of a popular assembly had long been a bone of contention between the two factions.

The address to Tonyn was signed by two hundred and twenty-nine inhabitants and refugees. It opened with the usual statement found in such addresses that the signers were sensible of the many blessings they had enjoyed under the mild, just, and auspicious government of the king and were convinced that it had ever been the governor's study to promote the true interest and welfare of the province and the service of his royal master. With deepest concern and indignation they regarded the petition to the throne, which was highly derogatory and injurious to the governor's character. They acknowledged with warmest gratitude the seasonable and vigorous efforts he had made to put the province in a respectable state of defense previous to a daring invasion by rebels, to which they owed under God the preservation of their laws, their liberty, and their lives. A closing paragraph stated that the refugees were peculiarly sensible how much they owed to Tonyn's goodness and made acknowledgment for the kind relief and support many of them had received at his hands.[74a]

In March, 1778, Drayton sold his property in East Florida with the purpose of leaving the province. About April 1, Tonyn suspended him from the office of chief justice for the second time as "the head of a faction against administration." Not long thereafter he removed to South Carolina, and settled at Magnolia Gardens or Drayton Hall, near Charleston.[75]

Tonyn dealt more severely with Dr. Turnbull. After his reinstatement, the latter wrote to the former on August 7, 1778, that he intended to live

---

[74a] C. O. 5/559, pp. 527-580, 595-600, 605-614.

[75] C. O. 5/546; Carita Doggett, *Dr. Andrew Turnbull and New Smyrna Colony*, pp. 145-151. See also Additional Notes, in Volume II. of this work, p. 316.

henceforth in St. Augustine and would serve as secretary and clerk of the council. However, Tonyn denied him the right to exercise those offices, though permitting him to receive the salary. Further, he alleged that Turnbull was evading the payment of a large indebtedness on the New Smyrna estate, despite the fact that he had previously admitted that the doctor's reverses had left him without the means of payment. Nevertheless, on February 17, 1780, an order was issued requiring Turnbull to pay £4,000 bail. Being unable to do so, he was taken into custody by the provost marshal and kept a prisoner for a year and seven months. The property at New Smyrna was divided among the heirs of the original proprietors, only a small part falling to Dr. Turnbull. In letters to Lord Germain, Tonyn did not hesitate to charge Turnbull with disloyalty to England.[76]

In the early autumn of 1778, negroes, horses, and other property in Georgia were being continually carried off by "Tonyn's banditti," who came from East Florida in small companies of five or six each. Three members of such a party were killed during the week preceding September 9 by Georgia scouts. When captured, these raiders claimed treatment as prisoners of war on the ground that they were soldiers in the king's service. Some of them had commissions. The Indians were also an annoyance. Once the banditti approached within two or three miles of Savannah and carried off one or two negroes, and they collected horses from all parts of Georgia.[77]

For several months there had been an apprehension in Georgia that the troops in East Florida were getting ready for an invasion. General Howe had voiced this fear to his council of war at Fort Tonyn in July, 1778, when he gave certain reasons in justification of it. Those reasons were: the movements of the enemy in Florida, the posts occupied by them and others which they were trying to secure, the positions of their armed vessels and men-of-war, the number of insurgents who were taking arms in Georgia and South Carolina and concentrating in East Florida, and the information that was being brought from St. Augustine by deserters, spies, and others.

[76] C. O. 5/558; Carita Doggett, *Dr. Andrew Turnbull and New Smyrna Colony*, pp. 171-173. See also Additional Notes, in Volume II. of this work, pp. 325-327.

[77] *Letters of Joseph Clay*, Savannah, Ga., 1776-1793, pp. 101, 106, 109.

Howe thought these signs pointed to an immediate invasion.[78] However, the movement did not begin until in November.

Just what the refugees who were entering East Florida during this period were costing the provincial government, cannot be determined accurately, because the general account for the extraordinary expenses created by them includes sundry expenses incurred for the care of prisoners of war. The total outlay for these two classes of persons during the year and a half from June 25, 1777, to December 25, 1778, was £2,363. The presence of the prisoners of war involved a large expenditure for the repair of prisons and for other measures of safety. These and other items connected with their custody amounted to about £1,515. The sum of £392 was expended solely for the benefit of refugees, and of the residue, amounting to about £1,457, a fraction went to the care of prisoners of war. Probably this fraction was small, inasmuch as the refugees were far more numerous, many were in destitute circumstances, and hundreds had entered the military service of the province.[78a]

A glance at the exports of East Florida during the years 1776, 1777, and 1778 will show what the productive occupations of the inhabitants, including the rapidly increasing number of refugees, were. It will also show the attempts made to cultivate certain products, supposed to be especially adapted to the soil and climatic conditions of the province, and will explain the increased export of certain items as in part due to the influx of loyalists and their slaves. As one would expect the products of the forests maintain the lead, and hunting, cattle raising, and barter with the Indians supply the next important items for export in the form of deerskins, raw hides, and some tanned leather. During the year 1776, the shipments included over fifty thousand feet of pine boards and timber, nearly eighty-seven thousand oak staves, seven thousand six hundred pine staves, nearly fifty-three thousand feet of mahogany, forty-two and one-half tons of camwood, thirty thousand shingles, one hundred and ninety barrels of tar, fifty-six barrels of turpentine, nearly fifty-eight thousand three hundred casks of indigo, twenty thousand casks of deerskins, fifty-five hundred casks of tanned leather, three hundred and forty-five raw hides, twenty-eight calf skins,

---

[78] C. C. Jones, *Hist. of Georgia*, II. 298.   [78a] C. O. 5/559, pp. 125-128.

eight hundred and sixty barrels of rice, eight hundred and fifty casks of coffee, seventy-eight puncheons, casks, and barrels of rum, but only one hogshead of sugar and one of molasses, several hogsheads, barrels, and pipes of Madeira wine, over sixty-five thousand oranges and two casks of orange juice, forty-six barrels of flour, ninety-three gallons of honey, eight tons of elephants' teeth, one case of raw silk, and eight negroes.

During 1777, the forest products show a large increase over the preceding year. The items are five hundred and fifty-three thousand feet of pine boards and timber, four hundred and nineteen thousand oak staves, fifty-two thousand feet of mahogany, one hundred and twenty-four thousand five hundred cypress shingles, four thousand hoops, one hundred and twenty handspikes, twenty-two hundred and forty-one barrels of tar, and four hundred and seventeen barrels of turpentine; the indigo drops to fourteen thousand and seventy casks; the shipment of skins and hides falls to fourteen thousand eight hundred casks of deerskins and one hundred and forty raw hides; the quantity of rice is increased to eleven hundred and sixty-seven barrels and twenty-one half barrels; the coffee mounts to thirty-seven hundred and fifty casks, and fifty-eight hundred and seventy casks of cocoa are added; the rum drops to one-sixth of the former amount; there are five hogsheads, barrels, and casks of sugar, but the molasses jumps to one hundred and forty-eight hogsheads, and the list is concluded by over nineteen hundred bushels of salt, two tons of ivory, four boxes of tortoise-shell, three boxes of medicine, and six bales and boxes of dry-goods.

During the third year of this period the exports were: four hundred and sixty-eight thousand eight hundred feet of pine boards and timber, three hundred and twenty thousand oak staves, forty-eight thousand five hundred feet of mahogany, four hundred feet of cedar and red bay, forty-six thousand cypress shingles, over twenty-three hundred hickory handspikes, over eighty-one hundred barrels of tar and about nineteen hundred and eighty barrels of turpentine, twenty-nine thousand two hundred and sixty casks of indigo, nearly thirty-four hundred and seventy casks of deerskins, two hundred and thirty raw hides, and fifty-two sides of tanned leather, four hundred and fifty-five barrels, thirty-three half barrels, and thirty-four bags of rice, nearly forty-three hundred casks of coffee, eleven casks of sugar, two hundred and six hogsheads of molasses, thirty-one puncheons of rum, eight hogsheads, quarter casks, and pipes of Madeira wine, three hogsheads of claret wine, five thousand oranges and sixteen hogsheads of orange juice, five barrels of vinegar, sixty-seven hundred bushels of salt, three hundred and one hogsheads of tobacco, sixteen bags of cotton, two casks of old copper, forty-nine bags of ginger, ten casks of sarsaparilla, six thousand casks of pimento, two casks of pinkroot, twenty-five and one-half tons of logwood and lignum vitae, and over two hundred and twenty-five bales, boxes, kegs, and chests of dry-goods.[78b]

[78b] C. O. 5/559, pp. 461, 465, 469.

Chapter V.

The expeditions from St. Augustine to Sunbury, Savannah, and Charleston, November, 1778-April, 1780.—Colonel Archibald Campbell's expedition to Savannah.—The diversion against Sunbury from St. Augustine.—General Prevost's coöperative expedition to Savannah from East Florida.—The surrender of Fort Morris at Sunbury.—The expedition of Colonels Campbell and Hamilton to Augusta.—Colonel Mark Prevost's excursion to Hutson's Ferry and his appointment as lieutenant governor of Georgia.—The defeat of General Ashe at Briar Creek.—The appointment of Colonel Thomas Browne and Alexander Cameron as superintendents of Indian affairs.—Conditions in East Florida.—General Prevost's expedition to Charleston.—The return of his troops to Georgia in successive detachments.—The defense of Savannah against d'Estaing's fleet and Lincoln's army.—Colonel Fuser's defensive measures in East Florida.—Chief Justice James Hume and his villa of Oak Park in East Florida.—The fear of a Spanish attack on St. Augustine.

THE British expedition from New York to Savannah in November, 1778, gave the troops of East Florida, including the provincial regiments, the opportunity to coöperate. Brigadier General Prevost had been notified of the expedition by General Clinton under date of October 20. The fleet and transports with three thousand men on board under the command of Lieutenant Colonel Archibald Campbell, arrived at Tybee Island on December 27. With Campbell were Colonel Alexander Innes and Captain Moses Kirkland, both under orders to render every assistance in their power to the commanding officer.[79]

A little after mid-November, two detachments were sent forward from St. Augustine by Brigadier General Prevost, one of seven hundred and fifty men under the command of his brother, to devastate the country through lower Georgia and to form a junction with Lieutenant Colonel Fuser's detachment at Sunbury, which they were to reduce. The orders issued were that the cavalry should proceed to the Sapello and there await the infantry. Thence they were to march together to attack Sunbury in conjunction with Lieutenant Colonel Fuser's command of two hundred and fifty men of the 4th Battalion, 60th Regiment. Fuser's command was to go by inland

[79] *Hist. MSS. Comm., Am. MSS. in R. Inst.*, I. 314, 323, 339, 340, 359, 368-369; E. A. Jones (ed.), *Journal of Alexander Chesney*, pp. 106-107. See also Additional Notes, in Volume II. of this work, p. 351.

channel, with the armed flat *Thunderer*, while the privateers *Spitfire* and *Alligator* were to alarm the coast.

The land force was led by Lieutenant Colonel James Mark Prevost, and comprised all the cavalry, the grenadiers of the 2d Battalion and seventy men of the 3d Battalion, 60th Regiment, the East Florida Rangers and McGirth's men, and the South Carolina Royalists. Colonel Prevost set out with a hundred regulars, and at Fort Howe was joined by Daniel McGirth with three hundred provincials and Indians. On November 19, they entered the Georgia settlements, taking captives and plunder from the plantations as they went. Near Midway meeting-house they encountered a smaller force of Americans under General Screven and Colonel White. Screven was severely wounded and taken by the enemy. White and the remainder of the party retreated, while McGirth reconnoitered in the direction of Sunbury only to find that Fuser had not arrived there. After burning Midway Meeting-House, Prevost and his force retreated, destroying all buildings and carrying off quantities of booty as they marched.

On November 24, the day of the encounter at Midway, Lieutenant Colonel Fuser and his two hundred and fifty men landed at Colonel's Island, or Colonel's Bluff. Here they heard that a body of three hundred Americans had marched for Sunbury. Sixty of Fuser's party remained with his boats, and the rest proceeded to the same destination under the guidance of several of the East Florida Rangers. At night two detachments entered the town, which seemed to be deserted, its inhabitants having taken refuge in Fort Morris. The next day the armed vessels sailed up the Midway and helped to invest the place. Meantime, Captain Johnston of the rangers betook himself to the meeting-house under the cover of darkness to get news of Prevost. He returned with the information that that officer and his troops were on their way to the Ogeechee. Colonel Fuser summoned the fort to surrender, but received the laconic reply: "Come and take it." However, he forbade the storming of the fort and conducted his party back to the vessels, leaving an "astonished enemy." While embarking, Fuser received a letter by the hand of a ranger from Colonel Prevost, saying that he had retired to Newport with all his booty, had destroyed the bridges in his rear, and could not return to Sunbury. When he reached St.

Marys, Prevost had a public sale of his plunder, from which he took in £8,000. From there he led his force to St. Johns River. On the arrival of Fuser and his little fleet each charged the other with the failure of his own expedition.[80]

Colonel Fuser and his detachment had barely returned to East Florida when they received orders to wait at the south end of Cumberland Island for Brigadier General Augustine Prevost and all the troops of the garrison, except four companies of the 3d Battalion, 60th Regiment, which were to remain at St. Augustine. Prevost incorporated his brother's detachment with his own force, also Lieutenant Colonel Isaac Allen and three companies of the New Jersey Volunteers, who had parted company with Lieutenant Colonel Archibald Campbell's division from New York. Colonel Fuser and his men were added to Prevost's expeditionary force at the south end of Cumberland Island. The total force numbered about nine hundred officers and men, of whom over four hundred belonged to General Prevost's own regiment, the 60th, the remainder being composed of a detachment of the 16th, the provincial regiments, and a few artillerymen. James Mark Prevost, now a lieutenant colonel, was second in command.

The supplies for the army were conveyed in boats along the coast. As these were often compelled to make wide detours to avoid the armed vessels of the Americans, the troops were sometimes reduced to the necessity of subsisting on oysters found in inlets of the sea and on a very scanty supply of rice. On January 6, 1779, Colonel's Island, a few miles below Sunbury, was reached, and during the following two days the town was invested by the troops, artillery, and vessels. As Major Lane, the commander of Fort Morris, refused to capitulate when summoned on the 9th, General Prevost opened his batteries and the post soon surrendered. The garrison comprised about two hundred and ten officers and men. More than a hundred prisoners were brought in from the neighborhood by the mounted rangers. Lieutenant Colonel Allen and the New Jersey Volunteers were detailed to garrison duty at Sunbury, the name of Fort Morris was changed to Fort

---

[80] Butler, *Annals of the King's R. Rifle Corps*, app. II. 306-309; C. C. Jones, *Hist. of Georgia*, II. 305-311; Ramsay, *Rev. in South Carolina*, II. 3 ff.; Lee and Agnew, *Hist. Record of City of Savannah*, p. 45; McCrady, *South Carolina in the Rev., 1775-1780*, pp. 324-329.

George, and the prisoners were sent to Savannah by boat, the grenadiers of the 4th Battalion accompanying them as an escort by the inland passage. The rest of the army marched to Savannah by way of the Midway and Ogeechee rivers. General Prevost was escorted by a party of dragoons from Colonel Campbell's mounted infantry, while the country in front was scoured by some East Florida Rangers. Lieutenant Colonel John Hamilton and his Royal North Carolina Regiment seem to have arrived at Savannah in advance of the main body of the expeditionary force, which reached that destination about the middle of January, or more than a fortnight after Colonel Campbell had taken the town. At Savannah General Prevost's army was called the Florida Brigade. Lieutenant Colonel Fuser was at once sent back to assume the command at St. Augustine.[81]

After forming companies of riflemen and dragoons from the inhabitants who had come in to take the oath of allegiance, assigning them to patrol duty in the outlying country, and taking further precautionary measures, Campbell placed Innes in command at Savannah in order that he might himself lead an expedition up the river against Augusta. Lieutenant Colonel John Hamilton and his Royal North Carolina Regiment from East Florida formed a part of this expedition. Augusta was at once evacuated by its garrison of whig militia, and Hamilton with two hundred mounted infantry was soon detached toward the frontiers of Georgia. Disarming the disaffected and encouraging the loyalists, he also reduced a number of stockade forts and repulsed a body of militia under Colonel Andrew Pickens, who had advanced against him from Ninety-Six District. At Augusta, as at Savannah, people flocked in to take the oath and were embodied in companies for defense under officers of their own choice.[82]

It was after the occupation of Augusta by Campbell and Hamilton that Brigadier General Prevost and his men made their belated entrance into

---

[81] Butler, *Annals of the King's R. Rifle Corps*, I. 309-311; *Hist. MSS. Comm., Am. MSS. in R. Inst.*, I. 339, 340; Stedman, *Hist. of the Am. War*, II. 104; McCall, *Hist. of Georgia*, II. 179; C. C. Jones, *Hist. of Georgia*, II. 314-317, 327, 331-333.

[82] Stedman, *Hist. of the Am. War*, 1794, II. 115, 118-121; Sabine, *Loyalists of the Am. Rev.*, I. 100, 246, 325; McCrady, *South Carolina in the Rev.*, 1775-1780, pp. 336-338; C. C. Jones, *Memorial Hist. of Augusta*, pp. 75, 77, 79; Lee and Agnew, *Hist. Record of the City of Savannah*, p. 49.

Military Expeditions and Operations

Savannah. They had been delayed by various causes, but especially by the necessity of transporting their artillery and other "impedimenta" by boat through the inland water-courses of Florida and Georgia. Soon after the Florida Brigade had reached Savannah, Lieutenant Colonel James Mark Prevost undertook an excursion northward to Hutson's ferry with a body of light infantry and the St. Augustine Grenadiers. On the way he routed eighteen hundred whigs, killing about one hundred and taking two hundred prisoners. This success so impressed Campbell that, when he and Hamilton withdrew under orders from Augusta, he transferred his force to Lieutenant Colonel Prevost and returned to Savannah preparatory to his departure for England. He also secured that officer's appointment as the lieutenant governor of Georgia until Sir James Wright should come from the mother country to resume the governorship. James Robertson, a refugee at St. Augustine for the past year, now returned to Savannah and became attorney general, advocate general, and a colonel of the militia. Thus the royal government was revived in Georgia.[83]

Meanwhile, several American officers had planned a concerted movement against the British and loyalists on the mid-waters of the Savannah River. General Ashe had begun this movement by following Lieutenant Colonel Prevost's column down the river and taking his position on Brier Creek, sixty miles from Savannah. Prevost promptly divided his force and on March 3 attacked Ashe's command in front and rear. The Americans were driven from the field, and communication was kept open between the British posts and frontier settlements. About the middle of March, Brigadier General Prevost was at Ebenezer, where he expected a party of Creek Indians to join him.[84] After assuming command of the forces in Georgia,

---

[83] Stedman, *Hist. of the Am. War*, II. 115-116, 121; Lee, *Memoirs of the War in the Southern Department*, 1812, pp. 71-72, 77; McCrady, *South Carolina in the Rev., 1775-1780*, pp. 336-337, 339; *Second Report*, Bureau of Archives, Ont., 1904, pt. II. 113; H. E. Egerton (ed.), *R. Comm. on Loyalist Claims, 1783-1785*, pp. 61-62; *South Carolina Gazette*, February 24, 1779.

[84] Stedman, *Hist. of the Am. War*, II. 121-122; McCrady, *South Carolina in the Rev., 1775-1780*, pp. 344-345; H. Lee, *Memoirs*, I. 78-79; Ramsay, *The Rev. in South Carolina*, II. 16, 17; Ramsay, *Hist. of the Am. Rev.*, II. 115; C. C. Jones, *Hist. of Georgia*, I. 347-352; *Hist. MSS. Comm., Am. MSS. in R. Inst.*, I. 398-399.

General Prevost had employed Benjamin Springer, described in a report of the board of police to Governor Sir James Wright in May, 1780, as "a man of very indifferent character," to collect live stock and provisions for the army. Springer sent out a number of irresponsible men, as did also the commissary. The latter's agents carried off cattle wherever they could find them, while Springer's men plundered the plantations of loyalists and Americans without distinction. Quantities of live stock and provisions were carried into East Florida in the early months of 1779 by these disorderly people, the report states, and there "converted to their own private use & benefit."[85]

On March 25, 1779, John Stuart, the superintendent of Indian affairs, died, and General Prevost nominated Lieutenant Colonel Thomas Browne as his temporary successor. General Clinton appointed until further orders Allan Cameron, who had been Stuart's deputy. Both nominations were sent to Lord Germain, and he submitted them to the king with the suggestion that since operations were pending, both toward the Mississippi and the Atlantic, the southern district be divided. This was done, and on June 25, Germain wrote Clinton that Cameron was to be superintendent of the western division and Browne of the eastern. As the functions of the two superintendents were essentially military, these officials were subordinated to Brigadier General Prevost, or in his absence to the chief officer commanding the troops in the respective divisions.[86]

Since the reduction of Georgia by the British, tranquillity had reigned in East Florida. Governor Tonyn reported that the planters were busy with their accustomed labors and the merchants active in exporting goods. Nevertheless, the coasts of the province were still being subjected to the descents of privateers, three of which had overhauled the *Jason* and its convoy about May 1, 1779.[87]

By this date Augustine Prevost, now a major general with twenty-four hundred men, including the loyalist regiments from East Florida, was three days' march within the boundaries of South Carolina, in an effort to allure

[85] *Collections* of Georgia Historical Society, III. 290-291.
[86] *Hist. MSS. Comm., Am. MSS. in R. Inst.*, I. 419, 423, II. 131.
[87] *Ibid.*, II. 426-427.

General Lincoln and his troops from Georgia. As Prevost advanced he was joined by numbers of loyalists from Georgia and the Carolinas. From some of these he learned of the almost defenseless condition of Charleston. Passing through the richest settlements, the army was followed by hundreds of negroes bringing much portable property belonging to their masters. Camp fever raged among them, and numbers perished. The sick were forsaken, and died in the woods. On the evening of May 10, the British and loyalists reached Ashley ferry, crossed the river, and next day summoned Charleston to surrender. After refusing counter proposals, Prevost decided that the American lines could not be forced without a great loss of his men, recrossed the ferry, and encamped. Some days later he retired to the seacoast and occupied John's Island, but garrisoned a post on the mainland with fifteen hundred men to cover Stono ferry. The report of commotions in Georgia induced Lieutenant Colonel Prevost to leave this post on June 16 with the St. Augustine Grenadiers and the vessels forming the pontoon bridge to the island, and return to Georgia.[88]

During the next three days Lieutenant Colonel John Maitland evacuated the post at Stono, having to convey across Stono Inlet the garrison and its sick members, the Indians, the horses, and the baggage. Many of the negroes were left behind for want of transportation. Some were drowned while attempting to cling to the boats. In its reduced condition the garrison numbered eight hundred men. It included among the other regiments at least two of loyalists from St. Augustine, namely, the North and South Carolina Provincials under the command of Lieutenant Colonel Hamilton. From John's Island General Prevost wrote to General Clinton, giving the hot season as his reason for removing the troops to Beaufort and the neighboring islands. He spoke of drafting the second battalion of the South Carolina Royalists into the first on account of the depletion of the former, and said that the Royal North Carolina Regiment was in a similar condition. He added that Governor Tonyn had consented that the East Florida Rangers should no longer be distinct from the other provincial regiments.[88a]

---

[88] *Hist. MSS. Comm., Am. MSS. in R. Inst.*, I. 472; Stedman, *Hist. of the Am. War*, I. 123, 125, 126, 129; McCrady, *South Carolina in the Rev., 1775-1780*, pp. 351-353, 365, 382, 384-385.

[88a] See Volume II. of this work, pp. 375-376.

When early in July the troops reached Otter Island, the negroes were segregated. Here hundreds of them died of camp fever. In 1785, the island was still strewn with their bones. The three thousand who survived were shipped to Georgia and East Florida and were sold in the West Indies.[89]

Arriving at Beaufort, on Port Royal Island, on July 8, General Prevost learned that numerous inhabitants in the interior of Georgia, including some who had taken the oath of allegiance, had "infested the lower settlements" under arms, and that a party of the 60th Regiment on the Ogeechee had been intercepted and its captain killed. He therefore dispatched the East Florida Rangers and other regiments into Georgia and hastened back to Savannah, leaving a few troops under Maitland to protect Beaufort and the islands, most of whose inhabitants had already submitted themselves to the British. He found much sickness among the troops in Georgia, especially at Ebenezer, and feared that he might not save both the army and the province.[90]

At Sheldon, some fifteen miles from Beaufort, were General Lincoln and eight hundred continentals, watching the British garrison on Port Royal and Lady's islands. Lincoln now joined with Governor Rutledge and the French consul at Charleston in inviting Count d'Estaing, commander of the French fleet in the West Indies, to lay siege to Savannah. On September 4, 1779, six French vessels appeared off the bar at Savannah, but departed the next day. Four days later the whole fleet was sighted, and orders were issued to put Savannah "in the best posture of defense." Outlying garrisons were called in, including Maitland and his troops from Beaufort. In the dispositions made to man the redoubts the loyalist regiments from East Florida are mentioned, Lieutenant Colonel Browne and the Carolina King's Rangers being assigned to that on the left, Lieutenant Colonel Hamilton and the Royal North Carolina Regiment to that in the center, and the South Carolina Royalists to that on the right. Although the force in Savannah numbered scarcely more than twenty-five hundred men, and the besiegers fully seven thousand after Lincoln's army joined the three thou-

---

[89] *Hist. MSS. Comm., Am. MSS. in R. Inst.*, I. 437, 447-448, 472; Stedman, *Hist. of the Am. War*, II. 129-132; McCrady, *South Carolina in the Rev., 1775-1780*, pp. 384-390.
[90] *Hist. MSS. Comm., Am. MSS. in R. Inst.*, I. 473.

sand French troops on September 23, the assault, which was made on October 9, failed at every point. Count d'Estaing reëmbarked his men for the West Indies, while Lincoln and his army departed for Charleston.[91]

During the past ten or eleven months, East Florida had remained without any military protection, except that afforded by a garrison of two hundred men at St. Augustine under the command of Lieutenant Colonel Lewis V. Fuser. Late in September, 1779, this officer began to repair the fortifications, and a month later was employing half of his soldiers and three hundred negroes on the works. As ready money was required for this object, Fuser applied to James Penman. The latter told him that, although more than a year before he had advanced £3,000 for the South Carolina Royalists, his purse and his credit were available as far as they would go. Mr. Penman complained that, ever since General Prevost's departure to Savannah Lieutenant Governor Moultrie had denied that that officer's authority extended to East Florida, but had devolved upon Governor Tonyn. Fuser said that he himself expected little from Tonyn and Moultrie, except "fine promises, pompous writing and nothing done," and that all they had accomplished in the present emergency was to provide three small galleys.[92]

At Fuser's request Penman went, late in September, to Jericho on St. Johns River to obtain news from Georgia, keep the inhabitants on their plantations, help them devise ways of protecting themselves against small invading parties, and report the movements of the Americans in case they should advance against East Florida. On receiving word of the British success at Savannah, the planters took their negroes from the military works, following the example of Governor Tonyn, Lieutenant Governor Moultrie, and Attorney General Henry Yonge. In a letter of December 12, Fuser protested to General Clinton that his command was too small to defend East Florida in case of invasion, and intimated that he had so written to General Prevost. The latter appealed to Clinton for three hundred more troops for Fuser, together with ammunition and provisions. Very

[91] *Hist. MSS. Comm., Am. MSS. in R. Inst.*, I. 483, II. 26-27, 33-34, 47, 55; Stedman, *Hist. of the Am. War*, II. 134-135, 137; McCrady, *South Carolina in the Rev., 1775-1780*, pp. 396, 402, 405-407, 410, 412-417, 419.

[92] *Hist. MSS. Comm., Am. MSS. in R. Inst.*, II. 37, 38-39, 40.

soon Major General Alexander Leslie arrived at St. Augustine from New York and saw the situation for himself. Thence he went to Savannah, where he and Prevost decided to send the 60th, or Royal American, Regiment to reinforce the garrison in East Florida. This addition raised the number of troops at Fort George to four hundred and fifty. Fuser's death was reported on February 5, 1780. He had shown himself to be an intelligent and energetic officer and had commanded the financial resources of the merchant, James Penman, in behalf of the province. Nevertheless, he and Penman were rated by Tonyn as members of a "desperate faction," which included General Prevost and his brother, Spencer Man, and other men not less loyal than they. On the recommendation of General Prevost, Major Beamsley Glazier succeeded Fuser.[93]

During the winter of 1779-1780, there was almost a famine among the lower Creeks, who resorted in large numbers to St. Augustine and caused the governor to expend more than £1,000 for provisions and presents to be distributed among them. Tonyn had also to look after the Seminoles, who were equally dependent on St. Augustine.[94]

The departure of William Drayton from East Florida after his second suspension from the office of chief justice, led to the appointment of James Hume as his successor. During the early 1770's Hume had been a member of the council and acting attorney general of Georgia, but early in 1776 had been expelled from the province for refusing to obey the mandate of the provincial congress respecting the conduct of causes in the courts.[95] He arrived at St. Augustine in April, 1780, and a few months later bought his predecessor's villa of Oak Park. This estate, which was about four miles from the town, comprised one hundred and eighty acres, of which several about the house were utilized as a pleasure ground and garden, while some sixty acres were laid off in parks. Chief Justice Hume, like other loyalists of means in East Florida, made extensive improvements on his residential property, and acquired other tracts of land for cultivation. He set out many thousands of orange trees, besides lemon, lime, citron, shaddock, and other

---

[93] *Hist. MSS. Comm., Am. MSS. in R. Inst.*, II. 39, 40, 54, 63, 64, 71, 76, 77, 88.

[94] *Ibid.*, II. 130-131, 152.

[95] C. C. Jones, *Hist. of Georgia*, II. 142, 191; Egerton (ed.), *R. Comm. on Loyalist Claims, 1783-1785*, p. 63; *Second Report*, Bureau of Archives, Ont., 1904, pt. II. 1135.

fruit trees. By grant he obtained the Cypress Grove tract of twenty-five hundred acres on Six-Mile Creek, on which he employed a hundred negroes in clearing land, erecting quarters for the slaves and other buildings, planting Indian corn, cultivating a rice swamp, and boxing thirty-two thousand pine trees for turpentine. By grant he also acquired two other tracts of five hundred acres each, which he was unable to develop, and he bought a turpentine tract of three hundred acres, placing on it twenty-five negroes brought from Georgia.[96]

In the winter of 1780-1781, Governor Tonyn sent a Mr. Forbes with a flag of truce to Havana to gain information concerning the plans of Bernardo de Gálvez, the Spanish governor of Louisiana, who in March, 1780, had captured Mobile. Forbes left Havana on January 7, 1781, and arrived at St. Augustine a week later with alarming news, which related no doubt to the Spanish expedition that took Pensacola four months afterward. The news was transmitted at once to Lieutenant Colonel Alured Clarke at Savannah, who in turn imparted it to Lieutenant Colonel Nisbet Balfour at Charleston with a request for aid for the defense of East Florida. Clarke and Tonyn expected that the Spaniards would attack St. Augustine after their attempt on Pensacola. Clarke stated that the garrison in East Florida had two twenty-six pounders and numbered four hundred and fifty men, that he would soon go thither with a hundred more, and asked Balfour to send an equal number and some cannon. Clarke intended also to employ in the defense of the province such inhabitants as could be mustered. Balfour replied, promising his assistance. In April, Tonyn complained that most of the merchantmen of East Florida had been captured,[97] but did not attribute their loss to the Spaniards. However, the fear of Don Bernardo's troops proved to be groundless, though it was one that Tonyn could not shake off for months.

[96] See Volume II. of this work, pp. 37-45.
[97] Siebert, "The Loyalists in West Florida and the Natchez District," *Mississippi Valley Hist. Rev.*, II. 475-476; *Hist. MSS. Comm., Am. MSS. in R. Inst.*, II. 238, 240-241.

Chapter VI.

Later operations of the loyalist regiments from East Florida, March, 1780-April, 1781.—The second expedition of East Florida troops to Charleston.—Superintendent Browne's movement to Augusta.—The distribution of the provincials from East Florida.—Defeat of the South Carolina Royalists and other provincials at Musgrove's mills.—Superintendent Browne's defensive operations at Augusta.—His surrender and evacuation of the town.—Movements of the Royal North Carolina Regiment.—The South Carolina Royalists under Major Thomas Fraser and Colonel Benjamin Thompson.—Petitions for land from refugees and others.—The adoption of a resolution to hold an election of representatives to make laws for East Florida.—The impressment of negroes.—The danger of a Spanish invasion.—Defensive measures.

TO General Clinton's expedition, which captured Charleston in May, 1780, were due the second movement of the loyalist regiments from East Florida against that capital and their subsequent operations to the evacuations of Georgia and the Carolinas. While advancing upon Charleston, Clinton sent to New York for one reinforcement and to Savannah for another. The latter was commanded by Brigadier General James Patterson and included a body of Creek Indians. Lieutenant Colonel Browne was to remain behind with the other Indians until further orders. Patterson and his force, accompanied by Captain Moses Kirkland, crossed the Savannah River in March. It included the South Carolina Royalists under Lieutenant Colonel Alexander Innes, the Royal North Carolina Regiment under Lieutenant Colonel John Hamilton, and a part of the Carolina King's Rangers. On March 26, a detachment of Patterson's command led by Colonels Hamilton and Tarleton was repulsed near Stono Creek by Lieutenant Colonel William Washington and his troop of horse, Hamilton being taken prisoner. Superintendent Browne was detained at Savannah for more than two months looking after Indian affairs, awaiting his orders from Charleston, and trying to find means of transporting his supplies in case he should be ordered to march. At length he was sent up the Savannah River to Augusta with the remainder of the

Carolina King's Rangers and a body of Cherokee Indians. He had added a new company or two to his rangers before leaving Savannah.[98]

After General Clinton had sailed from Charleston on July 5, leaving Cornwallis in command, the latter dispersed a part of his force to cover the frontiers of South Carolina and Georgia. Camden was occupied by Lord Rawdon with a number of British and provincial troops, including some Carolina King's Rangers and the Royal North Carolina Regiment. At Prince's Fort, on a branch of the North Fork of the Tyger River, were Lieutenant Colonel Innes and his regiment of South Carolina Royalists, together with other bodies of provincials. In July, 1780, Cornwallis had written to Clinton that Innes had reported that he was under directions to return to New York as soon as possible. The question raised was whether he was to go immediately or remain two or three months longer. He remained, as will appear farther on. At Augusta Superintendent Browne continued on duty. Cornwallis appointed Colonel Robert Cunningham to command a brigade of loyal militia, newly organized, in Ninety-Six District. One of the regiments was placed in charge of Captain Moses Kirkland, whose commission as a major was dated July 6, 1780. He continued on service in his district until he joined Colonel John Harris Cruger to go to the relief of Browne and his force at Augusta in mid-September. When Lord Rawdon established a post at Hanging Rock, twenty-four miles from Camden on the road to Charlotte, he sent the Carolina King's Rangers thither as part of the garrison. This post was charged on August 6 by Colonel Sumter, and many officers and men of the rangers were killed or captured. About the same time General Gates and his grand army arrived from North Carolina, forcing Rawdon to call his outlying garrisons back to Camden. Cornwallis also came on summons and roundly defeated the Americans. Part or all of the Royal North Carolina Regiment took part in this battle, being in the rear division of Cornwallis's army.[99]

[98] *Hist. MSS. Comm., Am. MSS. in R. Inst.*, II. 92-93, 112, 403; Tarleton, *Memoirs*, p. 7; Lee, *Memoirs*, I. 155; Munsell, *Siege of Charleston*, p. 157; C. C. Jones, *Hist. of Georgia*, II. 448; McCrady, *South Carolina in the Rev.*, 1775-1780, pp. 447-448, 451, 561-563, 614.

[99] Lee's *Memoirs*, I. 169-176; Gregg, *Hist. of the Old Cheraws*, pp. 315-318; *Hist.*

Military Expeditions and Operations

On August 17, Lieutenant Colonel Innes and a hundred of his South Carolina Royalists, together with two other provincial companies, came from Ninety-Six District and reinforced the camp at Musgrove's mills. That night Colonels Shelby, Clarke, and Williams, with less than half the total strength of the encampment, approached, erected a breastwork of logs on a neighboring wooded hill, and next morning by stratagem drew Innes and most of his followers toward the breastwork. They drove them back, killed and wounded many, and rode off with a number of prisoners. Innes himself was wounded and was deserted by the militia that formed a part of his force. In the previous June the South Carolina Royalists had numbered three hundred and ninety-six men.[100]

After the battle of Camden, Cornwallis ordered that persons in arms with the British who deserted to the enemy should be hanged. Browne at Augusta carried this order into effect by gibbeting five of his prisoners without trial. Colonels Elijah Clarke and James McCall undertook to punish Browne and recover Augusta. On September 14, they broke up an outlying camp of Indians, drove them into McKay's trading house, called the White House, where Captain Johnston and his company of Carolina King's Rangers were stationed, and captured some of the soldiers and Indians. The party in the White House was greatly strengthened by Browne and the main body of his garrison and by a party of Cherokees, which crossed the river at night. Browne put the trading post in a state of defense, and summoned aid from Ninety-Six. On the appearance of Colonel Cruger and Major Kirkland with their force of regulars and militia on September 18, the Americans paroled their prisoners, including two officers and forty-one privates of the rangers, and retreated. Browne had been shot through both thighs, and took vengeance by hanging some prisoners in the White House. Until his recovery Kirkland took charge of the garrison at Augusta.

MSS. Comm., Am. MSS. in R. Inst., II. 158; McCrady, *South Carolina in the Rev., 1775-1780*, pp. 562, 614, 621, 623-631, 672; E. A. Jones (ed.), *Journal of Alexander Chesney*, p. 107.

[100] Savary (ed.), *Col. David Fanning's Narrative*, p. 14; Draper, *King's Mountain and its Heroes*, p. 115; McCrady, *South Carolina in the Rev., 1775-1780*, pp. 687-694, 697-698, 707-708; *Hist. MSS. Comm., Am. MSS. in R. Inst.*, II. 173; Notes from the Muster Rolls.

At the time of this episode the rangers alone numbered two hundred and forty-four men.[101]

Browne finally capitulated to General Pickens and Colonels Clarke and Lee on June 5, 1781, after a siege of seven weeks. The garrison of Augusta was first weakened by the capture of two of its companies by Lee at Fort Galphin, fifteen miles down the Savannah River. A quantity of Indian presents, consisting of ammunition, small arms, blankets, and other articles, was taken at the same time. Then many of the Carolina King's Rangers were killed, wounded, or captured when they attempted to escape with Colonel Grierson from their fort to Fort Cornwallis in the northern part of Augusta, where Browne and his contingent were stationed. The Americans now dug trenches of approach, and erected a "Mayham tower," from which their only useful fieldpiece raked the interior of the fort. Although Browne made three desperate efforts at night to capture the enemy's trenches and resorted to other defensive measures, he and his garrison were starved into submission by the protracted siege. They were permitted to march out with the honors of war. Browne and the other officers were paroled and sent down the river to Savannah under guard of an infantry squad. The other prisoners, about three hundred in number, were conducted with the American force by Pickens and Lee across the Savannah River to Ninety-Six, which was being invested by General Greene.[102]

At mid-August, 1780, the Royal North Carolina Regiment had a strength of four hundred and eighty men. From Camden it moved with Cornwallis and his army to Charlottetown, North Carolina, where the commander-in-chief received, about October 12, the distressing news of Colonel Ferguson's utter defeat on Kings Mountain. This information being promptly confirmed, Cornwallis began his retreat on the fourteenth, or just a week after the disaster. Hamilton's corps continued with the British army

---

[101] Lee, *Memoirs of the War in the Southern Department*, I. 207; E. A. Jones (ed.), *Journal of Alexander Chesney*, p. 107; C. C. Jones, *Hist. of Georgia*, II. 455-458; Schenck, *North Carolina, 1780-1781*, pp. 416-422; Notes from the Muster Rolls.

[102] McCall, *Hist. of Georgia*, II. 368-374; Tarleton, *Hist. of the Campaigns of 1780 and 1781*, p. 493; Ramsay, *Hist. of the Rev. in South Carolina*, II. 497; Lee, *Memoirs of the War in the Southern Department*, II. 92, 105-107, 109, 115; C. C. Jones, *Hist. of Georgia*, II. 477-495.

Military Expeditions and Operations

in its pursuit of General Greene during the winter of 1780-1781. After Major Craig's occupation of Wilmington, North Carolina, as a supply post for Cornwallis, with a force from Charleston late in January, Craig authorized Colonel David Fanning to raise recruits for Hamilton's regiment. Numerous volunteers were collected, the inducements being a bounty of three guineas and a grant of land to each one who would serve during the war within the provinces of North and South Carolina and Virginia. The Royal North Carolina Regiment was not in the battle of Guilford Court House in March, 1781, being with the baggage at Bell's mill on Deep River. After Wilmington was reached a large part of the regiment remained there until the evacuation of the place in the following November. At that time its rank and file totaled four hundred and fifty-eight men, including the detachment that accompanied Cornwallis to Petersburg and Yorktown. One hundred and fourteen of its men were in the surrender on December 19, 1781. At the evacuation of Wilmington the main body of Hamilton's corps returned with the remainder of Craig's force and a number of refugees to Charleston. Mustered in June, 1782, they numbered four hundred and fifty-one men.[108]

As early as July, 1780, Lieutenant Colonel Innes had informed Cornwallis that he had instructions to return to New York as soon as possible. In a letter to Clinton, Cornwallis asked whether Innes was to go immediately, or remain two or three months until his business had been attended to. By May, Innes was back in New York, having left the South Carolina Royalists in charge of Major Thomas Fraser. At Christmas the corps was stationed at the Quarter House near Charleston and comprised nine troops of cavalry, totaling two hundred and ninety men, under Fraser, and one company of infantry, numbering thirty-four men, under Captain Lindsay. In January, Benjamin Thompson, an American loyalist who had been an under secretary of state, came to Charleston from England. He brought with him his colonel's commission. About the time of Thompson's arrival Major Craig and his command were driven from John's Island into Charleston by a part of General Greene's army. The South Carolina Royalists lacked some of its officers, and had recently lost Captain Campbell in an

---

[108] See Additional Notes, in Volume II. of this work, pp. 340, 349, and references there given.

action against Colonel Francis Marion's men on the north side of Cooper River, though it had captured and killed about a hundred of them. Brigadier General Alexander Leslie now gave Colonel Thompson a chance to win his spurs by sending him out from Daniel's Island with a mixed force of infantry and cavalry, including four troops of the South Carolina Royalists. By mounting the foot soldiers on the dragoons' horses from time to time, Thompson's expedition traveled thirty-six miles almost without interruption. It fell in with Marion's command on the Santee on February 25, 1781, and drove the major part of it into the river, according to Thompson's report. It brought back a supply of cattle and other plunder and received the "best thanks" of Leslie, who praised Thompson's merit and the spirited behavior of the troops. In April, Colonel Thompson went to New York. About two months later the muster of the South Carolina Royalists showed but five troops of cavalry, numbering together two hundred and nine men, and the single company of infantry, which had increased to fifty-five men. The commanding officer of the cavalry was still Major Fraser, and that of the infantry, Captain Lindsay. Apparently the corps continued to have its headquarters at the Quarter House.[104]

At the meeting of Governor Tonyn and his council in mid-February, 1781, petitions for land were received from refugees and old settlers. The warrants of survey issued were for tracts ranging from one hundred to five hundred acres. The board then considered the expediency of calling a general meeting of the freeholders to elect representatives for the purpose of framing laws for the government of East Florida. A resolution was adopted in favor of issuing writs of election returnable in forty days.

Late in February, the governor was authorized by the board to make requisition on the inhabitants for a hundred negroes to be employed on the fortifications. This was done at the request of Lieutenant Colonel Glazier, the commanding officer, and of the engineer, and was in preparation against an attack of the Spaniards. Late in April, Tonyn complained of the interruption of correspondence between St. Augustine and New York on account of the capture of most of the merchantmen of East Florida. On May 1, he

---

[104] *Hist. MSS. Comm., Am. MSS. in R. Inst.*, II. 389, 406; Ellis, *Life of Rumford*, pp. 125-130; Rivington's *Gazette*, April 17, 1781. See also Additional Notes, in Volume II. of this work, p. 375.

told the council of three expeditions intended by the Spaniards, one against West Florida, another to the island of New Providence, and the third against East Florida. He reminded them that late in March Bernardo de Gálvez's fleet and troops were at Pensacola "in full force," and that the Seminole warriors were in St. Augustine now by the joint action of Colonel Glazier and himself. The board decided that the Seminoles should be employed for the defense of the province. The question of prohibiting the exportation of provisions and of requiring the inhabitants to provide themselves with a supply for four months, was postponed until the governor should submit it to the general assembly with the recommendation that a law be passed empowering him to issue a prohibitory proclamation in cases of necessity.[105]

[105] *Hist. MSS. Comm., Am. MSS. in R. Inst.*, II. 270, 285; C. O. 5/572, Council Minutes, February 27, 1781.

Chapter VII.

The first general assembly of East Florida, March-November, 1781.—The election of members of the commons house.—The administration of oaths and the naming of the officers of that house.—The governor's speech.—The addresses of the two houses and Tonyn's reply.—Early enactments.—Tonyn's message on the conquest of West Florida by the Spaniards, and the defensive measures recommended by him.—The report of a committee on the causes of the backwardness of East Florida, and its recommendations.—The term of laws.—The impressment of negroes.—The contest between the two houses over the negro bill.—The prorogation of the General Assembly.—Tonyn appeals to both houses to resume consideration of public affairs.—The dissolution of the assembly.—Defensive measures by the council.—Its authorization of a second general assembly.

A ROYAL writ commanded all of the inhabitants of twenty-one years of age, or over, who possessed fifty acres of land, to appear at the court house in St. Augustine on March 13, 14, 15, and 16, 1781, twenty days' notice having been given, to elect nineteen "fit and discreet persons" severally possessed in their own right of five hundred acres of land within the province of East Florida to be their representatives. The members so chosen were to meet with the governor at the state house on March 27 and so qualify themselves to sit as the commons house in the general assembly, which would then and there meet for the transaction of legislative business. The nineteen members elected were: Robert Baillie, William Brown, Peter Edwards, Stephen Egan, Thomas Forbes, George Kemp, Jacobus Kip, John Leslie, Francis Levett, Benjamin Lord, William McLeod, John Martin, Philip Moore, William Moss, John Mowbray, John Ross, Thomas Ross, Robert Scott, and Robert Payne.[106]

The members of the council constituted the upper house of assembly, Lieutenant Governor John Moultrie being the president of that body. Governor Tonyn directed the master of chancery to attend the commons house and administer the oaths to the four members-elect mentioned in the return to the writ of election, and to deliver to them a *dedimus potestatem*

[106] C. O. 5/572, Journals of Commons House of Assembly, March 27 to November 12, 1781.

to swear the other members. They subscribed to the oaths of allegiance, supremacy, and abjuration, and to a declaration that there was no transubstantiation of the bread and wine in the sacrament of the Lord's Supper. The master of chancery also informed the commons house that the governor had appointed Peter Edwards to be its clerk, and Stephen Haven to act during Edwards's absence from the province.[107] By order of the governor it chose its own speaker. William Brown was elected by a unanimous vote. It named John Love as messenger and doorkeeper, and, like the upper house, it adopted certain rules and regulations fixing the number of members who could meet and adjourn and the size of a quorum to transact business.

On March 29, the two houses met together to hear the governor's speech, in which he said that he was happy that during his administration East Florida had arrived at such a state of affluence that he could fulfil the king's promise in his proclamation of October 7, 1763, by establishing a provincial legislature for ordaining laws and ordinances, under such regulations and restrictions as obtained in other colonies, for the good government and public welfare of the province and its inhabitants. Henceforth the council would be the upper house of assembly. Although grand juries of East Florida had represented that a provincial legislature would be beneficial to the community, and the council had concurred in that view, he had thought it better to suffer a few inconveniences than lose the support and patronage of their sovereign in a time of general revolt, when this colony, like others, might prove to be unworthy and ungrateful. But the increase of property in the province due to the growth of commerce and planting, and other considerations, impelled him to call the assembly. In view of the wicked and obstinate rebellion he asked the houses to pass an act recognizing their allegiance to the "blessed prince" on the throne and acknowledging the supremacy of parliament. The governor also asked the legislature to make provision for defraying a reasonable part of the expenses of the imperial government and for the administration of the province, since the king and parliament, with "astonishing and unprecedented condescension,"

[107] C. O. 5/572, Journals of Upper House of Assembly, March 27 to November 12, 1781.

had relinquished their just right of taxation. He had ever represented to the secretaries of state the loyalty of the inhabitants, and he now returned his thanks to the gentlemen who had served in the militia at the repeated invasions of East Florida. As a defensive measure he recommended the passage of a militia act.

On March 31, the president and members of the upper house called on the governor and presented an address, in which they thanked him for his speech and affirmed their loyalty to the crown and parliament. The address of the commons house was of the same tenor, but expressly signified its willingness to contribute to the support of the home government. On April 2, an address of thanks from Governor Tonyn was read to the lower house, in which he expressed his confidence that the regard of its members for justice and the constitution would induce them to contribute their share toward the general expenses of the government in proportion to the circumstances of their constituents. He added that he had done all in his power to render the province a happy asylum for those gentlemen whose firm attachment to government had led them to relinquish their possessions rather than sacrifice their allegiance, but that what he had done still fell short of their merits and distresses. Copies of the addresses thus exchanged were ordered to be printed, and one copy posted at Payne's corner in St. Augustine and another at the bluff on St. Johns River.

In April, both houses passed an act, introduced by Attorney General Henry Yonge, for punishing anyone who should deny the force of the laws of East Florida, and early in May they passed a measure for the better establishment and regulation of the militia. Other measures enacted were a bill for the better regulation of taverns, punch houses, and retailers of spirituous liquors; a bill empowering the governor, or commander-in-chief, to prohibit the exportations of provisions on certain occasions for the time being; a bill for explaining the jurisdiction of the court of common pleas, for altering the style thereof, for choosing and summoning grand and petit jurors, and for other purposes; a bill for the speedy recovery of small debts and damages and for electing constables, and a bill for the better control of pilots and for regulating the pilotage of vessels into the several ports of East Florida. The law to prohibit the exportation of provisions and that for regulating the pilotage of vessels were both intended to safeguard the province in case of invasion.

On June 27, Governor Tonyn sent a message to the two houses to inform them that West Florida had surrendered to the Spaniards about May 10. He added that this unfortunate event would seriously affect East Florida, and that a short bill should be passed enabling him to call into service the negroes requisite for completing the military works. The commons house asked what wages might be expected from the engineer for the labor of these negroes, and if that officer would supply the provisions needed for them. The governor answered that the provisions would be furnished, but that the engineer had no fund for the payment of the wages. However, both houses concurred in passing the bill requested. It was at this time that the governor announced his intention to embody the militia immediately under the militia act mentioned above, because an invasion was expected.

Earlier in June, a special committee of the commons house of assembly, of which Robert Baillie was chairman, made a report on the causes of the slow progress of the province in population and in cultivation of the land. After examining various records of warrants of survey, royal orders in council, and grants of land from the offices of the surveyor general, attorney general, and register, they reported that about one million acres had been laid out and granted in very large tracts, mostly of twenty thousand acres each, to persons who had never made any attempt to settle on, or cultivate, any part of their respective tracts. They maintained that this was one of the principal causes which had effectually retarded, and prevented, the settlement and improvement of East Florida. Some members of the committee, many years resident in the province, had observed that the proprietors of these tracts, living in Europe, were not only ignorant in most cases of the agricultural methods of this part of the world, but also that they generally sent over agents, or managers, equally uninformed. Even after these agents had gained a few years of experience and observation, they were still bound by orders from their employers to follow methods of culture unsuitable to the soil and climate of East Florida. Thus large sums of money had been thrown away.

Some members of the committee, who had formerly lived in Georgia and South Carolina, believed that jealousy of this desirable country in those provinces had given rise to false representations of the physical and climatic conditions of the province. Further, the fact that the promising settlements on St. Marys River, which enjoyed easy and safe navigation for vessels of large tonnage, had been laid waste by the rebels some years ago and remained defenseless ever since, seemed a sufficient reason for the lack of inhabitants in that fertile region. If a town were laid out on St. Marys, made a free port, and given protection, the population, cultivation, and trade of East Florida would be greatly promoted. Again, the settlement of the province had been retarded by the high quit-rents stipulated in the land grants. Although these had never been demanded, they had been represented as a lien on the property.

In view of the persecution, distress, and ruin of many of the loyalists in the adjacent provinces, the committee recommended that a law be enacted to encourage such persons to come and settle in East Florida by affording them a few years' respite from such a debtor's law as bound them in those colonies. The rebellion had made it impossible for them to pay immediately. Another measure of relief would be to compel the grantees of the many large, uncultivated tracts of land to sell or resign them, in order that they might be regranted and distributed in small tracts among a number of poor, distressed, and industrious settlers. These measures would tend to promote the growth of population, agriculture, and prosperity of East Florida and add to its strength.

On July 3, the commons house took under consideration the above report, added two members to the original committee of seven, and directed them to inquire of the law officers what measures the house could take to break up the large tracts of land.

The journals of the house do not disclose what information they obtained, but we know from other sources that in most cases the conditions specified in the grants had not been complied with and that, therefore, these large grants were subject to reversion to the crown. This was the position taken by Governor Tonyn, who proceeded to regrant some of them in parcels of from fifty to five hundred acres to refugee loyalists.

Late in June, 1781, the commons house of assembly asked the governor what his instructions said about his signing bills, unless they were declared to be in force for the term of two years. He replied that laws granting money raised by import duties, tonnage, or excise must continue for one year and other laws for two years, except in emergency cases, where the law provided for a service in its nature temporary and contingent.

The commanding officer and the engineer of the garrison were pushing the repairs of the fortifications on account of the danger of an invasion, and made a requisition on the governor for the labor of two hundred negroes. He consulted the council as to the action to be taken, and was authorized to demand immediately from the inhabitants one-tenth of their working slaves for a period of six weeks.

Two months before this, that is, late in April, the commons house had passed a bill for the better governing "of negroes and other slaves" and to prevent their abduction from their masters and employers. This bill was amended in certain respects and passed by the upper house on June 6, but was not returned for some days to the lower house. On July 16, the latter adopted a motion to refrain from business, except that of providing a sum toward the expenses of the empire and considering ways and means for defraying the internal expenses of the province, until bills already passed by the commons house should be returned by the other. On July 25, the commons house voted not to proceed to any business until it should receive an answer from the upper house respecting the negro bill. The latter replied that it was willing to relinquish all of its amendments, except the one requiring that negroes on trial for capital offenses should be under the protection of the law and have the best security for their life and limbs. It declined to acquiesce in according to justices of the peace jurisdiction over life and death, since they could not in all cases direct a jury or decide according to the spirit and forms of criminal law. The next action of the commons house was to vote to proceed to no business until the negro act should pass and to send a message to the governor requesting an adjournment for a month or six weeks. In his reply Tonyn asked for a moderate grant of revenue for the defense of the empire, but the house, after some debate, adopted a resolution declaring the impropriety of doing so, or of taxing its constituents, before a law should be passed establishing their right and property in slaves, who might be justly deemed the riches of East Florida.

The upper house now adopted a series of resolutions in justification of its position, these resolutions being presented by Chief Justice Hume for the committee which had considered the abstracts from the minutes of the lower house. The upper house also adopted an able address to the governor, evidently written by Mr. Hume, in which it was charged that the commons house had assumed to itself the whole power of legislation, thus destroying the balance of the constitution and leaving no alternative, except that of yielding or suspending business. On August 1, the upper house attended upon the governor and presented its address. It received a polite answer from him, expressing his confidence in the good intentions of both houses and his hope for a cordial reconciliation between them. He then adjourned the two chambers, in accordance with their expressed wish.

The chief contention between the two houses was over the jurisdiction of justices of the peace in the trial of slaves in capital cases. The upper house maintained that it was conformable to the principles of humanity and English law, besides being advantageous to the owners, that such of their negroes as were charged with capital offenses should have the fullest chance for their life and limbs by being tried by a jury before the justices of the general court in St. Augustine. The commons house contended that trial by justices of the peace avoided the delay, inconvenience, and expense that would arise from a form of procedure in which the culprit and witnesses must be taken from distant parts of the province to the capital. The dispute was carried on with much warmth on both sides, and with an assumption of authority by the commons house at the expense of that of the other house, though the latter remained firm in its support of the constitution and its own rights.[108]

Four weeks later, at the close of August, the upper house sent a message to the commons house proposing to take up the negro bill for further consideration, and received a reply that it would agree to an amendment which it submitted. The exchange of messages continued through the early days of September. On the tenth of that month the commons house charged

[108] C. O. 5/547, f. 23.

the other with evasion, claimed that its negro bill breathed more humanity than any of a like nature passed in the sister colonies, professed its attachment to the king and its eagerness to restore cordiality between the two houses, but also its inability to concur with the proposal of the upper house. Accordingly, the latter sent an address to Governor Tonyn stating that it had sought in every way an accommodation with the commons house, which had resorted to unconstitutional methods to enact its negro bill, and that the upper house relinquished every prospect of reaching an understanding or of being able to proceed with the public business. On September 17, the upper house adopted a resolution that it could not, consistently with its honor and dignity, transact any business with the other until the latter's message charging it with evasion was revoked, or expunged. Simultaneously Governor Tonyn sent a message proroguing the general assembly until October 17.

On the seventeenth, the governor addressed both chambers. He appealed to them to resume the consideration of public affairs, and complete on loyal and constitutional principles the enactment of such provincial laws as they thought most needed. He commended the laws passed at the last session as bearing the marks of their loyalty to the government and their regard for the British constitution. The salutary effects of those laws, he added, were manifest in the state of the fortifications, which were nearing completion. At the end of October, the upper house still insisted that it could not do business with the commons house until the latter retracted its objectionable message of September 10. On November 12, Governor Tonyn delivered his last speech to the two houses, stating that he had used every means in his power to accommodate, or remove, the disagreement between them; that he had flattered himself the commons house would see, and acknowledge, that its resolutions of July 26 were hasty and unconstitutional and its message of September 10 to the upper house was expressed in a style unsuitable to the transaction of business. He had anxiously deliberated how to restore the constitution and preserve the reputation of East Florida for loyalty. He would have dissolved the houses earlier, but feared in this alarming crisis, when the other colonies were in rebellion, that our enemies would greedily seize the surmises of the legislators' disaffection and industriously propagate them. With no prospect of an accommodation between them, he declared the two houses dissolved on November 12, 1781.

On November 16, he signed a few grants, and received about a score of petitions for tracts of land and for town lots from refugees and others. Fearing an invasion, the council authorized the governor to issue a proclamation prohibiting the exportation of provisions of all kinds and laying an embargo upon all shipping within East Florida, in as much as a number of seamen would be wanted for the galleys and armed vessels for the defense of the province. In view of the fact that another requisition had been made by the commanding officer and the engineer for one hundred and fifty more negroes for the military works, the council adopted a resolution that the inhabitants should send immediately to the fortifications at St. Augustine such an additional number of slaves for a month as would make with those already sent one-fifth of their working negroes. The governor asked the opinion of the board concerning the expediency of convening another general assembly. Its recommendation was that a writ be issued for electing representatives to meet as a commons house in an assembly to be held at St. Augustine on January 7, 1782.

In the midst of the contest between the two houses over the negro bill notification was sent from the war office in Westminster, under date of November 2, 1781, that Governor Tonyn had been promoted from the rank of colonel to that of major general. At the end of the same month, the governor was still expecting an invasion by the Spaniards, and the province was being put in condition to receive them. The work on the fortifications and the new galleys was almost finished, and they were supplied with heavy guns just arrived from England. The militia had been given arms and assigned to town duty, without a proclamation of martial law, and St. Augustine had a sufficient stock of provisions to withstand a siege. Tonyn had full confidence that the garrison would receive a further reinforcement in case of need.[109]

Governor Tonyn wrote to the board of trade in London at the end of the session that the same gentlemen who constituted the last commons house of assembly would in general be reëlected to the next one, which would be

[109] *Hist. MSS. Comm., Am. MSS. in R. Inst.*, II. 345; C. O. 5/547.

convened on January 7, 1782, and explained the chief object at issue between the two chambers. The board of trade replied on February 22 that it thought the magistrates of the vicinage and a jury of freeholders fully competent to decide with justice and equity cases brought before them, that the inconveniences mentioned by the commons house seemed insuperable and a sufficient justification for adopting the mode of trying slaves usual in the other provinces, that in its opinion the upper house was not well founded in its opposition to the negro bill, and that dissolution was not likely to effect agreement between the two houses, especially as Tonyn thought that the same members would be reëlected to serve in the assembly. The board of trade, therefore, recommended that, in case the contest should be renewed, the upper house should agree with the other in establishing the jurisdiction of justices of the peace for the trial of slaves.[110]

This recommendation undoubtedly decided the question. As the bill was finally enacted it contained clauses providing that justices of the peace, or any three of them, with the aid of a jury, were empowered to determine causes in which a slave was accused of a crime or offense for which capital or other punishment might be inflicted. The act was assented to by the governor on May 31, 1782. It was very long and detailed, and constituted a kind of code for the better management of negro and other slaves.[111]

[110] C. O. 5/564.   [111] C.O. 5/624.

Chapter VIII.

The exodus of refugees from Savannah to East Florida, May-August, 1782.—The coördinated evacuations of Georgia, South Carolina, and East Florida.—General Alexander Leslie at Charleston in charge.—The postponement of the evacuation of East Florida.—Remonstrances against the evacuation of that province.—General Leslie arranges for the conveyance of the loyalists from Savannah to East Florida. —Many remain and transfer their allegiance to the United States.—Governor Wright's protest against the surrender of Georgia.—Discontent of the Georgians in East Florida.—Governor Tonyn and the General Assembly aim to keep East Florida under the king's protection.—Land and provisions for the newcomers.

THE evacuation of Georgia, South Carolina, and East Florida by the British at the close of the Revolution was a coördinated movement conducted by Lieutenant General Alexander Leslie at Charleston under orders from General Sir Guy Carleton at New York. This movement came to a sudden head in East Florida during the latter half of the year 1782, imposed great hardships and added losses on thousands of loyalists, and spent itself in a prolonged evacuation of the Florida peninsula that lasted two and a half years and cast throngs of homeless people into the Bahamas, the southern states, and the lower Mississippi Valley, and smaller numbers into Nova Scotia and the British Isles, Jamaica, several islands of the Spanish main, Dominica, and "other Foreign Parts." Only four hundred and fifty whites transferred their allegiance to the new Spanish government in East Florida, keeping two hundred negroes with them.

Already before General Clinton's retirement from command, he had notified Governor Tonyn in March, 1782, to address his future military requests to Leslie. Carleton supplemented this order on May 22 by informing Leslie that the governors of East Florida and Georgia and the officers commanding at St. Augustine and Savannah were to obey his orders. In a secret communication he added that a day or two later Leslie might expect a fleet of transports for use in removing the troops and stores, together with such loyalists as chose to depart from Savannah and St. Augustine. Leslie was to render assistance to the local authorities and prevent destruction, seeing to it that even the fortifications remained uninjured. Carleton added that Charleston would have to be evacuated soon, but requested that secrecy be observed as far as possible.[112]

When the program of evacuation was put into execution Savannah came first and East Florida last. The explanation of the delay in the latter case is to be found primarily in the advice of Captain Keith Elphinstone of the ship-of-war *Perseus*, who suggested to General Carleton the desirability of postponing the removal of the loyalists from Florida until after the surrender of Savannah and Charleston, so as to have the necessary shipping available to give the Floridians time to make their arrangements after Tonyn should be informed a few months later. Captain Elphinstone's advice was valued by Carleton as that of one who had come into contact with some of the officers of the southern provinces, and knew something of the situation there. After passing this advice on to Leslie, Carleton authorized him to give such orders as he might think best under the circumstances.[113]

Leslie, in his turn, sought light on the question of the immediate evacuation of East Florida. He communicated with James Penman, long a resident of St. Augustine and one of its leading merchants, who had given large financial support to the commanding officers of the garrison there during the war. Penman was opposed to the immediate evacuation of the peninsula, if he was not averse to an evacuation at any time. In a long letter he informed Leslie what he thought would be the evil consequences of withdrawal, and urged the importance of East Florida "as a frontier against Spanish attacks." This letter was written on June 5. On the day before, however, Leslie had written to the governors of East Florida and Georgia to inform them of the intended evacuations. He sent his letters by the hand of a trusted messenger to insure secrecy, but the news leaked out in Charleston within a few days through the inadvertence of a naval officer, who gained the information from orders received from Admiral Digby.[114]

A series of remonstrances followed in rapid succession, which were

---

[112] *Hist. MSS. Comm., Am. MSS. in R. Inst.*, II. 426, 494, 495.

[113] *Ibid.*, II. 500. See also Additional Notes, in Volume II. of this work, p. 313.

[114] *Hist. MSS. Comm., Am. MSS. in R. Inst.*, II. 513, 520.

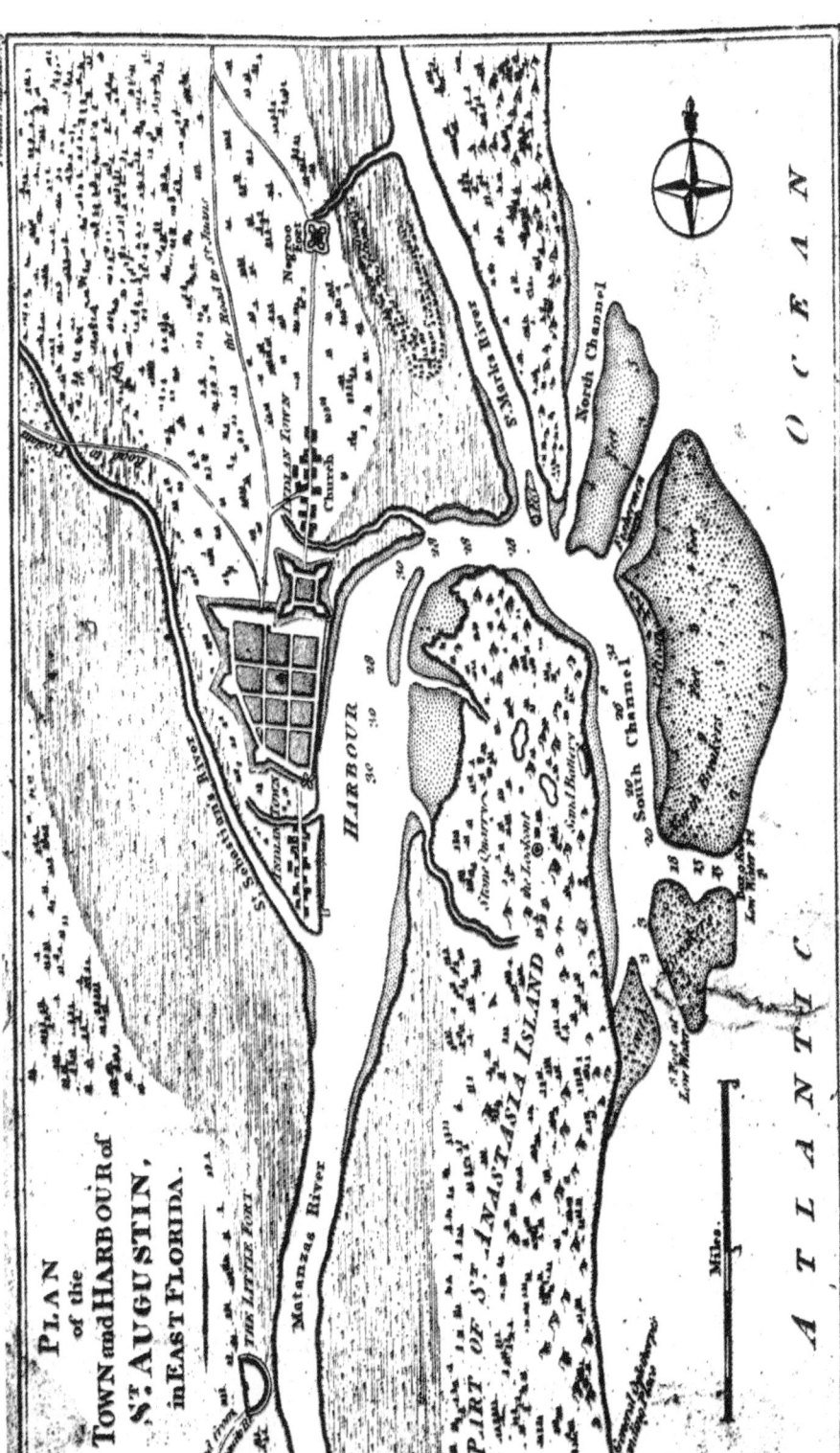

addressed to Leslie. The first, dated June 12, was a memorial from some of the "inhabitants of South Carolina" protesting against the proposed evacuation of East Florida. The next came from some "proprietors of lands" in the latter province who were living in Charleston, and represented the misfortune that would befall them if East Florida were surrendered. The third was an address from the general assembly of Georgia, and protested against the evacuation of both Georgia and East Florida. It has been preserved in two forms, one asking that the garrison of St. Augustine be brought to Savannah and the other suggesting that East Florida "be kept as an asylum for refugees."[115]

Governor Tonyn had received Leslie's letter about the evacuation on June 18, and had immediately communicated its contents to the general assembly, then in session at St. Augustine. On the following day that body adopted and transmitted an address to the governor thanking him for communicating Leslie's letter with its intimation of directions from the commander-in-chief for the withdrawal of the troops from St. Augustine and its dependencies, and the expected arrival of transports to carry off the governor and such inhabitants as he might recommend. As East Florida contained only loyalists, many of them refugees, and had been held out as an asylum for the well-affected from other colonies, those who should depart would go in a state of indigence and looking for new habitations, while those who remained would be left without government, laws, or arms, and surrounded by enemies, savages, and lawless banditti. The addressers, therefore, asked Tonyn if he meant to embark with the garrison, and if he would not apply to Lieutenant Colonel Beamsley Glazier, the commanding officer at St. Augustine, for provisions and military stores to enable them to make a defense, and to General Carleton for a military force in place of the garrison, should the latter be removed.

On June 20, another address followed from the two houses urging Tonyn to entreat General Leslie to send the refugees at Charleston to East Florida, together with provisions, arms, and ammunition, thus strengthening the province and preserving it to the king. As Georgia was also to be evacuated, they requested Tonyn to make it known there that a "vast pro-

[115] *Hist. MSS. Comm., Am. MSS. in R. Inst.*, II. pp. 524, 525, 527.

portion" of the inhabitants meant to remain and defend East Florida. Tonyn answered immediately that he had written to the commander-in-chief and General Leslie in the most pressing terms for arms and ammunition for the inhabitants, a detachment of troops, a naval force for St. Johns River, and a supply of provisions. He would suggest further, he added, that the province would be a convenient asylum for more refugees, whose coming would greatly strengthen it.[116]

On June 20, the upper house adopted resolutions in favor of supporting the governor with their lives and fortunes in defense of East Florida and preserving it to the king. This was followed by an address to the crown from both houses embodying the essence of the joint address to Tonyn and of the resolutions, and imploring their sovereign's immediate aid and protection as being entitled to his peculiar regard. At this time also Governor Tonyn wrote two letters, bearing the same date, to General Leslie. In one he confessed that he lacked words in which to express his astonishment over the intended evacuation, or his "sympathy for the greater part of the inhabitants who must remain" in East Florida. He enclosed the address of the general assembly with the hope that the request contained therein for arms, ammunition, and cannon, would be granted. He urged the importance of preserving the province to the crown. In the other letter Tonyn referred again to his deep concern about "the impending distresses of the loyal inhabitants who must remain," and asked for troops as well as arms and military stores. For the defense of St. Johns River, whence naval stores "of great consequence to Britain" were exported, he desired some armed vessels. From the king's ministers he had received no orders to relinquish East Florida, he said, and he hoped that measures would be taken to preserve it.[117]

On June 21, Tonyn wrote to General Carleton, enclosing the resolutions of the upper house of assembly and commending the determination therein expressed to defend the province to the last extremity, and the conduct of the inhabitants in general. He ventured to suggest that the commander-in-chief countermand the order for the withdrawal of the garrison from St.

---

[116] *Hist. MSS. Comm., Am. MSS. in R. Inst.*, II. 528, 529; C. O. 5/560, fols. 751, 757, 759, 761, 765.

[117] *Hist. MSS. Comm., Am. MSS. in R. Inst.*, II. 529, 530.

Refugees from Other Colonies 105

Augustine, and that he take East Florida under his own protection. As some of the inhabitants were already planning to emigrate to Jamaica, he proposed that transports and a convoy be provided for them. At the request of the people these dispatches were carried to New York by a messenger, who was to bring back Carleton's reply.[118]

At Charleston there was still much doubt among the populace about the removal of the troops, but Leslie was confident that many there would go with their negroes to Jamaica and others to St. Augustine or St. Johns Bluff in Florida. He had done nothing toward the evacuation but order the Carolina King's Rangers, which had been embodied in that province, to return thither. He soon reached the conclusion that the transfer of the unfortunate loyalists from Savannah to East Florida would afford them relief and refuge in a country where their slaves would still be useful to them, and he saw the need of supplying provisions for their subsistence. As he expected most of the Georgia loyalists to remove to East Florida, he arranged for their conveyance under a convoy and "recommended them in the strongest terms" to Governor Tonyn.[119]

It was already near the end of June, and the evacuation of Savannah was but a fortnight away. For some time past Savannah had been the place of refuge for loyalists from the outlying parts of Georgia. Many of these had first resorted to Ebenezer and other posts, where they had helped to construct the defenses and had carried arms. Later they had retreated to Savannah in the spring and summer of 1781 with the garrisons, and had served in the militia or worked on the fortifications. Here their wives and children had joined them. They had been promised the royal favor and protection in a letter from Lord George Germain, which had been received by Governor Sir James Wright early in February, 1782. But by mid-June Carleton's order of May 23 had arrived, announcing that "transports might be daily expected" to remove not only the troops and stores but also the governor and all those loyalists who might choose to depart with their effects.[120]

The number of the loyalists was about fourteen hundred, of whom five hundred were women and children. Probably there should be added to this

[118] *Hist. MSS. Comm., Am. MSS. in R. Inst.*, II. 531.
[119] *Ibid.*, pp. 543, 544, 546.   [120] C. C. Jones, Jr., *Hist. of Georgia*, II. 515, 524.

number at least five hundred loyal militia. There were besides several thousand negroes, three hundred and fifty Indians, and thirteen hundred regular troops. Of these, according to a return received at St. Augustine from General Leslie on July 18, 1783, giving the number of refugees and their negroes only who went to East Florida, the figures are:

	Whites	Blacks
Men	503	799
Women	269	705
Children	270	452
Total	1,042	1,956
		1,042
Grand total		2,998

Not all of the loyalists left Georgia, for assurances of protection were given by General Anthony Wayne and Governor John Martin that British subjects, especially merchants and traders, might remain under certain conditions. This arrangement included those militia men who would enlist in the Georgia regiment of infantry for a term. These people were assembled, and those found worthy of citizenship were required to take the oath of allegiance. They were also promised that every effort would be made to pass an act of oblivion for all offenses that might have been committed, except murder. Complying with these conditions, many loyalists of Savannah ceased making preparations to leave, and transferred their allegiance to the United States. The others, with their families and personal property, retired to Cockspur and Tybee Islands and encamped until time for the embarkation. Chief Justice Anthony Stokes tells us in his *Narrative* that he left Savannah on June 22, 1782, and reached the shipping on the following day, that the season was extremely hot, the water on the barren island of Tybee unwholesome, and the other natural inconveniences there without remedy, and that many of the loyalists died on that island before the embarkation.[121]

[121] C. C. Jones, Jr., *Hist. of Georgia*, II. 516, 517; *Narrative of the Official Conduct of Anthony Stokes . . . His Majesty's Chief Justice, and one of his Council of Georgia . . .*, 1784, pp. 93, 96; C. O. 5/560, pp. 805-810.

Refugees from Other Colonies

Governor Wright was at Tybee on July 6, and protested thence to Sir Guy Carleton against the surrender of Georgia. He declared that Sir Guy could not conceive of "the distress and misery" brought on the loyalists and of the great property they were giving up, besides "one of the most valuable" of the provinces, when a reinforcement of four hundred or five hundred men would have held it and when promises of the king's protection and support had recently been given to these people. On July 11, the British troops evacuated Savannah. During the next fortnight the transports were taking on the refugees, their negroes and effects, and some provisions, and were sailing away to various destinations. Chief Justice Stokes sailed with the fleet that left on July 24 for New York. As there were not enough of the king's ships to accommodate all who were ready to go, Lieutenant Governor John Graham hired five small vessels to take the negroes, provisions, and other possessions of some of the loyalists. On July 20, Graham, who was one of the superintendents of Indian affairs, wrote from Tybee Island to Carleton for instructions concerning his future relations with the Indian nations and reported that two hundred Choctaws, who had been with the garrison at Savannah for six months, were already embarked for St. Augustine. One hundred and fifty Creeks, who had defeated a party of Americans near Savannah on their way to that place, followed the example of the Choctaws. In the fields crops of rice, Indian corn, peas, and potatoes remained unharvested. In the hurry of their sudden departure, as Governor Wright complained later, the departing loyalists had been able to take with them only sufficient provisions for six weeks' subsistence. The governor, with some of the civil and military officers, sailed for Charleston, South Carolina, as did also a part of the troops and the East Florida Rangers. The other part of the garrison, together with Brigadier General Alured Clarke, went to New York. Jamaica was the destination of a number of the refugees and their slaves, more than two thousand of the latter being transported to that island. However, most of the loyalists from Georgia and a large part of their negroes were taken to East Florida.[122]

[122] *Report on Am. MSS. in R. Inst.*, III. 11, 26, 28, 30, 64-65, 163, 222, 352, IV. 147, 166; McCall, *Hist. of Georgia*, II. 420; C. C. Jones, Jr., *Hist. of Georgia*, II. p. 518; Siebert, *Legacy of the Am. Rev. to the British West Indies and Bahamas*, Ohio State University Bulletin, April, 1913, p. 7.

Many were doubtless induced to go there by Governor Tonyn's proclamation, which had been published in Savannah, offering protection, grants of land, and other advantages.[123]

In a memorial addressed to Carleton by the refugees themselves from St. Augustine, July 31, 1782, it was stated that at least four thousand persons, white and black, had removed from Georgia to East Florida. This memorial shows unmistakably that they did not come willingly to the latter province, on account of the distressing prospect of having to pass through a second evacuation in the near future. They voiced their fear to Carleton and besought his protection and countenance in such an event, while suggesting Jamaica, or some other of the West India Islands, as the only place where they could employ their slaves advantageously.[124] The number of refugees from Georgia, as given by Governor Tonyn over two months later, was considerably smaller than that named in the memorial. Some of the most prominent and wealthy Georgians had already gone, or were going, to Jamaica. That fact doubtless was at the root of their continued discontent, which probably irritated Tonyn, who spoke disparagingly of them. He seems to have considered them as a disturbing element. He said that they numbered about fifteen hundred whites and one thousand negroes, that they included "a few respectable families" but were for the most part exceedingly indolent backwoodsmen, that about four hundred of them might be found capable of bearing arms and serviceable in completing the provincial corps, but that their appearance was against them. He did not fail to mention that their families were in distress and exceedingly dissatisfied.[125]

Though displeased with the Georgians, Tonyn was gratified with the altered decision about East Florida. On July 15, Carleton had written to Leslie approving his delay in evacuating St. Augustine. Leslie had passed the word on to Tonyn, and on July 23 the governor had sent a message to the houses of assembly saying that the commander-in-chief had permitted the troops to remain, that Admiral Digby had ordered a sloop-of-war and two galleys as an additional defense, and that Leslie, aware of the "com-

---

[123] See Volume II. of this work, pp. 310, 311.
[124] *Report on Am. MSS. in R. Inst.*, III. 44, 45.
[125] *Ibid.*, pp. 163, 164.

Refugees from Other Colonies

modiousness of this province as an asylum for refugees" had early concurred with Carleton's wishes. At the end of July, Tonyn sent a letter of thanks to Carleton, and expressed the hope that "the attention due to subjects so distinguished for their loyalty" and the "commodius asylum" afforded by East Florida would induce the king to keep it under his protection. On August 16, the general assembly replied to the governor's message in resolutions of thanks for the steps he had taken to keep the troops and secure an additional naval force, by which the province would be rendered a safe resort for many refugees. It also asked him to convey the assembly's thanks to Carleton and Leslie, and declared its desire to remain under the protection of the British empire.[126]

The white population of East Florida was more than doubled by the influx of the Georgians, and the black population was increased by one-fourth or more. These new people must be fed and housed and enabled to care for themselves. The promise of grants of land for those who wished to settle was easily fulfilled by breaking up some of the great tracts granted under conditions never complied with by the original grantees. Tonyn regarded such tracts as forfeited or vacant land, which he could parcel out to actual settlers. He explained his policy to Major Nicholas Welsh, one of the Georgians, who had arrived fully two months ahead of his fellows.[127] As the supply of provisions brought from Savannah at the evacuation soon ran low, the issuance of rations was begun as early as November, 1782. Already for several weeks Superintendent Browne had been on St. Johns River in search of provisions and lands for the newcomers. He was well aware also that the refugees lacked plantation tools. While some of the Georgians settled in St. Augustine and in the town of St. Johns Bluff, the greater number sought habitations in the country, along St. Johns River, on the Matanza, or as far away as Doctor's Lake, about thirty miles southward from the bluff, and doubtless in the region traversed by the three roads radiating from the capital. The documents printed in the second volume of this work show surprisingly few who obtained grants of land. This suggests that most of them merely "squatted" on vacant land, and built log cabins

---

[126] *Hist. MSS. Comm., Am. MSS. in R. Inst.*, III. v, vi, 19, 35, 45, 73.
[127] See Volume II. of this work, pp. 9-12.

or abodes "walled and thatched with palmetto (yucca) leaves." On October 11, 1782, Tonyn issued a proclamation giving notice of the cessation of hostilities and prohibiting the inhabitants from entering Georgia in a hostile manner and molesting the people therein.[128]

The richest and most notable Georgian who removed to East Florida in 1782 was Lieutenant Governor John Graham. He had served as a lieutenant colonel of the loyal militia, and since the middle of January had been superintendent of Indian affairs in the western division of the southern district. He had brought with him two hundred slaves to clear land and make settlements on five tracts of five hundred acres each at the head of the Matanza River. The grants for these plantations had been issued to him and his four sons individually. All of the tracts were apportioned out of a township of twenty thousand acres originally granted to Levett Blackburn. After employing Lieutenant Colonel John Douglas, another refugee from Georgia, as his superintendent and entrusting him with the task of clearing and planting his lands, Graham went to Charleston, South Carolina, at the end of November, 1782, and obtained leave from Lieutenant General Leslie to go to England for six months for his health's sake. He also secured Leslie's consent that Douglas should serve as the deputy secretary of Indian affairs during the interim. Douglas divided Graham's negroes into several large gangs and set them to work on the different tracts in November to clear, plant, build a reserve dam and the ditches for the cultivation of rice on one of the tracts, and erect houses, barns, and other structures to form several settlements. The slaves cleared a total of three hundred and forty acres and planted them with rice, provisions, and indigo. Douglas then received a letter from his employer advising him of the intended cession of East Florida to Spain, and later another letter to the same effect, but leaving him to continue in developing the properties if he thought best. Finally, in December, 1784, Douglas sent the negroes to South Carolina, where they were sold. In England, Graham petitioned for lands in the island of St. Vincent. He testified in December, 1783, that his salary as lieutenant governor had been stopped and that he expected his

---

[128] *Hist. MSS. Comm., Am. MSS. in R. Inst.*, III. 140, 164; Morrison (ed.), *Schoepf's Travels in the Confederation* (1783-1784), II. 231.

Refugees from Other Colonies

salary as superintendent would soon be terminated. Already his large landed properties in Georgia had been confiscated, and the commissioners of loyalists' claims figured his losses at a total of £18,631 10s and his debts at £3,783 2s 6d. He himself estimated his losses in East Florida at £3,542 9s 14d, or according to another set of figures at £2,270 18s 6d. His award on the Florida claim was £1,011 10s. The parties of Choctaws and Creeks who had accompanied Superintendents Graham and Browne from Savannah, did not remain long. The Creeks returned to their nation before the middle of November, 1782, and the Choctaws considerably earlier.[129]

[129] *Hist. MSS. Comm., Am. MSS. in R. Inst.*, II. 23, 252, 364, 373, 392, 425-526, III. 30, 179, 247, 334, 352, IV. 146, 147, 148, 166; *Second Report*, Bureau of Archives, Ont., 1904, pt. II. pp. 1126-1131; *Hist. MSS. Comm., Am. MSS. in R. Inst.*, III. 179, 222. See also Volume II. of this work, pp. 76-83; and Additional Notes, p. 336.

Chapter IX.

The influx of refugees from Charleston to East Florida, August-December, 1782. —The preparations for the evacuation of Charleston.—The first fleet to East Florida.—The strength of the province.—The removal of plundered negroes from Charleston.—The landing of troops and provisions in East Florida.—The new town of St. Johns Bluff.—The conditions in and around St. Augustine.—Victualing the refugees.—The deputation of Indians from the northern nations at St. Augustine.—Defensive measures in East Florida.—Withholding rations as a means of discipline.—Plundered slaves in East Florida.—Enumerating and locating the newcomers.—The committee of four principal refugees.—The Cunninghams.—The second fleet from Charleston.—The census of the refugees and the total population of East Florida.—The suspension of Judge Robert Catherwood from his offices.—Riots and other disturbances in the province.—Provisions of the act to regulate taverns, liquor shops, gaming places, and ferries.—The assize of bread in St. Augustine.—Plays for the benefit of distressed refugees.—Dr. William Charles Wells and The East Florida Gazette.—The necessity of keeping the Seminole Indians friendly.

SCARCELY had the last of the Georgians arrived in East Florida, when, by mid-August, 1782, a fleet of transports and victualers appeared at Charleston, and Lieutenant General Leslie began to prepare for the evacuation of that place. Already the loyal inhabitants had met and signified their intention of departing when the garrison should be withdrawn. They had also named their destinations, and recorded the number of their negroes and the quantity of their goods that were to be removed with them. This information was carried to Commander-in-Chief Carleton at New York by two delegated loyalists, Charles Ogilvie and Gideon Dupont, Jr., with a memorial requesting the postponement of the evacuation until the following spring, the notification of the governor of Jamaica to get ready for a large accession of people, and the issuance of orders to the board of police at Charleston to take cognizance of all debts owing to the loyalists, who should be permitted to indemnify themselves for their losses by carrying away the movable property of their enemies without the British lines. They also sent a memorial to Leslie, who had decided to forward the South Carolina Royalists, the Carolina

King's Rangers, the Royal North Carolina Regiment, or Volunteers, and the North Carolina Highlanders to St. Augustine, and bring thence to Charleston two battalions of the 60th Regiment. These arrangements were approved by Carleton, who directed Leslie to send some ordnance and stores to East Florida, and consult Tonyn concerning the needed supply of provisions to be sent with the loyalists going to St. Augustine. Merchants and other inhabitants who remained at Charleston, should make their own terms with the Americans.[130]

To Lieutenant Colonel Archibald Campbell, now governor of Jamaica, Carleton wrote desiring him to provide accommodation and subsistence for the great number of loyalists and negroes going thither. To Leslie he sent the memorial and other communications from Dupont and Ogilvie, and recommended that he alleviate as far as possible the distress of the departing refugees. To Tonyn he wrote under date of September 20, 1782, acknowledging the receipt of the general assembly's resolutions of August 16, which he answered by declaring that the evacuation of St. Augustine, or any part of the king's dominions, "must never be considered but as a measure of necessity." At the same time he requested full information as to the number and condition of the population in East Florida, their collective force, and the natural strength of the province. He explained that he needed this information for his own guidance.

In the second week of October, the first fleet of transports sailed from Charleston, carrying Lieutenant Colonel Archibald McArthur, who was to replace Lieutenant Colonel Beamsley Glazier as commandant in St. Augustine, the Royal North Carolina Regiment, the Carolina King's Rangers, the South Carolina Royalists, and the East Florida Rangers, Lieutenant John Wilson of the Engineers, and a supply of small arms, ammunition, and brass ordnance. A vessel was sent in advance to notify the authorities, and bring back the two battalions of the 60th Regiment. Leslie also decided to send as many provisions as could be spared from the magazines at Charleston.[131]

Meantime, Governor Tonyn forwarded a letter containing the informa-

[130] *Hist. MSS. Comm., Am. MSS. in R. Inst.*, III. 73, 91, 97, 109, 111, 112, 113, 125.

[131] *Ibid.*, pp. 149, 155, 160, 234. See also Additional Notes, in Volume II. of this work, p. 335.

Refugees and Defense Measures 115

tion called for by Carleton. He reported that the number of settlers before the arrival of the refugees from Georgia was about one thousand whites and three thousand negroes, that the loyalists from Savannah numbered approximately fifteen hundred whites and one thousand negroes, that he had been authorized by an act of the general assembly to arm every male inhabitant in East Florida in case of rebellion or invasion, that four hundred of the Georgians might bear arms and complete the strength of the provincial regiments, and that about five hundred negroes could be trusted with arms. Later he sent plans of the fortifications at St. Augustine and elsewhere in the province.[132]

As there were thousands of slaves within the British lines at Charleston, the citizens of South Carolina feared that these would be deported, as had been done before. About eight hundred had been employed in the engineer and ordnance departments. These negroes were in charge of Colonel James Moncrief, the commanding engineer, who owned lands in East Florida. In September, 1782, a Mrs. Butler, then in Philadelphia, had written to Carleton that about two hundred of her husband's slaves were in danger of being removed to Moncrief's properties. However, a month earlier, Governor John Mathews had informed General Leslie that if the slaves were carried off he would retaliate in several ways, which he specified. This warning induced Leslie to propose a negotiation looking to the mutual restitution of property. To this Mathews agreed. Accordingly, these gentlemen named a joint commission of four members, who signed an agreement on October 10. Leslie soon discovered, however, that the British officers were unwilling to give up their negroes. On October 18, he wrote to Carleton that officers who had seen long service in the south, regarded their slaves as their own property, pretended that they had been guides or spies, or had been promised their freedom by someone of rank, and were including them in the number of those to be carried away.[133] He added that the slaves were exceedingly unwilling to return to hard labor and severe punishment under their former masters, but that those paid for or removed by

---

[132] *Hist. MSS. Comm., Am. MSS. in R. Inst.*, III. pp. 163-164.

[133] *Ibid.*, III. 154, 161, 175, 177; Ramsay, *Hist. of the Rev. of South Carolina*, II. 375-379, 384; McCrady, *South Carolina in the Rev., 1780-1783*, pp. 658-662. Concerning Colonel James Moncrieff, see Volume II. of this work, p. 341.

permission should be sent to the island of St. Lucia. In consenting to ship these negroes to that island, Leslie was complying with orders. The government had employment there for several hundred blacks.[134] However, these blacks were but a small part of those taken from Charleston.

Governor Mathews and other citizens were still protesting against the plundering of their negroes at the very time that Leslie wrote his letter admitting the fact to Sir Guy Carleton. Their representatives found on transports bound for St. Augustine one hundred and thirty-six negroes, but only seventy-three of these were handed over. Other vessels displaying the royal pennant they were not permitted to visit. Colonel Moncrief is said to have taken with him the eight hundred slaves under his charge, and transports were furnished to some of the loyalists to convey a large number of the plundered slaves to East Florida.[135] Later on efforts were made at St. Augustine by Leslie's custodian of sequestered property to recover and restore some of these negroes, but with little success, as we shall see.[136]

The weather was stormy on the Florida coast in the latter part of October, 1782, and the bar at St. Augustine was unusually treacherous, thus delaying the landing of the troops, stores, and provisions at that point. Getting into port was much easier in St. Johns River, where larger ships could enter in safety on account of the greater depth of the bar, but it was the easiest of all at St. Marys. The troops were finally disembarked, and at the end of October the provisions were in the process of being landed both at St. Augustine and St. Johns Bluff. As most of the supply had been carried into St. Johns by mistake, it was necessary to send an officers' party and a galley thither to guard it. A vessel laden with clothing for the new garrison of provincials grounded on the bar at St. Augustine, and several men lost their lives in going to its assistance.[137]

All rentable houses both in St. Augustine and in the town of St. Johns Bluff must have been occupied before John Winniett had completed his first

[134] *Hist. MSS. Comm., Am. MSS. in R. Inst.*, III. 112.

[135] *Ibid.*, p. 177; Johnson, *Life of Greene*, II. 369; McCrady, *South Carolina in the Rev., 1780-1783*, pp. 660-661, 674.

[136] See *post*, pp. 122-124.

[137] Morrison (ed.), *Schoepf's Travels in the Confederation*, II. 226; *Hist. MSS. Comm., Am. MSS. in R. Inst.*, III. 192-193.

enumeration. Houses could still be bought when there was none for rent, and there were plenty of lots for sale at both places. With the coming of the loyalists from Savannah and Charleston many of them settled about the mouth of St. Johns River and built "an extensive place" six or seven miles up the river on Hesters or St. Johns Bluff, which rises precipitously seventy feet above tide water and fronts toward the mouth of the river. The site of this town was a tract of two hundred acres owned during most of the 1770's by William Hester. As early as June, 1771, Hester had sold a lot to a settler, and about 1779 conveyed the rest of the tract to Thomas Williamson. Williamson had divided it into town lots, each as a rule with a frontage of seventy-five feet and a depth of one hundred and twenty feet. He called the lots facing the water "bay lots" and named the two streets with which he provided the town Water Street and Prince's Street, the latter being at right angles to the former. The first dwellings erected were small log houses, but when the refugees began to flock in in the summer and autumn of 1782 numerous frame houses, with detached kitchens and other structures, were hastily built. The town which soon numbered about three hundred houses, according to Governor Tonyn,[188] had two taverns, a public house, a livery stable, a dry goods shop, a storehouse for "coarse and wet goods," a shop where plantation tools could be bought, and even a small free masons' lodge. During eight months the town had a "practitioner of Physick" in the person of Dr. Hugh Rose, who had come from Charleston and by his practice in his new location "cleared about 200 guineas." St. Johns Bluff was in a fair way to become soon "a place of some consequence," as Lieutenant Colonel McArthur, who had been made a brigadier general in January, 1783, wrote in the following May. It could be reached by larger vessels than St. Augustine, because the bar at the mouth of St. Johns River lay twice as deep as that before the provincial capital. The bar at St. Augustine was covered by a depth of not more than nine feet, was traversed by narrow tortuous channels, and was unprotected from the sweeping force of wind and wave. Beyond St. Johns Bluff and up the river the stretch of country contained many of the best plantations in the

---

[188] T. 77/20, No. 6; T. Frederick Davis, *Hist. of Jacksonville, Florida, and Vicinity*, Florida Hist. Soc., 1925, p. 13.

province, which produced among other things quantities of naval stores and lumber for export. The new town was expected to become the center of this trade. Squadrons of transports landed their throngs of refugees here, and numerous victualing ships unloaded great piles of barrels, boxes, and other receptacles filled with provisions of all kinds for the people who disembarked here and in large part for those who disembarked at St. Augustine.[139]

Religious services were conducted at this time both in St. Augustine and St. Johns by the Reverend James Seymour, who had been a missionary at Augusta, Georgia, from 1772 to 1780 under the auspices of the Society for the Propagation of the Gospel. As a loyalist Mr. Seymour had been subjected to "grievous losses and sufferings," including imprisonment. In 1780, he had fled with his family to Savannah, where he had endeavored to gain a livelihood by teaching school. Later he took his wife and children to St. Augustine. On account of the precarious state of health in which the Reverend John Forbes now found himself, Mr. Seymour became the officiating minister there and consented to remain until the Spanish governor should take possession. This information was contained in a letter from the missionary dated June 7, 1783. It also said that his former parishioners at Augusta had lately written to him proffering their service to have his name expunged from the confiscation bill if he would return and live among them. However, Mr. Seymour decided to go to the island of New Providence in the Bahamas and asked to be appointed the clergyman there. The society agreed to this arrangement and to continue his salary. Another letter from the missionary under date of February 14, 1784, showed that he was doing duty for Mr. Forbes, who had gone to Europe for the benefit of his health and who, it may be added, died soon after.

While Mr. Forbes remained in East Florida Mr. Seymour made frequent journeys to the more distant parts of the province and especially to St. Johns Town. Here the people treated him generously and invited him to stay among them, which he would have been glad to do had not the

---

[139] Morrison (ed.), *Schoepf's Travels in the Confederation*, II. 226, 227, 236; *Hist. MSS. Comm., Am. MSS. in R. Inst.*, IV. 97, 98, III. 192, 224. See also Volume II. of this work, pp. 33, 101, 105, 109, 174, 221; and Additional Notes, p. 309.

arrival of the terms of the peace terminated his hopes. His duties at St. Augustine had been rendered difficult by the great accession of loyalists from the Carolinas and Georgia and the lack of assistance. In fact, Mr. Seymour was now the only protestant clergyman in East Florida. Fortunately, his health was good and he was used to a warm climate, but he was barely able to keep his family alive on the salary of £60 received from the society, supplemented by the surplice fees and a small benefit from the garrison. He had recently baptized ninety-four children, married thirty-three couples, and conducted forty-seven funerals, besides attending several condemned criminals. The society testified to its appreciation of Mr. Seymour's arduous services by voting him a gratuity of £30. He wrote that he thought it both prudent and necessary to remain with Governor Tonyn and the garrison to the end of the evacuation of the province and then go to New Providence. He added that the governor had "always behaved to him with great attention and kindness." Mr. Seymour did not live to take up his intended work in the Bahamas. He died on his voyage thither.[139a]

The surplus population of St. Augustine spread out into new additions, and the neighboring country for a hundred miles around received numbers of the immigrant loyalists. Schoepf records that round about the capital stood "the hastily built cabins of these poor fugitives, walled and thatched with palmetto (yucca) leaves." He also tells us that it had become "so common at St. Augustine to see ships aground" on the bar there and on the coast generally that such disasters had "almost ceased to arouse sympathy or wonder" and that after the surrender of Charleston, "within two days no less than sixteen vessels, bearing refugees and their effects, went to pieces here and many persons lost their lives." He adds that "a great quantity of dismal remains of vessels" still protruded "on all sides from the sand and the water" when he was at St. Augustine in March, 1784.[140]

Before the arrival of the multitudes of loyalists the planters of East Florida had seldom, if ever, produced enough provisions for their own needs. The Georgians had brought scarcely a six weeks' supply for themselves, and the supply shipped by General Leslie from Charleston along

---

[139a] *Florida Historical Society Quarterly*, V. No. 4 (April, 1927), pp. 198-201.
[140] Morrison (ed.), *Schoepf's Travels in the Confederation*, II. 227-228, 231.

with the Carolinians was so much less than he had intended to send that only half the allowance allotted to individuals could be issued. The Georgians were given provisions for three months, the first importation of Carolinians for the same period, and the second importation had to be content with provisions for only six weeks. At the end of the first quarter the first two contingents were to receive only a month's supply in order that the last might get second delivery for another six weeks. If a new supply should not arrive by the end of these periods weekly issues would be resorted to, despite the great inconvenience of such an arrangement to the refugees. The original plan had been to furnish provisions to the Carolinians for a longer period than to the Georgians, but the latter protested in a memorial which they gave to Governor Tonyn to forward to Sir Guy Carleton. In it they represented their lack of supplies and prayed to be "put on as favorable a footing as the refugees from South Carolina," who were to have, they asserted, a full allowance for themselves and their negroes for nine months.[141]

Such was the food shortage in East Florida in January, 1783, when a large deputation of Indians from the northern nations came to St. Augustine from Detroit. This deputation included chiefs of the Mohawks, Senecas, Delawares, Shawnees, Mingoes, Tuscaroras, and other tribes, together with twelve hundred Cherokees and delegations of Creeks and Choctaws. Lieutenant Colonel John Douglas, deputy secretary of Indian affairs, mentions the presence of no other tribes than the Choctaws and Chickasaws, numbering together six hundred according to his statement. All told there were no less than two thousand Indians at this conclave. They came to learn the state of affairs in the south, to express their attachment to the British crown, to confirm the southern tribes in that sentiment, and particularly to promote a confederation among all the tribes. Fortunately they stayed only about ten days, departing on January 12, 1783, well satisfied with their entertainment. They caused a heavy drain on the store of provisions, for they were subsisted by Superintendent Browne and Deputy Secretary Douglas under authority from the governor and the commandant. While this visitation was notable for its large numbers and special

[141] *Hist. MSS. Comm., Am. MSS. in R. Inst.*, III. 320, 322, 317, 316. See also Volume II. of this work, p. 309.

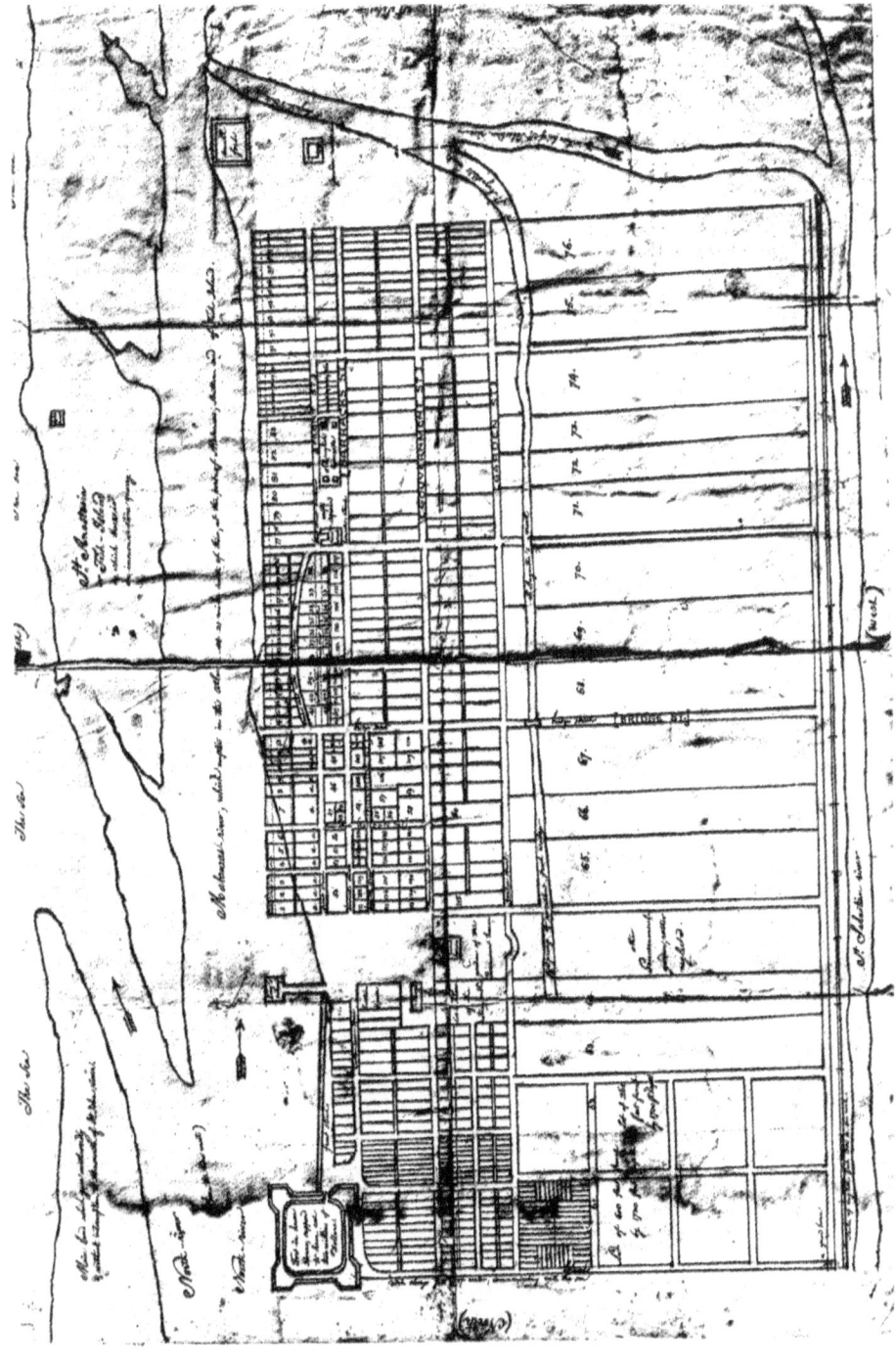

objects, it was the kind of experience the people at St. Augustine were accustomed to. Superintendent Browne, who had returned from Savannah at the evacuation about six months before, recorded that since his arrival more than three thousand Creeks had come down and that they still persisted in their visits, pleading "their poverty and their friendship."[142]

Brigadier General McArthur was now paying considerable attention to the defenses of East Florida, but was advised by Commander-in-Chief Carleton not to extend them too far. McArthur regarded the fort at the mouth of the Matanza River as the key to St. Augustine and used it at first as the headquarters for an officers' party and provided it with two eighteen-pound guns. A little later he replaced the squad by a captain and thirty men and stationed a large and a small galley in the harbor. He also stationed three galleys in the harbor of St. Augustine and in that of St. Johns River, while he sent an eighteen-pounder to the blockhouse near the bar of the river. Other defensive measures were planned by Lieutenant John Wilson, the engineer. McArthur thought it unnecessary to assign more than an officer, a sergeant, and ten men to Mosquito Inlet [now Ponce de Leon Inlet] eighty miles south of St. Augustine, in as much as there were in that neighborhood nearly a hundred men capable of bearing arms, who could occupy the blockhouse there in times of emergency to drive away privateers threatening their plantations. The commandant also urged Governor Tonyn to assemble the militia by companies, at least on Sundays. It was by letter of January 12, 1783, that Carleton appointed McArthur "to take the title of, and act as Brigadier General until a British officer of senior rank" should be sent to St. Augustine, or other orders given. Instructions were enclosed to define his new duties.[143]

The reduction in the quantity of provisions issued to the loyalists, resulted in the supply holding out "beyond expectations." But this was accomplished in part by declining to issue any provisions at all to twelve planters who had large gangs of negroes, and were best able to buy food for them. Thus it became possible to distribute rations for the fifth month to all needy refugees who had come with the first two fleets, and for ten

---

[142] *Hist. MSS. Comm., Am. MSS. in R. Inst.*, III. 322, 277, 325, 334, 367.

[143] *Ibid.*, pp. 224, 321, 327.

weeks to those who had come with the third, or last, fleet. Even so, there would still be enough provisions for the garrison until the end of June, 1783. An additional supply soon arrived from New York, and made possible an adequate distribution to the loyalists and their negroes until the following June.[144]

The threat to withhold rations from a planter served occasionally as a means of discipline in the case of unreasonable persons. Such a threat was used by Brigadier General McArthur to force a refugee by the name of Colonel Bull to consent to the removal of a guardroom that had been annexed to a house in St. Augustine, where half of the garrison's gunpowder had been stored, the house having recently passed into the possession of the colonel. Mr. Bull was informed that if he insisted on keeping the guardroom, though the powder had been removed to the Indian church, the provisions he had been receiving for his hundred and seventy-eight people would be stopped. Another refugee who was brought to terms by threatened deprivation of rations was Colonel Elias Ball, Sr., but in this case the dispute seems to have referred to the troops and stores. In a letter of April 5, 1783, General Carleton threatened to have these removed, at least such part as occasioned uneasiness. However, in May, General McArthur wrote that Colonel Ball had cried *peccavi* and received his rations.[145]

Back in the autumn of 1782, when the citizens of South Carolina were trying to prevent the plundering of their slaves by the departing British officers and the loyalists, Lieutenant General Leslie had evidently written to Governor Tonyn a word of warning about permitting such property to be shipped from East Florida to the West Indies. The governor had replied that he held the same views, and had given appropriate orders to the attorney general of his province. The next day Brigadier General McArthur complied with these orders to the extent of writing to Leslie that Lieutenant Wilson was sending back to Charleston twenty-eight negroes, "mostly rebel property."[146] The dispute about the ownership of plundered slaves in East Florida seems to have been more or less in abeyance during the absence in Tortola of John Cruden, the agent for property sequestered

---

[144] *Hist. MSS. Comm., Am. MSS. in R. Inst.*, III. 395.

[145] *Ibid.*, III. pp. 222, 224, 395, IV. 14, 90, 168.

[146] *Ibid.*, III. 222, 224.

by the British in South Carolina, but it was promptly revived by him when he appeared in St. Augustine in April, 1783. Near the end of that month Cruden was in correspondence with Dr. James Clitherall, a loyalist from South Carolina, who was trying to recover some slaves for their owners. At that time orders were received by Governor Tonyn from the secretary of state in England to make preparations in concert with Brigadier General McArthur for the evacuation of East Florida. Any desire the governor may have had to restore plundered negroes to their masters now disappeared, and near the end of May, Clitherall wrote to Cruden that the governor and his council were throwing every obstacle in the way of the latter's endeavors, aided by those of the loyalists, to do so. He added that the governor refused to surrender even those negroes who were without owners and had not been condemned by the court of admiralty; that gentlemen from South Carolina, then in St. Augustine, who had found their negroes willing to go back with them, were not allowed to swear to their property, far less to carry it away; that all this was being done under the cloak of friendship for the suffering loyalists, but that the negroes were to be kept until the governor and the council should see what the states would do in regard to the repeal of the confiscation acts, and that no opportunity was being missed to carry off negroes by persons who did not own them. On May 31, Dr. Clitherall demanded certain slaves, who were sequestered property, as the representative of Mr. Cruden, and was informed that the latter had no right to interfere. Gentlemen from South Carolina presented two memorials to the governor relating to property of other citizens of their state, especially property that fell under the positive orders of Sir Guy Carleton for restoration, but the governor failed to reply in writing, going so far as to assert that the commander-in-chief had no power over him and no right to direct him. Governor Tonyn and some members of his council insisted that they must first know that the confiscation laws of Georgia and South Carolina had been rescinded and the property of the loyalists restored before they would deliver up a single negro. A commissioner from South Carolina, who had been sent to St. Augustine to negotiate about the negroes, was placed on parole as soon as he landed and not permitted to write home. Dr. Clitherall did not conceal from the agent for sequestered property his own conviction that the governor was seeking to make profit by his confiscation of plundered negroes. On the contrary, he deplored that all public business was under the immediate control of a man "whose chief study is to inrich himself at the expence of the many." He expressed his opinion that such conduct on the part of the officials of East Florida only served to irritate the inhabitants of the neighboring states, insure adherence to the confiscatory measures, and bring ruin to many families.[147]

Lieutenant Colonel Glazier had appointed John Winniett commissary of refugees, and McArthur continued him in that office or changed his title to inspector of refugees, besides forming a committee of four of the principal refugees, namely, Colonels Elias Ball[148] and James Cassels[149] from South Carolina and Colonels John Douglas[150] and Josiah Tattnall[151] from Georgia, to take a census of the newcomers and their negroes and supply them with provisions. They were given two assistants.[152] John Winniett's first report included only those refugees who had arrived during the period from July to November 14, 1782. This showed two thousand one hundred and sixty-five whites—men, women, and children—and three thousand three hundred and forty blacks—also men, women, and children—or a total of five thousand five hundred and five.[153] The first fleet from Charleston seems to have brought in about nine hundred refugees. These included a number of persons described by Governor Tonyn as substantial merchants and planters, and also probably the provincial regiments. The merchants were accommodated with houses in St. Augustine, and the planters were placed on the lands left unimproved and unsettled by the original grantees. The small maritime force of the province was increased by the arrival of two galleys, but Tonyn asked for several more to provide an adequate defense and for a convoy to protect vessels engaged in the export trade. The refugees were in great need of plantation tools, and the governor exerted himself to supply them. McArthur called Leslie's attention to this urgent need, and asked him to send a supply from Charleston. At this time, or later, it was estimated that tools were necessary for five thousand refugees,

---

[147] *Hist. MSS. Comm., Am. MSS. in R. Inst.*, III. 419, IV. 57, 101, 113, 114-115, 194. See also Volume II. of this work, p. 351.

[148] See *post*, p. 126.   [149] See *post*, p. 126.
[150] See *ante*, p. 120.   [151] See *post*, pp. 125, 126.
[152] *Hist. MSS. Comm., Am. MSS. in R. Inst.*, III. 192.   [153] C. O. 5/560, f. 477.

and, curiously enough, the cost given included provisions for three hundred and fifty who had arrived before the evacuation of Georgia and South Carolina. The amount was £8,108 14s. As St. Augustine and St. Johns Bluff were crowded with the newcomers both McArthur and Tonyn employed every means to disperse them. Rations were now being distributed to both white and black refugees in large numbers.[154]

Of the committee of four prominent loyalists which supervised the enumeration of their fellow refugees and the distribution of provisions among them, Colonel Douglas of Georgia has already been spoken of. Colonel Tattnall had been a "planter and sawyer" in the same province, a mandamus councilor, and the commanding officer of a regiment of militia. In the early days of the Revolution he had been active in the defense of Savannah and the governor's house, and had assisted Governor Sir James Wright in his flight to the king's ships. For these acts of loyalty and as a hostage for certain prisoners held by the whigs he had been imprisoned for six weeks and then released on parole by exchange in March, 1777. Having denounced the committee of safety and its oath of abjuration, he had been ordered to quit the province within sixty days. He and a colleague, and doubtless others who had been ordered out of Georgia, had applied to Colonel Samuel Elbert for passes to go inland in open boats as there was no opportunity to go to sea within the time allowed. Colonel Elbert asked instructions of General Robert Howe about issuing the passports as he believed that the applicants intended to go to St. Augustine, adding that Tattnall and his companion claimed the privilege of going where they pleased "as prisoners under parole."

However, in December, 1777, Colonel Tattnall sailed with others to the Bahama Islands, and in the following June embarked for England. On the voyage he was taken prisoner by Count d'Estaing's fleet, carried to Philadelphia, and detained seven weeks. Thence he went by way of New York to England, where he landed in December, 1778. In March, 1780, he returned to Georgia as receiver general of the quit-rents at a salary of £100 a year, having been appointed by Lord George Germain. He also resumed his place in the council. Late in 1781, or early in 1782, he went

[154] *Hist. MSS. Comm., Am. MSS. in R. Inst.*, III. 220, 224; C. O. 5/560, f. 481.

to New Providence in the Bahamas, but was driven back to the mainland by the capitulation of the islands to the Spaniards early in May, 1782.[155] He remained at St. Augustine until the evacuation of East Florida.

South Carolina was represented on the committee of loyalists in the capital of East Florida by Colonels Elias Ball, Sr., and James Cassels. Both of these men seem to have come in the first fleet from Charleston in October, 1782, and both had been given commissions as colonels by Cornwallis in June, 1780. They evidently continued in service until the British lines had become contracted about Charleston. Cassels had landed at St. Johns Bluff, bringing thirty negroes with him. He soon rented a tract of uncultivated land on St. Johns River, employed his slaves in clearing and planting a part of it and in putting up a house and other buildings, and then departed from the province in April, 1784, leaving a crop on the place. He sold his negroes in South Carolina. Colonel Ball had lived on his plantation at Wambaw, in Ninety-Six District, South Carolina. His property, real and personal, had been confiscated by an act passed in the autumn of 1782. He estimated his losses in Carolina at £25,753, though the commissioners on loyalist claims cut this amount in half and awarded him £12,700. He carried with him to East Florida one hundred and seventy-five negroes. A few months after his arrival there he purchased a tract of fifty-seven acres "within the garrison," close to St. Augustine. Here he put about fifteen of his slaves to work, building a house and other structures and cultivating Indian corn. He employed the rest of them on unused land on the west side of St. Johns River about thirty miles from its mouth, where they cleared over a hundred acres, sawed lumber, and raised provisions. Thirty of his negroes died before he left East Florida in June, 1784.[156]

Several other prominent South Carolinians, who withdrew from Charleston to St. Augustine during the evacuation period, were Major William Cunningham, Colonel Patrick Cunningham, and Brigadier Gen-

---

[155] Egerton (ed.), *R. Comm. on Loyalist Claims, 1783-1785*, p. 318; *Collections* of Georgia Hist. Soc., V. pt. 2, pp. 62-63; C. C. Jones, *Hist. of Georgia*, II. 228, 372 n., 420-421.

[156] E. A. Jones (ed.), *Journal of Alexander Chesney*, p. 118; McCrady, *South Carolina in the Rev., 1780-1783*, p. 586. See also Volume II. of this work, pp. 15-18.

Refugees and Defense Measures 127

eral Robert Cunningham. The two latter were brothers, and the first named was their cousin. Robert Cunningham owned a plantation at Island Ford in Ninety-Six District and was the first district judge chosen for that division. Patrick had been early appointed deputy surveyor general of South Carolina. In July, 1775, Robert opposed the revolutionary measures passed by the provincial assembly, was already at the head of two hundred loyalists, and on August 23 advised his assembled neighbors at King's bridge on the lower Enoree River not to sign the whig association proffered to them by William Henry Drayton, a commissioner from the council of safety. On September 16, Captain Cunningham opposed the treaty signed by Drayton in behalf of a thousand men he had collected, and by Colonel Thomas Fletchall, Patrick Cunningham, and other leaders of twelve hundred loyalists. Robert and sixty of his followers remained on the field after all the others had dispersed. About five weeks later he was arrested at his house, taken to Charleston, examined by the congress, and committed to jail. Patrick and his party failed to rescue Robert on the way to Charleston, but captured some ammunition that was being sent to the Cherokees. He was caught in February, 1776, and soon lodged in jail. Both brothers were released after a few months. Thereafter they remained quiet until Sir Henry Clinton took Charleston in the spring of 1780. In the following June, Robert was made brigadier general of the brigade of militia of Ninety-Six District by Cornwallis, and Patrick was commissioned a colonel and commanded the Little River Regiment in this brigade. His brother was posted with one hundred and fifty men at Williamson's stockade, seventeen miles from Ninety-Six Court House, until his force was scattered in the autumn of 1781. Going to Charleston, he led forth five hundred men or more into the upper country, and in November routed Major Moore and his party near Orangeburgh. The two brothers were among the four thousand and more loyalists who left Charleston for East Florida at the evacuation. After a few months in the latter province Robert bought a tract of fifty acres on St. Marys River about one hundred miles from St. Augustine. He fenced his land, erected a log house and other buildings, cleared twelve acres, and planted "provisions." He departed from East Florida late in October, 1783. Patrick brought some negroes with him and employed them in cutting live oak. He remained in the province only two years.[157]

The most fearless and dreaded of the Cunninghams of South Carolina was Major William Cunningham. He had lived in Ninety-Six District and served on the whig side until the autumn of 1776. He fled to Savannah in 1778 in order to keep out of the reach of Captain William Ritchie, who had threatened to kill him for his defection. During his absence Ritchie abused his father and slew his brother John, who was a crippled epileptic. Cunningham returned home on foot, went to Ritchie's house, and mortally wounded him. Going to Charleston after its surrender, he came back to take vengeance on his former neighbors and to carry out Cornwallis's orders to put to death as traitors those who had renewed their allegiance to the crown and then had taken up arms against the British. In the summer of 1781 he operated in the upper country, captured Turner's station, and added recruits to his force. In November, he partly destroyed and partly dispersed Colonel Richard Hampton's men at Orangeburgh, took Colonel Hay's station, and executed the garrison. His force now numbered three hundred men, but separated into bands, two of which soon retired to Charleston. They formed a part of "Bloody Bill's" regiment of mounted militia. Returning to Ninety-Six District in June, 1782, he was overtaken by Captain William Butler near Corradine's Fort on Saluda River. Some of his men were shot and others captured in crossing the river, but Major Cunningham escaped to Charleston on his fast horse "Silver Heels." In October, he and five of his men made their way on horseback to St. Augustine. He bought "a small improvement" on St. Johns River on land claimed by Lady Egmont and cleared and planted fifteen acres. He finally left East Florida on May 1, 1785.[158]

[157] Force, *Am. Archives*, 4th ser., IV. 29, 40, 41, 42, 43, 63, V. 582, 646, 650; E. A. Jones (ed.), *Journal of Alexander Chesney*, pp. 64, 87-88, 104; Curwen, *Journal and Letters*, 1845, pp. 618-638; Moultrie, *Memoirs*, I. 96-100; Drayton, *Memoirs*, II. 343-344; *Hist. MSS. Comm., Stopford-Sackville MSS.*, II. 169; R. W. Gibbes, *Documentary Hist. of Am. Rev., 1764-1776*, pp. 200, 224; *Hist. MSS. Comm., Am. MSS. in R. Inst.*, I. 227; Egerton (ed.), *R. Comm. on Loyalist Claims, 1783-1785*, p. 56; Sabine, *Loyalists of Am. Rev.*, 1865, I. 348; *Second Report*, Bureau of Archives, Ont., 1904, pt. II. 800; McCrady, *South Carolina in the Rev., 1775-1780*, pp. 38, 43-45, 52 ff.; McCrady, *South Carolina in the Rev., 1780-1783*, pp. 24, 35, 27, 67; A. O. 12/109. See also Volume II. of this work, p. 315.

[158] Curwen, *Journal and Letters*, 1845, pp. 638-640; *The Royal Gazette*, September 12,

Refugees and Defense Measures

By Christmas, 1782, the South Carolinians, together with some North Carolinians who had been in military service at Charleston and had come with the first convoy, were forming their settlements in the country. Inasmuch as the final evacuation of Charleston had taken place on December 14, a second fleet under the convoy of the *Bellisarius* brought a much larger contingent of loyalists and negroes, which—according to Governor Tonyn—was supposed to comprise a thousand of the former and fifteen hundred of the latter. This fleet arrived on December 31, part of it putting into St. Johns River and part anchoring at St. Augustine. The latter squadron lost some vessels on the bar before the town, namely, the galley *Rattlesnake*, two provision ships, and six private vessels, four lives being lost with those last named.[159] Writing on January 3, Mrs. Elizabeth Lichtenstein Johnston said that out of the last fleet from Charleston sixteen small vessels had been lost on and about the bar and that six or eight were high on the beach. She thought it "amazing how such a place was ever settled." Many loyalists remained in Charleston, as did also the British merchants, who had petitioned for permission to stay six months in order to recover debts due to them and dispose of their effects.[160] Even so the enumeration at Charleston of the people who sailed for East Florida, dated December 13, 1782, shows two entries, one giving a total of twelve hundred and seventy-three whites —men, women, and children—and sixteen hundred and fifty-three blacks, and the other three hundred and forty-two whites and five hundred and fifty-eight blacks. This second entry seems to give the number that came in the first fleet from Charleston.[161] But these figures are low, as shown by a return received in St. Augustine from General Leslie on July 15, 1783.[161a]

November 18, 21, December 8, 1781; Johnson, *Traditions*, pp. 311, 548-549; Ramsay, *Revolution in South Carolina*, II. 272-273; Draper, *King's Mountain and Its Heroes*, p. 468; Johnson, *Life of Greene*, II. 301-302; McCrady, *South Carolina in the Rev., 1780-1783*, pp. 467-476, 490, 628, 631.

[159] *Hist. MSS. Comm., Am. MSS. in R. Inst.*, III. 276-277, 319; Massachusetts Hist. Soc., Miscellaneous Papers, 1769-1793 (MS.), V. 139; *South Carolina Hist. and Gen. Magazine*, January, 1910, p. 26; McCrady, *South Carolina in the Rev., 1780-1783*, p. 674, where the second entry is credited to West Florida; Elizabeth L. Johnston, *Recollections of a Georgia Loyalist*, p. 210.

[160] *Hist. MSS. Comm., Am. MSS. in R. Inst.*, III. 301, 373-374.

[161] See *ante*, p. 114.   [161a] C. O. 5/560, pp. 811-820.

This document is entitled "A Return of Refugees with their Families & Negroes, who came to the Province of East Florida, in consequence of the evacuation of the Province of Carolina." Its totals are as follows:

	Whites	Blacks
Men	1,117	1,281
Women	499	800
Children	402	482
Total	2,018	2,563
		2,018
Grand total		4,581

The total number of the refugees from both South Carolina and Georgia that arrived during the period of the evacuations can be computed from the figures given in the enumerations made by John Winniett, as follows:

	Georgia	Carolina	Total
Winniett's report, July to November 14, 1782[162]			
Whites	782	1,383	2,165
Negroes	1,659	1,681	3,340
			5,505
Winniett's report, November 14 to December 31, 1782[163]			
Whites	911	1,517	2,428
Negroes	1,786	1,823	3,609
			6,037
Winniett's report, December 31, 1782, to April 20, 1783[164]			
Whites			497
Blacks			1,336
			1,833
		Grand total	13,375

[162] C. O. 5/560, f. 477; Carleton Papers, XXX. no. 164.
[163] C. O. 5/560, f. 507; Carleton Papers, XXX. nos. 167, 168, 171.
[164] Carleton Papers, XLVII. no. 86.

Before the arrival of the fleet from Georgia in July, 1782, the figures giving the population of East Florida, according to Governor Tonyn, were:

	Whites	1,000	Negroes	3,000
Adding Winniett's totals	Whites	5,090	Negroes	8,285
		6,090		11,285

we arrive at the total population on April 20, 1783, namely, 17,375. From these last figures it will be seen that Brigadier General McArthur's statement in May, 1783, that the population of East Florida was about sixteen thousand and that the proportion between the two races was nearly three blacks to two whites,[165] was only crudely approximate.

Early in December, 1782, while John Winniett was gathering the figures for his second report of the numbers arriving from Georgia and South Carolina, and six months after Governor Tonyn had received notice from Lieutenant General Leslie of the proposed surrender of his province to Spain, the latter made public this distressing piece of news. He softened the pain of it as best he could by assuring the inhabitants that their welfare would be attended to by the British government and that he would cooperate with them in obtaining "compensation for their great losses and suffering."[166]

On January 2, 1783, Governor Tonyn read a letter to the council from Colonel John Skey Eustace, a commissioner under flag of truce from Georgia, charging Dr. Robert Catherwood, judge of the court of vice admiralty, with selling "expectations" of the award of certain captured negroes. Judge Catherwood was given a public hearing at his request, and incriminating evidence was produced in support of the particular charge and others. Accordingly, on January 23, the members of the council unanimously recommended that he be suspended from his offices of judge of the court of vice admiralty, assistant justice of the courts of common law, and member of the council until the royal pleasure should be known. Early in February, Tonyn sent the proceedings in this inquiry and the council's

---

[165] *Hist. MSS. Comm., Am. MSS. in R. Inst.*, IV. 97.
[166] *Ante*, p. 103; *London Chronicle*, July 22-24, 1783.

recommendation to the privy council in England, with a letter explaining that Judge Catherwood's indiscretions, especially his open avowal of taking extortionate fees "under the denomination of fees of indulgence," had excited a clamor against him, but that no attention had been paid to the rumors until a specific charge had been made.[167]

Turmoil prevailed in various parts of East Florida at this time. Loyalists and their slaves had been pouring in by the thousands, among them several provincial regiments who had returned from their campaigns in Georgia and the Carolinas; large delegations of Indians came and went; and numerous sailors from the transports and other vessels enjoyed a boisterous holiday on shore. The taverns, "punch-houses," liquor shops, and gaming places did a rushing business. Riots and other disturbances frequently occurred, especially in St. Augustine. Hence the general assembly passed an act on January 25, 1783, forbidding any person to sell beer, cider, brandy, rum, punch, or other strong liquors "in less quantities than two gallons at one time," except wine in case a license had been obtained for retailing it. A license must also be procured in order to conduct a public house supplied with a skittle-alley, shuffle-board, billiard table, or other gaming device under penalty of £10 for every offense, one-half to go to the informer and the other to the fund from the general tax.

A one-year license for a tavern, punch-house, restaurant, or liquor shop in St. Augustine, or within four miles thereof, cost £5 and for other parts of the province £10, for a skittle-alley or shuffle-board £20, for a billiard table £30, and for any other gaming place £10. The qualifications of the applicant were to be certified to by two or more justices of the peace. Any person without a license who supplied liquor to another, or with a license retailed it to slaves or Indians, or bartered it for goods of any kind to soldiers, sailors, indented servants, or Indian slaves was subject to a fine of £10. Keepers of taverns or liquor shops were forbidden to sell more than one shilling and sixpence worth of spirituous liquor to an "articled mariner" in one day, or permit him to drink in the place after nine o'clock at night. A breach of these regulations brought a fine of 20s. Ferry owners or ferry-men were prohibited from transporting fugitive seamen or soldiers

[167] C. O. 5/547; *ibid.*, f. 47.

who could not produce passes or certificates of discharge. If they were found guilty of wilfully so doing they were liable to a fine of £5.

Licenses for the sale of wine in less quantities than three gallons, to be drunk on the premises, were issuable at £3 each to persons who had no license for retailing spirituous liquors, but to those having such licenses at £2. Commissioners to issue licenses were to be appointed by the governor or the commander-in-chief. The provisions of this act were published in *The East Florida Gazette* of February 22 to March 1, 1783, by order of the police office.

Another law mentioned in the same issue of that paper shows that some of the bakers and sellers of bread in St. Augustine were guilty of sharp practices on the public. This law ordered a monthly "assize of bread" to fix the quality, weight, and price of that commodity in the provincial capital. The senior justice, Samuel Farley, was to publish at least once a month the market price of flour and the legal weights of the different sized loaves with their prices. When flour was 50*s* per hundred weight the six-penny loaf was to weigh one pound avoirdupois, but when flour was half that price a loaf of the same weight was to sell for threepence, a two-pound loaf for sixpence, and a four-pound loaf for a shilling. Bread exposed for sale was to be marked with the price and maker's name. Justices, churchwardens, or vestrymen were authorized to enter shops and bakeries, weigh loaves, and determine their quality, and in case they found the bread unsatisfactory confiscate and distribute it to the poor of the district, and fine the proprietor from one to five shillings for every loaf seized. Any person resisting search or seizure was to be fined £20.

As numbers of the refugees were poor or impoverished, aid was extended to them in various ways. They were granted land and supplied with food and agricultural implements. In overcrowded St. Augustine many had to rely more or less on charity. Some of the money for this purpose was raised by theatrical entertainments. An advertisement in *The East Florida Gazette* stated that on Monday evening, March 3, 1783, two plays were to be given at the theater in the state house for the benefit of the distressed refugees, one the "Beaux Stratagem," a comedy, and the other "Miss in Her Teens," an "entertainment." The characters were to be taken by gentlemen, and tickets were procurable at Mr. Johnston's store, formerly Mr. Payne's, at five shillings and ninepence each for seats in the pit and one shilling less for those in the gallery. The doors were to be open at six o'clock and the performance begin at seven.

The East Florida Gazette was edited and published by Dr. William Charles Wells in St. Augustine as a weekly newspaper. Wells' father, Robert Wells, had been a binder and seller of books and the printer of *The South Carolina and American General Gazette* in Charleston. He had made himself offensive to many of the Carolinians by the loyal sentiments expressed in the columns of his paper and had departed for Great Britain in the summer of 1775. Three months later he had been joined by his son, who had refused to sign the whig association. During the next few years young Wells had studied medicine in Edinburgh and London, and, after going as surgeon with a Scotch regiment to Holland in 1779 in the service of the United Provinces, he had returned to Edinburgh and taken the degree of M.D. Early in 1781, he made the voyage back to Charleston, became an officer of volunteers and, like his father, a bookseller and printer. At the evacuation of Charleston in December, 1782, he sailed for St. Augustine, taking his printing press and a pressman with him. There in the latter part of January, 1783, he began to issue the first newspaper ever published in East Florida. He became the captain of a company of militia or volunteers and the manager of a group of young officers who acted plays for the benefit of distressed refugees, among the plays being "Zara," "Douglas," and "The Orphan." Dr. Wells was one of the performers, but was not a success in comedy parts. On April 21, 1783, he issued a special number of his paper as *The East Florida Gazette Extraordinary*, which contained the news of the peace. In a letter written at St. Augustine on the preceding day Mrs. Elizabeth Lichtenstein Johnston, a refugee from Georgia, mentions the arrival of a packet from London "with the accounts of a peace being made, with terms most shameful to Britain," and adds:

The war never occasioned half the distress which this peace has done, to the unfortunate Loyalists. No other provision has been made than just recommending them to the clemency of Congress, which is in fact casting them off altogether.

Early in July, Dr. Wells visited Charleston under a flag of truce on busi-

Vol. I.
No. 5.

THE East-Florida GAZETTE.

NULLIUS ADDICTUS JURARE IN VERBA MAGISTRI. Hor.

From SATURDAY, FEBRUARY 22, to SATURDAY, MARCH 1, 1783.

POLICE OFFICE.

WHEREAS frequent riots and other disorders have happened in this province, and particularly in the town of St. Augustine, for want of regulations and restrictions in keeping taverns, punch-houses and retailing of spirituous liquors, whereby the peace and good government of the province has been disturbed, and the morals of many of the people have been corrupted; for remedy whereof, as much as may be, the General Assembly by an Act passed the 17th day of January last, directs, that no person or persons shall sell any beer, cyder, brandy, rum, punch, shrub or other strong liquors whatsoever, (except wine, where a licence is obtained for retailing the same) in less quantities than two gallons at one time, and to one person, or keep any skittle alley, shuffle board, billiard table, or any other publick gaming place, until he, she, or they shall have first obtained a licence, or licences from the Treasurer, under the forfeiture and penalty of ten pounds sterling for every offence, one half to the informer, and the other in aid of the general tax.

If any person not having a licence shall sell or dispose of on credit any spirituous liquor in less quantities than two gallons at one time to any one person, the sum shall be forfeited and he, shall in the person so credited or trusted be liable to any suit on that account.

Persons obtaining licenses to keep a tavern, punch-house, victualling house, or house of accommodation for the entertainment of strangers or to retail spirits or liquors in the town of St. Augustine, or within four miles thereof, shall pay five pounds; and for other parts of the province two pounds; for keeping a skittle alley twenty pounds, a shuffle board twenty pound, a billiard table thirty pounds; and for any other such gaming place ten pounds, all which licences shall continue in force one year only; the fitness and qualifications of persons who apply for licences to be certified by two or more Justices of the Peace.

If any person shall barter, exchange, give or lend any spirituous liquors or strong drink by any deceitful ways and means, in order to evade the intentions of the Act, not having a licence, or having a licence shall retail liquors to slaves (not having tickets) or to any Indian, or barter in exchange for the same with goods of any kind from a soldier, sailor, indented servant, or Indian slave, the offender shall pay a fine of ten pounds.

For persons crediting or trusting any mariner belonging to any vessel in this province, having signed the ship's articles, a sum exceeding five shillings, (except by leave of the master) shall forfeit the money or goods so credited or trusted, and if such mariner be harboured or kept by any person, in his or her house, the offender shall forfeit the sum of two shillings for every hour he is so continued.

Keepers of taverns or tippling houses, or any other person who shall sell spirituous liquor mixed or otherwise to any articled mariner to the amount of more than one shilling and sixpence in one day, or entertain, or suffer him to remain in his or her house to drink or tipple therein after nine o'clock at night (unless by leave of the master) shall forfeit the sum of twenty shillings.

If any person or persons keeping or attending any ferry shall wittingly or wilfully transport or suffer to be transported over such ferry, any fugitive seaman or soldier not having a certificate of his discharge, or a written pass from his officer, shall forfeit five pounds.

The Governor or Commander in chief for the time being is by the said Act authorised to empower Commissioners to grant licences to such persons as they shall think fit, to sell any kind of wines in less quantities than three gallons, to be drunk and spent within the house of the party so licensed: and such commissioners shall take for every licence the sum of three pounds, where such person has not a licence for retailing spirituous liquors; and

where a person has such licence the sum of two pounds; and if any one shall presume to sell any kind of wines in less quantities than three gallons, without having first obtained such licence, every person so offending shall forfeit and pay the sum of twenty pounds sterling.

To the end therefore that so useful and salutary a law may be strictly obeyed, if any person shall be convicted of the least breach thereof before the senior Justice, the party offending will be proceeded against with the utmost rigour by the said Act prescribed.

ASSIZE of BREAD.

FORASMUCH as the inhabitants of the town of St. Augustine, have been and yet are aggrieved and subjected to great and many inconveniences for want of some wholesome restrictions on the bakers of bread for sale, with regard to the quality, weight, price and assize of an article so absolutely necessary to their health and support; and whereas evil disposed persons have taken the advantage for their own unlawful gain and lucre to deceive and defraud his Majesty's subjects, and more especially the poor, being thereby greatly distressed: The legislature of this province, for remedy in future of a practice so encroaching and oppressive, has required the senior Justice, upon the best information he can get, to make publick once in every month or oftener if he shall think necessary, the ordinary or market price of flour, which shall be taken and deemed the market price from time to time of such flour, for one month after such publication, and also to set forth the separate different weights of each of the sizes of bread, that is to say, than when flour is at the rate of fifty shillings per one hundred weight, the sixpenny loaf shall weigh one pound averdupois [sixteen ounces] and the other sizes in proportion, diminishing or encreasing the weight of the said loaves according as the flour rises or falls, and according to the aforesaid proportion.

I have therefore enquired what is the present ordinary or market price of flour this day, and find it to be twenty-five shillings the hundred weight, so that for one month from the date hereof, the three-penny loaf is to weigh one pound, the sixpenny loaf is to weigh two pounds, and the shilling loaf is to weigh four pounds, to be made of good wholesome wheaten flour, without any mixture other than what shall be necessary to the well making or baking thereof, to be judged of by the Magistrate trying and examining the same.

And every baker or other person making bread for sale, or exposing the same for sale, must mark or imprint, or cause to be fairly marked or imprinted on every loaf, so by him or her made, the price of such loaf, together with the initial letters of his or her Christian name, and surname at length, that the baker and price thereof may be more distinctly known.

The Justices, Churchwardens, or Vestrymen, may in the day time enter into any house, shop, stall, bake-house, or ware-house, or of, or belonging to any baker or seller of bread, and there search for, view, try and weigh all and any bread of such person or persons, which shall be there found, and they may enquire into and examine all complaints concerning the above offence; and if any such bread so found shall be wanting either in goodness of its materials, or not duly baked, or wanting in its due weight, as by this assize is set, or not marked as aforesaid, or shall be compounded or made up with any other materials than what are by the Act allowed, then and in every such case it shall be lawful for the Justices, Church-wardens or Vestry, or any two of them, to seize and take the bread so found, and cause the same to be given and distributed to the poor of the district where such seizure shall be made, and also to impose a fine on any baker or seller of bread so offending a sum not exceeding five shillings, nor less than one shil-

ling for every loaf so found deficient and seized; and if any person whatsoever shall not permit or suffer such search or seizure to be made, or shall oppose, hinder, obstruct or resist the same, he, she, or they so doing shall for every such offence forfeit the sum of twenty pounds sterling.

SAMUEL FARLEY,
Police Office, Feb. 25, 1783. Senior Justice.

(BY PERMISSION)

On MONDAY, Evening the 3d of March,
WILL BE PRESENTED,
At the THEATRE,
In the STATE-HOUSE,

The BEAUX STRATAGEM,

A COMEDY.

To which will be added,

The ENTERTAINMENT of

MISS IN HER TEENS.

The Characters by Gentlemen, for the benefit of the distressed Refugees.

Doors to be opened at SIX o'Clock; Performance to commence at SEVEN; no money taken at the door.

Tickets to be had at Mr. JOHNSTON's Store, formerly Mr. PAYNE's.

PITT, 5s. 9d. GALLERY, 4s. 9d.

WHEREAS the senior officer of his Britannic Majesty's ships and vessels of war, at the port of Charlestown, having thought proper to transfer the appointment of Commissary for naval prisoners for the southern district, to St. Augustine, East-Florida: All commanders of privateers, tenders of marque, armed vessels of every denomination, and prize masters are hereby directed, that in future they do report and deliver their naval prisoners, at the Commissary for naval prisoners, office, St. Augustine.

Given under my hand and seal of office, at St. Augustine, East-Florida, this 26th day of February, one thousand seven hundred and eighty three.

CHARLES PRINCE, Commissary
Naval Prisoners Southern District.

By order of the Senior Officer.

East-Florida, St. Augustine, February 26, 1783.

Wanted to Charter,

FOR Government use, a VESSEL of about one hundred and forty tons burthen, well sheathed, and in every respect fitted for a naval prison ship. Any persons willing to furnish a vessel answering the above description, are to give in their proposals at St. Augustine, to Lieutenant CHARLES PRINCE, Commissary of naval prisoners or to

JAMES FRASER.

To be Sold and possession of the greatest part of the Premises immediately given.

THAT excellent HOUSE and LOTT, on the Bay, known by the name of Dessel's Quarter, pleasantly situated for a private family, and equally well for either wholesale or retail business; it is at present owned and occupied by JAMES WALLACE, to whom any one intending to purchase may apply.

The premises are extensive and well fitted with back store, kitchen, shed, &c. and room for further improvement.

TO BE SOLD,

A light, airy

POST COACH,

With harness compleat for a pair of horses.

Enquire of the Printer.

FACSIMILE OF THE FIRST PAGE OF ONE OF THREE ISSUES OF THIS NEWSPAPER DISCOVERED IN ENGLAND IN THE SUMMER OF 1926 BY MR. WORTHINGTON C. FORD

ness for his father's family. Nevertheless, he was arrested and kept in jail for three months in a room with a ceiling that admitted water freely whenever the rain fell. On August 13, Miller's *South Carolina Gazette* denounced him for returning and bringing with him a copy of his newspaper in which "the good people of these States are insulted." Governor Tonyn sent a commissioner in the person of Mr. Wyllie, who was later appointed chief justice of the Bahama Islands, to demand his release. The mission was successful, for the *South Carolina Gazette* of October 4 mentions that a sloop had lately sailed from Charleston for St. Augustine with Dr. Wells on board. In the following spring John Wells, the doctor's elder brother, returned from England, and "in consequence" of his arrival, as Dr. Wells tells us, he himself embarked at St. Augustine for Great Britain in May, 1784. John Wells may have continued for a brief time the publication of *The East Florida Gazette.* At any rate, he printed at least two books in St. Augustine in 1784, which bear the following titles:

(1) *The Case of the Inhabitants of East Florida. With an Appendix, containing Papers, by which all the Facts stated in the Case, are supported;* (2) *Essay II. By Samuel Gale. On the Nature and Principles of Publick Credit. Containing an Investigation of the Natural Laws and Principles of Circulation, Restorative of the Publick Credit of any State, in Case it shall have become decayed. Together with a Postcript, pointing out the Method of applying those Laws and Principles, Practically, to the Present State of the Publick Debts and Finances of Gt. Britain.* St. Augustine, East-Florida: Printed for the Author, by John Wells. MDCCLXXXIV. The latter is a folio publication of some fifty pages and the only copy known is in the New York Public Library. Mr. Gale was a refugee from Charleston, South Carolina, and went to London in 1784 where he printed four essays on the nature and principles of public credit during the years 1784 to 1787. He soon went to Nassau in the Bahamas and there married. Later he decided to remove to his native land, but died while preparing to do so. Meantime, Dr. Wells had returned to London. There he rapidly achieved eminence in his profession and in natural science. In 1816 he was awarded by the Royal Society the gold and silver medals established by another American loyalist, Count Rumford. As his practice was never large he lived

modestly in a small house in Serjeants' Inn, Fleet Street. He died on September 18, 1817, and was buried in the parish church of St. Bride in the same street, which contains the tombs of his father and mother.[167a]

With the prospect of the evacuation of East Florida confronting him, Governor Tonyn and the other inhabitants of the province were more than anxious not to offend their Indian neighbors, the Seminoles. The governor, therefore, regarded the omission of a sum for the purchase of presents for these Indians from the estimate of the provincial civil establishment as a vital matter. As the sum had been stricken out by the British government, he wrote late in April, 1783, to the appropriate committee of the privy council that such action would expose the settlements in East Florida to the depredations of the Seminoles and render it impossible to maintain the peace of the province, especially as those Indians were allies of the inhabitants and occupied lands more or less interspersed with those of the latter. He notified the committee that he had drawn bills on the treasury to pay for the presents distributed among the Seminoles.[168]

[167a] Louisa Susannah Wells, *Journal of a Voyage from Charlestown, S. C. to London* (1778) (New York Hist. Soc., 1906), app., pp. 83-90, 97-100; *Proceedings*, Am. Antiquarian Soc., XXIII. pts. 1-2 (1913), p. 369; Sabine, *Loyalists of the Am. Rev.*, II. 406-409; Elizabeth L. Johnston, *Recollections of a Georgia Loyalist*, pp. 210-211.

[168] C. O. 5/547, f. 135.

Chapter X.

The evacuation of East Florida, February, 1783-June, 1784.—The memorial of merchants and others in London.—The cession of East Florida to Spain.—Instructions to prepare for the evacuation.—Fears for the security of persons and property in East Florida.—The inclination of the Creeks and Cherokees to leave the country.—Governor Tonyn's arguments against the cession.—Consternation and lawlessness after the receipt of the news.—Claimants of plundered negroes in St. Augustine.—Lands for the refugees.—The choice of the provincial regiments as to where they should go.—The mutinous spirit among them.—Indecision among the inhabitants.—A vengeful spirit among the Indians.—Departures to England.—Major Andrew Deveaux's expedition to New Providence.—His operations, and the capitulation of Governor Claraco y Sanz.—The appraisal and public sale of property in East Florida.—Permission to emigrants to settle where they please.—Preparations for the movement to the Bahamas.—The accession of loyalists in Great Abaco Island.—The problem of tonnage needed for the evacuation.—Lieutenant Wilson's report on agricultural conditions in the Bahamas.—The proposal of Nova Scotia as a place of settlement.—The appointment of Brigadier General McArthur to command in the Bahamas.—Remonstrances against the removal of troops from East Florida.—The arrival of transports and victualers.—Inhabitants and the provincial regiments to leave for the Bahamas, Nova Scotia, and Great Britain.—Governor Tonyn forms two troops of horse to check banditry.—The first fleet with provincial regiments departs for Nova Scotia.—Further facilities for the evacuation.—Tonyn to remain, regulate the embarkation, and reconcile the Indians.—The special officers for the evacuation.—Three companies of the 37th Regiment arrive.—Steady exodus of loyalists, including four thousand for the Mississippi.—General McArthur writes of the arrival of refugees and provisions in the Bahamas.—Colonel David Fanning's activities in East Florida and his departure for the Mississippi.—Word brought by a packet from London on February 3, 1784, that the Floridas would not be retained.—What Schoepf saw of the evacuation.—The departure of transports for Nova Scotia.—A transport sails for Jamaica.—Emigrants from East Florida bound for the Bahamas and other destinations.

THE prospect of the cession of East Florida to Spain brought a response in England as early as February, 1783. On the tenth of that month a meeting was held in London of the merchants, planters, and proprietors of lands in the Florida peninsula under the chairmanship of Lord Hawke. This meeting presented a memorial to Secretary of State Thomas Townshend to the effect that the memorialists had experienced losses to the amount of £300,000 and upward from 1763 to the present in cultivating East Florida; that in 1777 and 1778 they had assisted at their own expense in defending that colony from the Americans and had suffered great loss; that their property had been given up as the price of peace and for the recovery of the Bahama Islands; and that they hoped for compensation in the latter.[169]

At the end of February, Lord Townshend sent a communication to Governor Tonyn in regard to the third article of the preliminaries of peace, by which East Florida was to be ceded to Spain. The governor was directed to give notice thereof to the inhabitants that they might lose no time in settling their affairs and preparing to comply with the terms of the article. In concert with the commanding officer of the troops he was to take measures for removing the artillery and other effects of the crown. The treaty terms relating to the loyalists were to be communicated to them, and every facility was to be given them in attempting to recover their estates.[170]

On April 7, General Carleton wrote to Brigadier General McArthur, enclosing a proclamation ordering the cessation of hostilities. He asked what were the intentions of the provincial troops and loyalists in East Florida, that is, whether they would remain or depart, in order that he might assist them. This letter was soon followed by the instructions, dated February 14, from the secretary of state in England to prepare for the evacuation of the province within the interval named in the eighth article of the treaty of peace. These instructions also required the recall of all officers and traders from the Indian tribes. Superintendent Browne and others feared that the enforcement of the latter stipulation would arouse the resentment of the Creeks and Cherokees.[171] Only a few days before the commons house of assembly had appealed to the superintendent to exert his influence in keeping the Indians quiet and maintaining their friendship, this appeal being supplemented at the end of April by another from William Brown, the speaker of the house. Simultaneously the agents of the English noblemen who owned lands and slaves in East Florida, applied to

---

[169] C. O. 5/560, f. 781.   [170] C. O. 5/560, Governor of East Florida.
[171] *Hist. MSS. Comm., Am. MSS. in R. Inst.*, IV. 16, 17, 57, 62.

Superintendent Browne to provide for the security of persons and property in the present crisis. With a view to preventing possible depredations by the Indians, the superintendent decided to send for the principal chiefs of the Creek nation and to keep them at St. Augustine until the evacuation was accomplished. This would leave their bands of warriors without leaders and render them inactive.[172]

Fortunately the Indians were too loyal and too well provided with presents to show resentment on account of the pending evacuation. However, Brigadier General McArthur wrote on May 19, 1783, to the commander-in-chief that the minds of the red men appeared to be "as much agitated as those of the unhappy loyalists" at the prospect, and that the Indians had proposed to abandon their country and accompany their friends. At that time he was expecting a large delegation of the Indians. Superintendent Browne gave further proof of their loyalty by writing for vessels to remove the Creeks, who were "determined to follow the fate of their English friends." They wished to go to the Bahama Islands, which numbers of the loyalists had already chosen as their destination. The Cherokees were also ready to depart. Schoepf reports that the Cowdriver, one of the latter's old warriors, "assured Governor Tonyn that if the great man over the water would give them large canoes and land for hunting, most of the men of his nation would be willing to withdraw with the Governor."[173] Already Superintendent Browne had sent orders recalling the officers and traders from the Cherokee and Creek nations. Sir Guy Carleton was opposed to the removal of the Indians, because he believed that the Bahamas were poorly adapted to their mode of life and that they would soon tire of their situation there. He therefore urged that they be dissuaded from going, although he agreed to furnish conveyance for those who persevered in their demand. In a letter written to Lord Townshend in mid-May Governor Tonyn deprecated the necessity of giving up East Florida. Surveying the conditions in the province, he found that a great part of the original planters, after expending large sums of money and overcoming many difficulties, had reached comfortable circumstances. In the midst of general

---

[172] *Hist. MSS. Comm., Am. MSS. in R. Inst.*, IV. 40, 89.
[173] *Ibid.*, pp. 58, 88, 89, 119; Morrison (ed.), *Travels in the Confederation*, II. 240.

revolt they were distinguished for their allegiance. The recent accession of nearly twelve thousand loyalists from other provinces had created general confidence that Florida would remain a British possession, and had induced the refugees to build houses and clear plantations. Such settlements extended more than a hundred miles on each side of St. Augustine, great additions had been made to the town, and two villages had arisen on St. Johns River, in one of which two hundred commodious houses had been built during the last six months.

These people were now under the necessity of encountering fresh difficulties and seeking new habitations in some remote part of the British dominions, instead of submitting to the arbitrary power of a foreign prince, or supplicating their late enemies for admission to citizenship. There were serious objections to the several regions proposed for the emigrants to remove to. The West India Islands were already populated, subject to unremitting heat, and required more capital to form plantations than the refugees in general possessed. The Bahama Islands were mere rocks fit only for fishermen. Nova Scotia was too cold for those accustomed to a southern clime and unsuitable for the owners of slaves. The inhabitants were at a loss where to go. Meantime Tonyn advised them to raise their crops in confidence that the British government would "provide a commodious residence for them." He feared that the American states, though disposed to retain the property already confiscated from the loyalists, would encourage the industrious refugees to return and settle.

The news of the cession did not incite the Indians to depredations, but did plunge the people of East Florida into a state of mingled consternation, dissatisfaction, and confusion that enabled small bands of white men to commit numerous lawless acts. Horses and cattle were stolen from the plantations far and wide, and even from barns and pastures in St. Augustine; robberies were committed on the roads; houses were plundered, and negroes were carried off or enticed away. Numerous evidences of this state of lawlessness are to be found in our documents, and show that it lasted during two and a half years, that is, from the receipt of the news of the cession to the departure of Governor Tonyn and other civil officials in November, 1785. The first theft of horses and cattle was attributed to some of the

Greek inhabitants, but the systematic plundering was done by small bands of malefactors who had engaged in similar operations in Georgia during the closing years of the war. They had their lurking places on the frontier of East Florida and made their inroads from that quarter, being sometimes joined by the lower sort of people of no property. The loyalists called them "banditti." Tonyn was greatly worried by them, and often refers to them in his correspondence.

Meanwhile, as early as May, 1783, there had been a "considerable influx of transient people" from Georgia and South Carolina at St. Augustine to recover their plundered negroes. Tonyn had permitted various loyalists to go to those states for the purpose of reclaiming their confiscated estates and recovering debts. However, they had not been permitted to land, having been attainted during the Revolution. The governor therefore felt justified in retaining the slaves of the visitors from South Carolina and Georgia until time should discover whether or not those states meant to fulfil their treaty obligations respecting the loyalists. To this end he had admitted a commissioner from South Carolina and sent one of his own thither.[174]

It will be recalled that at the time of transmitting the proclamation announcing the cessation of hostilities, early in April, 1783, Sir Guy Carleton had asked about the intentions of the provincial troops and loyalists in East Florida, in view of the impending evacuation of the province, the news of which was received from England in the course of the same month.[175] Carleton had recently suggested that lands be granted to these people by Governor Tonyn with a view to their remaining in the province. When the governor replied to this proposal on May 15, which he had anticipated by granting lands to a number of the refugees in the hope that East Florida would be permanently retained by the British, he said that he agreed with Carleton in giving every encouragement to the loyalists by gratuitous grants, but regretted that the cession of the province to Spain would prevent him from affording a settlement to "those brave men."[176]

Already one of the provincial regiments at St. Augustine had expressed

[174] C. O. 5/560, f. 717.   [175] *Ante*, p. 138.
[176] *Hist. MSS. Comm., Am. MSS. in R. Inst.*, IV. 75.

its intentions. On May 10, Lieutenant Colonel John Hamilton had reported to Brigadier General McArthur that the officers and men of his regiment, the Royal North Carolina Volunteers, had resolved to embark for some British settlement as soon as ordered to do so, either to Britain, Halifax in Nova Scotia, or the West Indies, and that a few of the men and non-commissioned officers preferred to be discharged before they should embark, "fearing they might be separated from their families." On May 16, Major Thomas Fraser reported for his corps, the South Carolina Royalists, that both the officers and men wished to go to some British settlement as soon as they should be informed that provision had been made for them, that they desired to receive their discharge at St. Augustine, and that about one-fourth of them intended to return to their families on the continent. Finally, on May 19, Superintendent Thomas Browne wrote to McArthur that the members of his regiment, the Carolina King's Rangers, declined to choose where they would go on being disbanded until informed what they might expect in the different countries which had been suggested as places of refuge.[177]

The anxiety prevailing among the people of East Florida during those appalling days had given opportunity for speculation and the spread of wild rumors concerning their fate. One of these rumors had received credence among the men of the provincial regiments, namely, that they were to be sent to the East and West Indies without their consent. By May 1, they had been ready to mutiny, and had demanded their immediate discharge. The persons who were responsible for starting this report were punished, and the regiments had become again quiet and obedient.[178]

When Brigadier General McArthur transmitted to Sir Guy Carleton the letters from the commanding officers of the provincial regiments, he wrote that the members of those organizations were "extremely anxious to know what lands or gratuities" would be allowed to those who chose to go to Nova Scotia, although they dreaded the climate there. He added that both the refugees and old settlers had such antipathy to remaining under the Spanish government, and that most of them had talked of leaving East Florida, but knew not whither to go. Meantime, they had seen the violent

[177] *Hist. MSS. Comm., Am. MSS. in R. Inst.*, IV. 84, 88.
[178] *Ibid.*, p. 90.

Evacuation of East Florida

resolutions against the return of loyalists adopted in many of the states, and those who had been counting on going back to one, or another, of those states had been worse upset in their plans. In the last mail, private letters had been received from London, which hinted vaguely that the British government was likely to exchange Gibraltar for Porto Rico and the two Floridas, and until this report was silenced by the arrival of later letters a large majority of the population could not decide what to do. By May 20, however, a number of the old settlers and a few refugees had given in their names as having decided. They were encouraged to sign for an early departure by a proclamation issued by the governor. Ninety had thus far chosen the island of New Providence in the Bahamas, eighty-five, Jamaica, and forty-seven, England. The decision of these people and any others who might follow their example, created an unexpected demand on the store of provisions, as Brigadier General McArthur promised to furnish an eight weeks' supply for those going across the Atlantic, a six weeks' supply for those leaving for Jamaica, and a three weeks' supply for those going to New Providence.[179]

Fortunately a number of victualing ships had arrived at St. Augustine and St. Johns Bluff by May 19, 1783, with more provisions, which McArthur wrote "would have made the poor refugees happy were it not for the sad alternative of seeking a new asylum or living under the Spanish government." However, the squadron had lost one of its vessels, the *Eliza* with a cargo of over a thousand barrels of flour, beef, pork, oatmeal, and peas, and sixty casks of rice, on a shoal near Beaufort, North Carolina. John O'Halloran, who had been on the doomed ship, reported that the captain would scarcely be able to save any of its cargo or rigging owing to the rapaciousness of the people at Beaufort. As soon as Carleton learned of this disaster, he promised to make good the loss of provisions and furnish a supply for those emigrants who were going to England and New Providence.[180]

Delegations of Indians were at St. Augustine in the closing days of April and on to the middle of May. Governor Tonyn, Brigadier General McArthur, and Superintendent Browne held a conference with them, and

[179] *Hist. MSS. Comm., Am. MSS. in R. Inst.*, IV. 92, 93.   [180] *Ibid.*, pp. 92, 96, 165.

regretted the drain on the public stores caused by their presence. Among these Indians were the Cowdriver and other chiefs, who are said to have sworn vengeance against the king for giving away their country and to have declared that on the departure of the English they would claim their own and kill every Spaniard who should thrust his head beyond the lines of St. Augustine. The correspondent, who wrote this to Captain Robert Bisset, then in London, added that the inhabitants of East Florida were in the utmost confusion and were at the mercy of bands of plunderers, that they were so enraged over the cession that he was afraid of serious trouble whenever the Spaniards should come to take possession, that the troops were mutinous and several soldiers had been killed the night before, their plan being to burn the barracks, plunder St. Augustine, seize the fort, arm the negroes, and put to death those whites who should oppose keeping the country. The writer of this letter quoted the unruly soldiers as saying they would rather die than go to Nova Scotia for their discharge, and he further remarked that St. Augustine was full of citizens from Georgia and South Carolina seeing about the reclaiming of their plundered negroes.[181]

The safe arrival of seven victualers in May under convoy of the *Bellisarius* and *Narcissus* made it possible to subsist the loyalists until the end of September, 1783. This encouraged Governor Tonyn to try to keep them in East Florida throughout that period. At the close of it such crops as they had planted could be harvested, and they would thus have enough food to carry with them in their migration until they should find "some suitable retreat."[182] By May 20, Major Manson of the Royal North Carolina Regiment and Captain William Wylly of the Carolina King's Rangers were planning on making the voyage to England, the former for the sake of his health and the latter to solicit the government in behalf of the officers of his regiment who had empowered him to do so. About the same time a sergeant and eight men mutinied against their superior officer and deserted from the Mosquito blockhouse. They were soon captured by a party of refugees serving in the militia. This party was rewarded by Brigadier General McArthur, who gave them fifty guineas, this sum being doubled by the garrison at St. Augustine.[183]

[181] *Hist. MSS. Comm., Am. MSS. in R. Inst.*, IV. 75, 83.
[182] *Ibid.*, p. 83. [183] *Ibid.*, pp. 94, 107-108.

In a letter written at the end of May to Lieutenant General Leslie, Brigadier General McArthur said that some of the principal inhabitants of East Florida were sending their wives and children to England by the transports then at St. Augustine, while others were departing for Jamaica and New Providence. He also referred briefly to the success of "little Major" Deveaux's expedition from St. Augustine in taking possession of the island of New Providence. Andrew Deveaux was a refugee from Beaufort, and was highly qualified by temperament and experience to accomplish this exploit. In the early part of the Revolution he had pillaged General Stephen Bull's plantation and set the torch to Sheldon church in what is now Beaufort County, South Carolina. After other adventures Deveaux had become a major in the loyal militia of Beaufort. Later in the war he had sailed with three small vessels and a party of soldiers from Stono River, and gathered forage as far as Ossabaw, Georgia. Late in February, 1782, he had managed to thwart a part of General Anthony Wayne's expedition in its attempt to destroy the forage and rice on Hutchinson's Island, opposite Savannah, and on Governor Wright's plantation about a mile northeast of the town. On the evacuation of Savannah Deveaux had gone to East Florida.[184]

Already in February, 1783, he was collecting volunteers for his expedition against New Providence in the Bahama Islands. Among those who agreed to join him was Colonel David Fanning, who received from the daring leader the articles of agreement that were to be signed by the volunteers. They provided that Deveaux was to furnish the men with arms, ammunition, and provisions for the expedition, that he was to be in sole command, even after the expedition, and that the volunteers were to rendezvous in St. Augustine on March 15 and be ready to go on board ship on three hours' notice. Those who wished to settle in the Bahamas were to be provided with land. All prizes taken on land or sea were to be divided among the officers and men according to rank, after deducting the expense of the expedition. Those guilty of disobedience of orders, or of mutiny, were to forfeit their prize money and suffer imprisonment in proportion to

[184] McCrady, *South Carolina in the Rev.*, *1780-1783*, pp. 610-611; C. O. 5/560, in folder at end of volume.

their offense. Ten shares were to be reserved by Lieutenant Colonel Deveaux and Captain Wheeler for deserving men and other shares for wounded men and the widows and orphans of any who might fall in the expedition. The volunteer raising the most men was to be second in command. Any who were unwilling to remain in the islands after their conquest were to be given passage to Jamaica or St. Augustine.[185]

These articles were exposed for signature at St. Augustine on March 3, 1783, the signers agreeing to forfeit to Deveaux, his heirs, or assigns, £10 in case of failure to comply with any of them. Colonel Fanning succeeded in raising thirty young men for the expedition, and with them awaited Deveaux's arrival at Halifax Inlet until he heard that he had sailed. Deveaux embarked at St. Augustine on April 1 with sixty-five men in two armed brigantines, commanded by Captains Dowd and Fennell, and sailed for Harbor Island, where he recruited for a few days, securing negroes principally. He thus increased his force to two hundred and twenty men, of whom not more than one hundred and fifty had muskets. With these Royal Foresters, as they were styled, he landed on New Providence Island near the eastern fort, which guarded the harbor of Nassau on that side, at nightfall. Finding the garrison asleep, except one sentinel whom he seized, Deveaux with about one hundred and fifty of his men carried this fort at daylight on the fourteenth, while Captains Wheeler and Dowd with a detachment of seventy Foresters captured three formidable galleys lying abreast of the fort. The invaders then climbed the heights in the upper part of Nassau, set up men of straw to increase their apparent numbers, some of the troops being disguised and painted as Indians, and Colonel Deveaux summoned the "grand fortress" to surrender, giving a pompous description of his force. Governor Claraco y Sanz put him off with a reference to a peace that had been signed. On April 18, Deveaux erected a battery of twelve-pounders on each of two commanding hills, within musket shot of the "grand fortress," and hoisted the English colors on both. Spanish shot and shells were ineffectual to prevent this, and a well-directed shot at the governor's house from a fieldpiece brought the governor to terms. He signed articles of capitulation by which he and his garrison marched out

---

[185] Savary (ed.), *Col. David Fanning's Narrative*, pp. 58-59. See also Volume II. of this work, p. 349.

Evacuation of East Florida

with all the honors of war, the troops were to be sent to Havana and the governor to Spain, the Spanish vessels in the harbor were to be surrendered, and the Spanish merchants were given two months in which to settle their accounts. Despite the fact that New Providence was garrisoned at the time by seven hundred Spanish regular troops, Governor Claraco experienced the humiliation of surrendering four batteries with about seventy cannons and four large galleys, all of which Deveaux sent to Havana with the troops. The victor had made his conquest possible by first capturing a fort with its thirteen cannons, three armed galleys, and about fifty men.[186]

Some days later the news of this gallant and astonishing exploit reached St. Augustine. Brigadier General McArthur sent a newspaper containing an account of it to Sir Guy Carleton and wrote of it as "a very splendid action lately performed by Major Deveaux of the Beaufort militia," but added that "unluckily he was nine days too late." Already on April 9, England had signed a treaty with Spain by which the Bahamas were restored to the former. The success of Deveaux and his plan to grant land to those of his followers who desired to settle there, undoubtedly stimulated many of their fellows to do the same. Naturally these people wished to learn about the conditions in the islands, and some of their number soon went to New Providence to gather information.[187]

Meantime, numerous loyalists were preparing for the inevitable surrender of their possessions in East Florida. Committees were busy appraising the lands, houses, and other property of their neighbors; William Slater and John Champneys were appointed by Governor Tonyn to conduct public sales of these estates, which soon glutted the market and could only be sold at low figures, or not at all. Many of the people became so needy and the price of necessities so high that the heads of government found it necessary to have ready money for current payments.[188]

---

[186] Malcolm, *Historical Memorandum, relating to Forts in New Providence*, 1913, pp. 22-26; Sabine, *Loyalists of the Am. Rev.*, 1864, I. 377; Fairbanks, *Hist. of Florida*, p. 237; McKinnen, *West Indies*, pp. 249-252; Bacot, *The Bahamas*, pp. 45-47; Forbes, *Sketches*, p. 53.

[187] *Hist. MSS. Comm., Am. MSS. in R. Inst.*, IV. 93, 128.

[188] *Ibid.*, 108, 203, 233. See also Volume II. of this work, pp. 9, 11, 12 and note, 13, 14, 19, 21, 22, 70, 71, 91, 126, 131, *passim*.

By June 5, 1783, John Cruden, the agent for sequestered property, was in New York about ready to sail for England. His brother James was also in New York and sent John's papers to Sir Guy Carleton on the day before he went on board ship to return to St. Augustine. Carleton wrote to McArthur at this time that every man in East Florida should have the liberty to go where he pleased to settle, and that McArthur should give permission to any who might choose to live under Spanish rule or return to the United States. He also wrote to Governor Tonyn urging him to form a militia. As a matter of fact the governor had been for some time organizing such a body, but had been lately stimulated to greater efforts by the lawlessness that had broken out in the province. The militia now numbered eight regiments of more than two hundred men each, but McArthur insisted that they had never been properly mustered.[189]

On June 16, the commandant wrote to Carleton that the vessels with refugees and other inhabitants for Jamaica and New Providence would sail in a few days and that the vessels for England were getting ready, but that in the event of a favorable report concerning ungranted lands in Providence many of the refugees would settle there. He also mentioned that a delegation of Creek Indians was said to be on the way to St. Augustine, and that he would have to provide them with powder from the magazine as that was the only commodity he had that would be useful to them.[190] The party of Creeks arrived about a week later as an escort for the commissary and some traders from their nation, and McArthur found it necessary to purchase certain supplies for them. They did not stay long, and departed in so amiable a mood that McArthur hoped to convince them that their emigration with the loyalists would be "the greatest evil that could befall them."[191] In fact, they and the other Indians accepted the advice given them.

The ship for Jamaica sailed on June 25 and that for New Providence probably about the same date. The two transports for England did not leave until July 9. The acquisition of the Bahamas and the prospect that the habitable islands among them would soon be occupied by loyalists from

---

[189] *Hist. MSS. Comm., Am. MSS. in R. Inst.*, IV. 96, 125, 159, 164, 168.
[190] *Ibid.*, p. 158. [191] *Ibid.*, pp. 165, 203, 233.

East Florida and others from New York, led Sir Guy Carleton to suggest, under date of June 20, that Lieutenant John Wilson, the acting engineer at St. Augustine, be sent to examine into the military state of New Providence. Just a month later Lieutenant Wilson sailed for that island. At the end of July, Carleton decided to include the Bahamas as a part of the Southern District, and instructed McArthur to consider them under his command until further orders. As Carleton had been receiving numerous applications from refugees at New York to settle in those islands, and as he knew nothing of the conditions there, including the amount of ungranted land, he requested McArthur to extend Lieutenant Wilson's investigation so as to include all the Bahamas. Carleton explained that he had recommended to the British government that the lands ungranted, or escheated, in the Bahamas, be given free of all expense to those loyalists who had lost their estates through their allegiance and should settle there. His letter is dated July 29. A month later Lieutenant Wilson returned to St. Augustine, and the gentlemen who had preceded him to New Providence seem to have returned at the same time. The report made by the latter was "not very favorable." They said, according to McArthur's account, that the soil was rocky and that there were "no tracts of land contiguous where any considerable number of negroes could be employed." McArthur added that Lieutenant Wilson confirmed their statement. Meantime, the acting engineer was very busy finishing his plan of the harbor, town, and environs of Nassau, in order that it might be forwarded to Carleton.[192]

Meanwhile, a large number of loyal refugees had associated in New York for the purpose of settling in the island of Great Abaco, the largest of the Bahama group. On June 28, 1783, Richard Blake, the chairman of their committee, addressed a memorial to General Carleton asking the appointment of a few companies of militia for the island and stating that the associators expected many other loyalists to join them from St. Augustine. Another memorial from the associators, written about the same time, reported the number of loyal inhabitants of East Florida who were emigrating to Abaco as being upward of fifteen hundred. The number of

---

[192] *Hist. MSS. Comm., Am. MSS. in R. Inst.*, IV. 170, 203, 233, 247, 248, 294, 339, 340.

those who went from New York to Abaco was fourteen hundred and fifty-eight. A few days later Carleton enclosed in a letter to McArthur a list of persons to whom he had granted commissions as the officers of eight companies of militia, who had gone, or were going, to the Bahama Islands. He added that these commissions were only to be in force until the governor should make further regulations. These companies of militia were organized in Great Abaco. Provisions were sent from New York and the British West Indies to Brigadier General McArthur at Nassau on New Providence Island in sufficient quantity to subsist the refugees for six months.[198]

On September 10, 1783, Governor Tonyn wrote to Rear Admiral Robert Digby chiefly about the tonnage necessary for the final evacuation of East Florida. He was unable to give him an exact estimate, and no one could have done so. Instead, he gave him the number of the population, about sixteen thousand he said, of whom it was imagined nearly ten thousand would emigrate, but it was impossible to guess in the fluctuating state of the people's minds what shipping would be wanted. About twenty thousand barrels of tar and turpentine were to be exported, and the merchants wished to take with them their considerable stock of goods. The officers of the civil government and other gentlemen, with their families, were going to England. Some people with negroes preferred Jamaica and the Windward Islands, and many the Bahamas. Tonyn solicited Digby's protection and accommodation for alleviating the distresses of these faithful subjects, and requested their conveyance to such parts of the British dominions as they might select.[194]

On September 12, Lieutenant Wilson received the instructions of Lieutenant Colonel Robert Morse, the chief engineer, to pay a second visit to the Bahamas and view all the islands. As soon as he could make up the accounts of his department he again set off, and in his round collected the information for a more accurate and reassuring report than that previously

---

[198] *Hist. MSS. Comm., Am. MSS. in R. Inst.*, IV. 224, 351; Stark, *Hist. and Guide to Bahama Islands*, pp. 172-173; Siebert, *Legacy of Am. Rev. to British West Indies and Bahamas*, pp. 18-19.

[194] C. O. 5/560, f. 583.

given by the gentlemen who had confined their observations to New Providence. Without attempting to conceal the fact that the islands were rocky and their surface was rough, Wilson's report called attention to the three kinds of soil on the islands, namely, one kind adapted to the growth of cotton, another to the cultivation of all sorts of vegetables, and the third to the production of guinea corn. Lieutenant Wilson attributed the uncultivated state of the Bahamas to the indolence of the inhabitants, who contented themselves with whatever nature produced without the expenditure of human effort. They did not clear the land, but planted small patches of yams, guinea corn, and sugar cane, and left these uncultivated. Pineapples, oranges, lemons, limes, cocoa, and other fruits common to the West Indies would grow in the Bahamas. The soil had never been subjected to a fair test, such as it would now be put to by the new settlers.[195]

This favorable report, together with statements in Carleton's letters that numbers of loyalists at New York were going to the Bahamas, inclined many of the inhabitants of East Florida to go thither. Carleton was willing that such emigrants should be provided with conveyance and the same assistance as those going to other places. Late in August he wrote to Superintendent Browne and Brigadier General McArthur, mentioning Nova Scotia as one of the destinations to which the troops might be sent from St. Augustine. To Browne he suggested that the extra officers in the Indian Department "provide without delay for their future maintenance," since the troops were soon to be withdrawn. If any of those officers should prefer to settle in Nova Scotia, or any other part of the king's American dominions, they should be recommended for lands like other officers. He thought that Browne should remain at St. Augustine as superintendent of Indian affairs after the removal of the troops. Writing to McArthur, Carleton emphasized the advantages held out to those troops who should become settlers in Nova Scotia, and promised that vessels would be sent from New York to convey them to Halifax, or any other part of Nova Scotia where their lands might be located and they would be disbanded, or they might go to the Bahamas. In the latter case, however, McArthur must furnish the conveyances. The men discharged at St. Augustine should be paid to

---

[195] *Hist. MSS. Comm., Am. MSS. in R. Inst.*, IV. 291.

the day of their discharge, and receive a fortnight's additional pay in advance. The royal artillery should remain on duty at St. Augustine until the final evacuation. On the departure of the troops McArthur should repair to New Providence, and assume immediate command of the Bahama Islands until further orders, or until the arrival of a governor appointed by the British government. Carleton bestowed a deserved recognition on McArthur by recommending him for appointment as governor of the Bahamas.[196]

Just as remonstrances were made when the removal of the garrison was proposed in the summer of 1782, so now a protest was forthcoming. On September 11, Governor Tonyn wrote to General Carleton that disasters were feared if the troops should be removed before the final evacuation of East Florida. He enclosed a memorial and petition, bearing the same date, signed by Chief Justice James Hume and other principal inhabitants, remonstrating against the expected disbanding of the provincial troops and warning the governor of "the accumulated distress to which not less than ten thousand" loyalists would be subjected by the dissolution of the civil government unless they were supplied with shipping to carry them to other British settlements.[197] At the same time an address was presented to Brigadier General McArthur by the members of both houses of the general assembly and other principal inhabitants. It extended thanks to McArthur for his uniform and unexceptionable conduct, but protested against the proposed removal of the troops and the discharge of the soldiers. It asked that some of the troops be kept in service to prevent rapine and murder, and that ships and provisions be supplied for those inhabitants wishing to go elsewhere. It closed by saying that neither the Bahamas nor Nova Scotia would suit people with negroes.[198]

In part, at least, the prayers of these petitioners were answered, for on September 12, a fleet of transports and victualers arrived at St. Augustine. Two days later a number of the inhabitants applied for conveyance to the Bahamas. Among these were Superintendent Browne and a large proportion of his Carolina King's Rangers. He asked for them the privilege of keeping their arms and accoutrements, already promised to those going to

---

[196] *Hist. MSS. Comm., Am. MSS. in R. Inst.*, IV. 291, 293, 294.
[197] *Ibid.*, p. 348.　　　　　　　　[198] *Ibid.*, pp. 356, 358.

ACTING ENGINEER AT ST. AUGUSTINE DURING
THE CLOSING MONTHS OF THE REVOLUTION

Evacuation of East Florida

Nova Scotia. Browne still believed that many of the Indians would insist on accompanying him. Nearly two-thirds of the South Carolina Royalists wished their discharge at St. Augustine, while more than half of the Royal North Carolina Regiment chose to go to Nova Scotia and about forty to Great Britain. Carleton gave instructions that those bound for Nova Scotia be furnished provisions, that the Royal Artillery be provided for until the end of June, 1784, and that the most needy refugees be supplied out of what was left.[199]

On July 13, 1783, six men of the Royal North Carolina Regiment had deserted, but had been caught after their leader had been killed. A month later the Creeks were expected to visit St. Augustine in great numbers. The officials felt the importance of keeping the Indians in good temper. Early in October letters were received in Savannah from St. Augustine, which said that about four hundred of the soldiers of the provincial regiments would leave for the Bahamas and Nova Scotia, that General McArthur would go to New Providence, and that the artillery would remain in possession of the castle until the Spaniards should arrive.[200]

In October, a few days before the embarkation of the soldiers for Nova Scotia, Governor Tonyn authorized the formation of two troops of horse to check banditry, although no provision existed for this service and the expense was heavy. He commissioned Colonel William Young and Captain Alexander Stuart, refugees from Georgia and South Carolina, respectively, as the commanding officers of the two troops, and gave them orders to protect the persons and property of their fellow provincials. Tonyn feared that the withdrawal of the garrison would give a free reign to banditry. However, St. Augustine was less than a week without a garrison, but the bandits continued their operations until the final evacuation by the British. Horses and negroes seem to have been their favorite booty. The inhabitants generally were in a panicky condition, which was continually affected by changing rumors. In the face of widespread banditry and disorders among the troops the administration felt largely helpless.[201]

---

[199] *Hist. MSS. Comm., Am. MSS. in R. Inst.*, IV. 188, 420-421; Siebert, *Legacy of Am. Rev. to British West Indies and Bahamas*, pp. 21-22.

[200] *Hist. MSS. Comm., Am. MSS. in R. Inst.*, IV. 35, 356, 402, 403; *Gazette* of the State of Georgia, Savannah, October 9, 1783.

[201] C. O. 5/560, f. 717, f. 847.

On October 3, such of the troops as chose to remain were disbanded at St. Augustine, and a week later, others embarked for Halifax. Quietness prevailed and the militia turned out "with great alacrity," but a few days before a dreadful gale had raged, "which caused a general alarm" as the tide had risen above Payne's corner.

On October 28, the first fleet for Nova Scotia received on board Brigadier General Robert Cunningham and part of the officers and men of the South Carolina Royalists and the Carolina King's Rangers. They had been mustered in St. Augustine late in the previous April. A few officers of both regiments carried with them several slaves. Under royal instructions the members of these and other regiments were granted lands in Nova Scotia at the rate of two hundred acres to every non-commissioned officer and one hundred to every private, exclusive of what the members of his family were entitled to. The grantees were freed from the payment of fees and quit-rents for the first ten years, and were furnished rations for one year. They were also permitted to keep their arms and accoutrements. The South Carolina Royalists received their lands at Stormont, on the east side of Country Harbor, and the Carolina King's Rangers at St. Marys Bay.[202]

Governor Tonyn was promised four thousand tons of shipping from England and an additional number of transports from the Leeward Islands and Jamaica to execute the evacuation. By a letter of December 14, 1783, from Whitehall, the governor was informed that negotiations had been undertaken for the purchase of land in the Bahamas, so that tracts could be granted to the refugee settlers and that land would also be appropriated to their use in the West Indies. Supplies of provisions were to be sent to both groups of islands in proportion to the numbers going thither. Tonyn was further advised that the captains of the transports were to take their orders from him, that the emigrants should be classified according to their destinations, and be embarked in appropriate companies. He was warned that the shipping would not be sufficient to accommodate all in a

[202] Elizabeth L. Johnston, *Recollections of a Georgia Loyalist*, p. 214; see Volume II. of this work, p. 375; Notes from the Muster Rolls; *Collections* of Nova Scotia Hist. Soc., 1896-1898, X. 25-26; Rev. W. O. Raymond, "The U. E. Loyalists" in *St. Croix Courier* (New Brunswick) series, 1892, LXVI.

single embarkation, and that the vessels must therefore be ordered to return for additional voyages. As most of the inhabitants would look to Tonyn for advice and assistance in selling, or removing, their property, he was asked to remain, regulate the embarkations, and prevent confusion as far as possible. He was to act by virtue of the respect accruing to him rather than by real authority, as his governorship would terminate with the actual cession. He would best meet the king's wishes by continuing in East Florida during such part of the eighteen months accorded in the treaty for the evacuation as he thought necessary. Finally, he was instructed to use every means to reconcile the Indians to the new situation, and to direct Superintendent Browne to distribute any remaining presents among them.[203]

William Brown, the speaker of the commons house of assembly, was now appointed the commissioner of evacuation, and kept the books in his office in which the emigrants' names were entered, as also the number of their slaves, and the destinations to which they were bound. The management of the transports was entrusted to Robert Leaver, who received his orders from Governor Tonyn, gave orders to the masters of the vessels, assigned groups of passengers to their respective ships, and on occasion forbade the carrying on board of possessions for which space could not be spared. The regulation of the small craft, which had to be called into requisition for the shipment of much of the personal effects, was in the hands of Lieutenant John Mowbray of the provincial navy. The record of all expenses and expenditures connected with the evacuation was kept by Peter Edwards, who thus became the clerk of the public accounts in addition to being the clerk of the crown and of the commons house of assembly and the secretary to Governor Tonyn.[204]

On November 1, only a few days after the embarkation of the provincial troops, three companies of the 37th Regiment arrived in East Florida from New York. As the Royal Artillery, under the command of Captain Henry Abbott, remained at St. Augustine until the final evacuation, the inhabitants would still have the protection of a garrison. General McArthur probably went to assume command of the Bahamas in December, 1783. Before taking his departure he designated Captain Abbott to deliver the

[203] C. O. 5/560, f. 721.   [204] C. O. 5/561, f. 329, and *post*, pp. 170, 174.

barracks and public buildings at St. Augustine "in the best order" to the Spaniards. The stream of loyalists continued to flow out of the province, most of them embarking on board the government transports in Amelia Harbor at the mouth of St. Marys River. Numerous small groups, however, took their departure in sailing vessels, which they bought or hired to take them to the lower Mississippi, Jamaica, or the Bahama Islands. By January, 1784, there were hundreds of loyalists from East Florida in the Bahamas, some with their families and more or less of their negroes. Inhabitants of Charleston were still negotiating with some of those who remained for the purchase of their negroes and offering the best of security as an inducement. Seven transports had recently arrived at St. Marys from New York for the use of the loyalists and another came soon afterward. Such government vessels carried the passengers without charge, thus saving them a great expense. It was an item that did not escape the notice of Mrs. Elizabeth L. Johnston, who wrote that her father-in-law, Dr. Lewis Johnston, would be able to have "his family transported passage free." He was at the time undecided about his destination as between Scotland and Jamaica, the latter being attractive "from the flattering accounts" the loyalists there gave of their large crops of indigo. In the following month, according to Governor Tonyn, four thousand of the inhabitants started from East Florida for the back settlements on the Mississippi.[205]

One of those who set out for the Mississippi country was Colonel David Fanning, formerly a settler on Raeburn's Creek in North Carolina. He had landed in Matanza Inlet late in November, 1782, with two hundred and fifty exiles from Charleston. Later he had removed to Halifax River. Early in March, 1784, he presented a petition from the people living near Mosquito Inlet [now Ponce de Leon Inlet] to Governor Tonyn. It was signed by Captain Thomas Young and a few others on behalf of their neighbors, and begged that a schooner be sent to carry them to the transports at St. Marys. Many of these persons seem to have been occupying the unburnt buildings at New Smyrna. As Tonyn had no vessels then in government service, he sent word back that the petitioners must get to the shipping

---

[205] C. O. 23/26; *Hist. MSS. Comm., Am. MSS. in R. Inst.*, IV. 356; Elizabeth L. Johnston, *Recollections of a Georgia Loyalist*, pp. 215-218.

as best they could. Fanning returned to the inlet and addressed the inhabitants, voicing sentiments widely held among the loyalists at that time. He told them that they were being sacrificed to the indignation of their enemies, expelled from their country, "thrown on the wide world friendless and unsupported," that the king's promises of support and protection had been broken, and that the national faith had been "basely bartered for an inglorious peace." His own hopes of receiving anything from the government for losses and services had vanished and he intended to leave with a small party in open boats and settle near Fort Natchez on the Mississippi. Together with his wife, two young negroes, and seven other families, all in sailboats, he set out on March 20, 1784. After journeying down the coast a hundred and sixty miles, he and his own family sailed on ahead as far as Key West, where they were detained by a gale. They were informed here that their boats were too small to cross the Gulf of Mexico, and that some families from St. Augustine had been recently killed by Indians. Fanning and his little party now sailed back to Boca Chica, and took passage for New Providence. Arriving at Nassau, they stayed nearly three weeks, and then embarked for New Brunswick.[206] Probably many of those who started for the settlements on the lower Mississippi, went by overland routes.

As late as February, 1784, the people still living in St. Augustine were "quite sanguine in the expectation" that the two Floridas would be retained by Great Britain, but a packet arrived from London on February 3 which brought an official communication that "dashed their hopes and made their disappointment unspeakable." The day, according to Mrs. Elizabeth Lichtenstein Johnston, was one of "sad confusion" and "occasioned many long faces." In March, the traveler, Johann David Schoepf, spent a few days in St. Augustine before leaving for New Providence on a sloop crowded with emigrants, negroes, and cattle. At St. Augustine he noted that preparations were being made to transfer the possession of East Florida to the Spaniards. Ships were "continually going out, with goods and passengers, to the West Indies or Nova Scotia." He thought that the refugees were in even a worse situation than the other inhabitants, because the little property they had saved had been invested in lands and houses which they were

---

[206] Savary (ed.), *Col. David Fanning's Narrative*, pp. 38, 42. See also Volume II. of this work, pp. 350, 351.

compelled to give up once more. He rightly concluded that few of all the residents in East Florida would be willing to "exchange a mild British rule for the Spanish yoke, even was there no question of religion." Only the Minorcans, by reason of religious affinity with the Spaniards, were inclined to remain, and some of the Greeks would probably stay, Schoepf thought.[207]

Such scattered references as one may find in the testimony of East Florida loyalists before the British commissioners on loyalist claims, show that transports sailed from one or another of the Florida harbors with emigrants for Nova Scotia in April, June, and October, 1784. In July of that year, the transport *Argo*, with loyalists and a few negroes on board, arrived at Halifax on its way to Chedabucto, afterward known as Guysborough. It was probably concerning the *Argo* and its passengers that Governor John Parr wrote from Halifax, on July 29, that "a Transport arriv'd a few days ago from St. Augustine, with 260 miserable Wretches, without a shilling, naked, destitute of almost every necessary of life." He added that he had "taken proper care of them." In 1784, also, other vessels from St. Augustine carried to Halifax one hundred and ninety-four negroes, old and young, in a destitute condition. They were distributed throughout the interior of Nova Scotia.[208]

At the end of July, 1782, some of the Georgians at St. Augustine had memorialized General Carleton to express their preference for the West Indies as the only region where they could employ their slaves to advantage. They added that there were no less than four thousand people, white and black, from Georgia in East Florida. Notwithstanding this representation only eighty-five persons had registered at St. Augustine near the end of May, 1783, to go to Jamaica. As the transport did not sail for that island until June 25 it probably had a much larger passenger list. Brigadier General McArthur promised a six weeks' supply of provisions for those going

---

[207] Elizabeth L. Johnston, *Recollections of a Georgia Loyalist*, p. 221; Morrison (ed.), *Schoepf's Travels in the Confederation*, II. 240-241.

[208] *Hist. MSS. Comm., Am. MSS. in R. Inst.*, II. 274, 276, 371, IV. 348; *Second Report*, Bureau of Archives, Ont., 1904, pt. II. 791-801; E. A. Jones (ed.), *Journal of Alexander Chesney*, pp. 74-78; Egerton (ed.), *R. Comm. on Loyalist Claims, 1783-1785*, pp. 272-273; *Acadiensis*, January, 1907, p. 32; *Report* of Public Archives, Canada, 1921, app. E, p. 7.

to Jamaica. The policy of the British government was to grant lands to the emigrant loyalists, and Governor Tonyn was advised early in the year 1784 that land would be appropriated in the West Indies for this purpose. So far as one can tell from the fragmentary evidence refugees left East Florida for England in the spring of this same year, and doubtless they were leaving for other destinations about the same time.

On May 10, 1784, Tonyn wrote to Governor John Maxwell of the Bahama Islands, recommending to his favor and protection the loyalists who were going thither to settle. The transport then sailing was laden with only three months' stores for twenty-seven hundred emigrants, whereas it was computed that altogether nearly five thousand had chosen to settle in the Bahamas. This total doubtless included the associated loyalists from New York. Tonyn did not forget to mention that considerable numbers of the people under his jurisdiction had selected the West Indies, the Bay of Honduras, Nova Scotia, and Europe as their respective destinations. In keeping with instructions from the ministry the governor requested that all of the inhabitants emigrating to the Bahamas be put upon the royal bounty, and that Maxwell inform him what he could furnish to East Florida in the way of provisions for the purpose of hastening the evacuation, the prolongation of which threatened a shortage.[209] Dr. Lewis Johnston and his family had expected to sail from St. Marys River by the middle of April, 1784, but did not leave there until May 30. After crossing the Atlantic, their transport lay in the cove of Cork for a week before finally dropping anchor in the port of Greenoch on July 18, much later than they had anticipated.

[209] C. O. 23/25, May 10, June 5, 1784; Elizabeth L. Johnston, *Recollections of a Georgia Loyalist*, p. 224.

Chapter XI.

The completion of the evacuation under the governorship of Zespedes, June, 1784-November, 1785.—The arrival of the Spanish governor, Zespedes.—His first proclamation.—His appointment of justices of the peace.—His second proclamation.—The comments on this by Chief Justice James Hume and the reply of Zespedes.—Continued banditry under Spanish favor.—Tonyn insists on the fulfilment of the terms of the treaty of peace.—Thievery by the banditti.—The numbers of British subjects in East Florida in October, 1784.—Few sales of property to the Spaniards.—John Cruden and his scheme to recover the revolted states for England.—The prolongation of the evacuation.—Complaints of the bread supplied on shipboard at St. Marys.—Voyages of the transports.—Marriages before emigration.—The merchants' address to Zespedes asking an extension of time.—Causes of delay.—Some of the Minorcans remain.—The total number of the emigrants.—The imprisonment of British subjects by the Spaniards.—The last division of transports nearly ready to sail.—Its departure ordered by Zespedes.—Expenses of the final evacuation.—Adverse winds and the accident to Tonyn's ship Cyrus.—Conveyance of Tonyn and other civil officers to England by the Two Sisters and the Ann.—Disastrous effects of the evacuation in East Florida.—Tonyn's efforts to reconcile the Indians to the Spaniards.—The return of William Augustus Bowles from the Bahamas and his adventures in East Florida.

ON June, 1784, Governor Zespedes arrived at St. Augustine with the officers of the Spanish civil and military departments and a small body of soldiers. He stationed detachments from his garrison in the town of St. Johns Bluff and at other places. His secretary was Captain Don Carlos Howard. Governor Tonyn promptly supplied the new governor, who supplanted him in authority, with a general survey of the conditions in East Florida, and particularly called his attention to the plundering operations of the parties of "banditti" that had been adding to the misery of the inhabitants in the country and in town.

On July 14, Zespedes issued his first proclamation, in which he announced his assumption of the government in the name of his Catholic majesty, assured the populace of his protection, declared that the banditti must retire from the province, and in keeping with the terms of the treaty of peace extended full liberty to the British subjects still remaining to withdraw with their effects during the rest of the period of eighteen months originally specified. All this was decidedly encouraging to Governor Tonyn, his fellow officers, and the British subjects. They felt that the new administration was well disposed toward them, and was acting favorably for their interests. Governor Zespedes also appointed justices of the peace to decide disputes among the adherents to the British crown, one of these being Francis Philip Fatio, long a resident, who began to style himself judge and to assume cognizance of questions that had arisen some time before the accession of the new governor. Complaints were soon made to Tonyn of Fatio's methods. Fatio was a foreigner, had a very imperfect acquaintance with the language, laws, and constitution of Great Britain, and was of obnoxious character in the community, according to Tonyn, who added that he decided cases by whim and caprice. The English governor objected especially to Fatio's exercise of retroactive jurisdiction, believing that British subjects could not be legally detained in East Florida, except for debts contracted and criminal acts committed under the Spanish government. Tonyn argued that it could not be supposed that the treaty of peace, after rendering the immediate payment of debts impossible for persons divested of their principal property, should expose them to the chance of perpetual imprisonment without the opportunity of retrieving their fortune in the future.[210]

Early in August, Zespedes issued his second proclamation. Before its promulgation Tonyn applied to Captain Howard for a copy, which he submitted to Chief Justice Hume for his opinion. Mr. Hume wrote that by the fifth article of the treaty the Spanish monarch guaranteed that the British and other inhabitants under Tonyn's administration might sell their estates and retire from East Florida with their personal effects within a prescribed period of time in full security whithersoever they might think proper, except on account of debts or criminal prosecutions. This article in Hume's opinion meant that every person, white or black, slave or freeman, who had enjoyed British protection at the time of the Spanish governor's arrival, had the full right to withdraw. He therefore objected to the clause in the proclamation ordering every negro who could not produce a cer-

---

[210] Fairbanks, *Hist. of Florida*, p. 239; C. O. 5/561, December 6, 1784.

tificate of manumission to take out a written permit within twenty days to work for the public, or hire himself to private persons, under the penalty of becoming the property of his Catholic majesty. Hume held that this clause would operate against those negroes who had joined the British standard by invitation of generals, or commanders, and had thus become free, though many of them could produce no certificate of manumission. It would also operate against those whose masters were not British subjects, since there were many plundered negroes in East Florida. Moreover, the clause required those persons employing negroes, for whom they had no title deeds, to enter them at the secretary's office, or be criminally prosecuted. Hume asserted that five out of every six slaves in the province were held without title deeds, that purchasers of negroes were never given bills of sale, and that masters could show nothing better than parole sales and possession. He objected also to the severity of the penalties designated in other clauses, and to making the judge a party to a suit by awarding him a part of what was condemned. Such an arrangement was wholly foreign to the British constitution.[211]

Governor Zespedes did not take kindly to having his proclamation passed upon in this gratuitous manner, and he did not hesitate to say so. He also pointed out the words in his proclamation which limited the clause, ordering negroes without a certificate of manumission to procure a license to work, to vagrant blacks, with which East Florida then abounded. He insisted that the Spanish government had no wish to meddle with negroes having masters, but that it would look after those having no acknowledged master, or no right to freedom, since they were a pest to the public tranquillity. Further, the Spanish administration must know what negroes enjoyed their freedom under the proclamation of some military officer. Zespedes denied that before, during, or since the war, simple possession was a sufficient proof of ownership under the laws of any nation. His policy was to restore slaves to their proper owners, and to give liberty to those who were the slaves of uncertain owners. In defense of the provision giving a share of what was condemned to the judge, he argued that laws esteemed good and necessary in one country might not be so in another. There were,

[211] C. O. 5/561, July 26, 29, 1784.

said Zespedes, four classes of negroes in East Florida, namely: 1. those absolutely free; 2. those deserving their liberty by virtue of military proclamations during the war; 3. those belonging to British subjects; and 4. those strolling about St. Augustine and the province. Of the last class those who presented themselves within the proper interval should be considered free by virtue of the Spanish governor's second proclamation, but those failing to do so should be considered vagrants. The clause relating to individuals who held negroes without sufficient proof of ownership, required that they register them and explain possession at the office of the secretary to the commanding general. Such proof, if not in writing, might be by witnesses or word of mouth. The second proclamation operated only against those persons who had appropriated blacks that ought to be free by virtue of British proclamations.[212]

The taking over of the provincial administration by Governor Zespedes by no means reduced banditry in East Florida. On the contrary, it encouraged it. Governor Tonyn had informed his Spanish successor shortly after his arrival of the "infamous character" of Daniel and James McGirth, John Linder, and probably others, and had been assured that they would be apprehended and sent to a place whence they could no longer annoy the inhabitants. At the close of July, Colonel William Young wrote to Tonyn that he had learned that Linder and his banditti were collecting on St. Marys River for the purpose of robbing the plantations on the west side of the St. Johns; that he had proceeded against them and found Linder, James McGirth, George Philips, and William Whaley at Daniel Melyar's house; that he had fired on them as they broke out, had killed one man, and taken Whaley prisoner; and that the others had escaped into a neighboring swamp. He had then confiscated some of their effects. He was told that James McGirth had been recently sent into Georgia to pilot back a body of rebels with the object of attacking his own station and robbing Tonyn's plantation.[213]

The first proof of the favor these renegades were now to enjoy is shown by the fact that Governor Zespedes enclosed a memorial from the McGirths and Linder in a letter of August 5, saying that they were attacked

[212] C. O. 5/561.   [213] C. O. 5/561, July 30, August 5, 1784.

in a house on Nassau River by Colonel Young and his troop on the night of July 27, and that they desired the return of certain articles Colonel Young had carried off. The Spanish governor not only approved their memorial, but also alleged that if Lieutenant Colonel Antonio Fernández, who was stationed at the pass of St. Nicholas on St. Johns River, had not arrived opportunely, many of the people on the river would have joined Linder and his party and taken vengeance for the bad faith of the Spaniards in failing to afford protection by plundering the plantations of British subjects. Tonyn did not credit this statement, which had evidently come from Colonel Fernández himself. As for the articles carried off by Colonel Young, Tonyn placed them at the disposal of the Spanish governor. He also defended Young's conduct on the score that it afforded protection to the British settlements. He reminded Zespedes that Young and his troop of light horse were in British pay and under the sole authority of the Spanish administration. One of the reports brought to Young was that the rebels from Georgia intended to attack and take St. Augustine.[214]

Late in September, Tonyn again protested to Governor Zespedes on account of the repeated crimes of McGirth and his gang. He expressed his astonishment at the favorable treatment accorded them, especially Daniel McGirth, who had found a secure sanctuary and place of triumph. Although burdened with horrid crimes, McGirth was suffered to range through the country and among the people, who were distressed by his atrocious deeds. He had stolen negroes in his possession, some of them the property of Samuel Farley, Esq., and others that belonged to the British crown and had been taken from the provost marshal. Farley's suit for his slaves had been stopped by the order of Zespedes on advice from Francis Philip Fatio. Mr. Farley had been appointed an arbitrator by the Spanish tribunal erected for the benefit of the British subjects, but had refused to take the oath. Tonyn demanded that McGirth and his accomplices be tried, and that the negroes in their possession be delivered up. In a letter of October 11, the British governor described Daniel McGirth as a man who had been outlawed by his country, and said that he would have plundered

---

[214] C. O. 5/561, July 30, August 5, 7, 1784.

the whole province had it not been for Colonel Young and his troop, of whom Zespedes spoke doubtfully as being an unauthorized band of men not even militia, whereas they were regularly raised, commissioned, and paid. Tonyn did not fail to mention that one Johnson and other "associated villains" from Georgia had appeared on the frontier with a number of stolen horses at the invitation of the banditti to barter their ill-gotten possessions and promote wicked designs.[215]

As for the terms of the treaty of peace being left altogether to "the undoubted good faith" of the Spanish monarch, Tonyn was prompt to remind Zespedes that he was himself under command from the court of St. James's to see that the provisions of the peace were duly fulfilled and that he proposed to receive and report all complaints from the British subjects and transmit also any other matters which in his opinion militated against the treaty. Among the items reported by him to Lord Sydney were the excessive penalties and confiscations imposed on those who did not take out Spanish passes for their persons and effects, thus impeding the free departure of inhabitants from East Florida. These penalties were included in the second proclamation of the Spanish governor.

Despite Tonyn's vigorous and repeated complaints, the notorious thieves continued to pass to and fro through the province, armed with swords and pistols, terrorizing people but enjoying the protection of the Spanish government and retaining their stolen property. The information supplied by Tonyn was ignored, and all examinations and prosecutions were stifled under various pretexts. Tonyn so wrote to Zespedes himself. To Lord Sydney, however, he wrote in another vein, professing to believe that his complaints had produced good effects, and that without them the treatment of the British subjects would have been unsupportable.[216]

Meantime, the bandits had been stealing indiscriminately from planters, householders in town, and government officials. In December, 1783, they had carried off three horses belonging to Francis Levett, a former provost marshal. Early in 1784, they had taken two coach horses of James Hume, the chief justice, from his servants out on St. Johns road. About the same

---

[215] C. O. 5/561, f. 229, September 24, October 11, 1784.
[216] *Ibid.*, December 4, 6, 1784.

time they had stolen a horse near St. Johns Bluff from Captain Peter Edwards, the clerk of the crown and of the commons house of assembly. They had taken a mare from its pasture in St. Augustine and some negroes from St. Marys beach, all being the property of John Fox, who was employed by Tonyn as a public accountant before the final departure. Johann Schoepf, the traveler, thought that the British authorities were responsible for these disorders. He found it unsafe to go far from St. Augustine, and was so warned by the governor. Colonel Young testified that in 1784 he apprehended Daniel McGirth and Daniel Cargill for stealing Francis Levett's horses, and that he heard Cargill swear that one Bellew had taken a sorrel stallion belonging to Levett. Roger Moore and his gang of thieves were also active in this period. Captain Stuart stated that he succeeded in dispersing the banditti who infested the frontier of East Florida, and received the thanks of Governor Tonyn for his services. Another refugee who coöperated in the measures taken to suppress lawlessness was John Cruden. In an address from the loyalists to the governor, the great services of Cruden are mentioned as those of one who had prevented the overrunning of the province by a band of desperate men. Tonyn was praised for his selection of Cruden, but the address does not specify the kind of services rendered. However, dispersions and arrests by Tonyn's troops of horse were largely ineffectual against the protection enjoyed by the malefactors under Governor Zespedes. Instances of thievery might be given that were chargeable to Spaniards and Greeks. As various kinds of valuable property, including slaves, were taken to St. Marys beach for shipment, the departing loyalists were constantly missing some of their possessions when these were to be carried on board ship.[217]

Despite the departure of multitudes to the Bahamas and Jamaica, to the Mississippi country, and back to the states since the latter part of June, 1783, there still remained between forty-five hundred and five thousand British subjects in East Florida, although nearly four hundred of these were already embarked on transports and ready to sail. The books of Wil-

---

[217] Morrison (ed.), *Schoepf's Travels in the Confederation*, II. 241; Treas. 1/622; E. A. Jones (ed.), *Journal of Alexander Chesney*, p. 92; Fairbanks, *Hist. of Florida*, p. 239. See also Volume II. of this work, pp. 44, 48, 182, 220, 230, *passim*.

liam Brown, the commissioner for evacuation, showed the following numbers as being still present on October 16, 1784, and a little later:

Whites	551
Blacks	1,133
	1,684
Entered on the books since	263
	1,947
Passes obtained since, and their holders embarked on the *Polly*, *William and Mary*, and *Elizabeth* transports for New Providence	119
Governor Graham's negroes since embarked	270
Persons named in the commissioner's books still to take out passes	1,558
	3,894

The above estimate was exclusive of the persons on the estates of Lady Egmont and Mr. Egan, those under the care of Major Ross and Mr. Fatio, those in Colonel Young's troop of horse and their families, and the Minorcans. Commissioner Brown noted also that many persons had not yet entered their names at his office.[218]

In a letter of November 30, Governor Tonyn explained to Lord Hawke that he had continued one of his two troops of horse in British pay for the protection of the plantations from the banditti until the emigration of the negroes could be completed. Their removal was "violently opposed" by the Spaniards. Tonyn also claimed that by persevering in his protests to Zespedes against infringements of the treaty of peace he had procured many of its benefits for the British subjects. This is a favorite theme of the English governor in his later correspondence. Few sales had been made to the Spaniards, and those only of houses in St. Augustine, which brought less than one-quarter of their value, Tonyn says. There was no prospect of obtaining even that proportion for valuable tracts of land in the country, because the Spaniards who had arrived belonged to the military and civil

[218] C. O. 23/26; C. O. 23/25; C. O. 5/561, f. 317.

departments. For these reasons the loyalists would have to depend chiefly on the justice and benevolence of the British government for the compensation of their losses. In order to ascertain these losses Tonyn had appointed David Yeats, the clerk of the council, and Mr. Leslie (probably John Leslie of Messrs. Leslie, Panton & Co.) to superintend and register the transfers of property made by individuals.[219]

From the closing days of October to mid-December, if not later, John Cruden was at St. Marys River. How he occupied himself during these weary weeks before his departure for the Bahamas, we do not know. He had been an active loyalist from the outbreak of the Revolution. As a member of the firm of John Cruden & Co., merchants of Wilmington and other localities in North Carolina, he had engaged at great risk to supply the loyalists of his province with provisions when they took up arms, had been appointed lieutenant colonel of a regiment of volunteers and paymaster of the North Carolina provincials, had advocated the restriction of trade among the Americans in a letter from New York, dated January 28, 1778, and had served as commissioner "for the seizure, superintendence, custody and management of captured property" in South Carolina for two years and three months before retiring to East Florida at the evacuation of Charleston. On June 18, 1784, Cruden wrote to the Hon. A. Maclaine at Wilmington, proposing a wild scheme for the recovery of the revolted states. Maclaine wrote to a friend twelve days later that he could not believe that Cruden could be "intrusted by any person in power to offer emoluments and rewards to American citizens to betray their country." He thought the scheme the "production of a madman." On October 28, Cruden wrote from St. Marys River to Lord Dartmouth about his plan for the restoration of America to England. "America shall yet be ours," he declared, "but the House of Brunswick do not deserve the sovereignty of it." Writing from the same place on December 12, he recounted his services on behalf of the crown and told of his great distress after having twice sacrificed his fortune. In East Florida, Cruden had disapproved of the conduct of William Brown, the commissioner of evacuation, in having aided and abetted one Dobbins, the master of a transport, in shipping a cargo of

---

[219] C. O. 5/561, f. 337.

mahogany to Charleston, thus enabling Dobbins to enrich himself and buy a vessel. John Cruden soon went to Nassau on the island of New Providence. His uncle, John Cruden, the elder, the head of the house of John Cruden & Co., located with his wife and infant son in Exuma, one of the Bahama Islands.[219a]

As many embarrassments had intervened to retard the evacuation far beyond Tonyn's expectation it would be impossible to complete it before March 19, 1785, which was the end of the term fixed by the treaty. The application for a prolongation of the term would be requisite, but such prolongation could not be obtained in East Florida, Tonyn thought. He had already written to Lord Sydney concerning these matters. He enclosed some particulars from Governor John Orde of Dominica in answer to a recommendation of some emigrants, who intended to settle in that island.

At the beginning of December, Robert Leaver, the agent for transports, was on board the *Two Sisters* in St. Marys River, and was receiving written complaints from the loyalists and a general complaint from the masters of the other transports about the bad quality of the bread. The shipmasters requested Mr. Leaver to order a survey, or investigation, of the matter. Leaver found from his printed instructions that he could only make a survey under orders from his commander-in-chief, and asked Tonyn to direct him. There was a convenient opportunity to bring a fresh supply of bread from Charleston in the transport *Amity's Production*. A visit to the different transports revealed the fact that their bread was in much the same state. If not all the new bread could be supplied at one time then fifteen or twenty tons should be on hand by January 1, and if the rest were provided by March 1, it would be in time for the remaining ships.[220]

Instead of the transports having lain inactive at St. Marys for several months, as Governor Maxwell had written to Brigadier General McArthur, by the opening days of December several of them, filled with passengers, had made repeated voyages to the Bahamas, while those with settlers for the West Indies and Jamaica, with a few exceptions, had made one voyage out and back, and were again filled with emigrants and their

---

[219a] E. A. Jones (ed.), *Journal of Alexander Chesney*, pp. 91-93; *State Records of North Carolina*, XI. 450, XVII. 156, 157; *Hist. MSS. Comm., Am. MSS. in R. Inst.*, II. 183.

[220] C. O. 5/561.

effects and nearly ready to sail. The personal property remaining to be shipped far exceeded in quantity every former computation, because Spanish purchasers were wanting. The only Spaniards in the province were those employed in the civil and military departments. Settlers from other parts of the Spanish dominions were not to be admitted until the British subjects should have left. Hence there was but little market for the houses and lands, as well as the personal effects of the departing loyalists. Only in cases where Spaniards wished to acquire their old homes did they purchase houses from the British inhabitants. Governor Tonyn agreed to sell his slaves to the newcomers at £55 each in ready money, but did not do so. Other inhabitants sold only a few of theirs, and carried the rest away with them. The Spanish government forbade the sale of lands for which no grants had been issued by the British authorities. Such lands and houses as were sold brought very low prices, and in a number of instances the purchase money was not paid. No property was sold at public vendue after July 18, 1785, which had been named as the last day for that purpose. Just before that date most of the sales were made under the condition that if East Florida were restored to Great Britain within a given time the transferred property would be returnable at the same price, with the cost of any improvements added. However, not all sales at vendue were genuine transactions. For example, the property of John Champneys, one of the venduemasters, was auctioned off on the date mentioned to Francis Philip Fatio in a "friendly sale," in which no money changed hands. It was understood, however, that Fatio would sell the property later for the owner.[221]

At the end of December, several of the British subjects wished to marry before their departure, and Tonyn applied to Zespedes for permission for Mr. Leslie to perform the ceremonies, since there was no Anglican clergyman at hand to do so. Zespedes replied that he considered it foreign to his functions and profession of faith to interfere with the espousals of subjects who professed any religion different from his own.[222]

At mid-February, 1785, by arrangement with Captain Howard, Tonyn sent to Zespedes an address signed by twenty-eight British subjects, mostly

[221] T. 77/20; Fairbanks, *Hist. of Florida*, p. 238. See also Volume II. of this work, pp. 13-14, 116, 185, 191.
[222] C. O. 5/561, f. 371, f. 375.

merchants who wanted more time to dispose of their goods, on behalf of themselves and others, asking an extension of time beyond the eighteen months allowed by the treaty for the evacuation. A few days later the Spanish governor answered that in view of a stipulation providing for such a contingency, which he quoted, there could be no doubt that such prolongation ought to be granted, but inasmuch as the stipulation provided that it should be proportioned to the value of the possessions of the inhabitants, every individual desirous of profiting by the clause ought to present a memorial giving the value of his possessions.[223]

Various causes had delayed the completion of the evacuation beyond the few months which Tonyn had expected at the beginning would be required. One of the most important of these causes was the slow process of transporting the personal property from the scattered and distant plantations down the rivers and coastwise in small craft to the shipping in St. Marys River. Another cause was the purchase of a further supply of provisions in East Florida for the emigrants. With a view to hastening the departure of the people still remaining, Tonyn published an advertisement that the last transports would leave on February 20, 1785, though he expected it would require a month longer for them to be in readiness to sail. A month before the advertised date he had written to Lord Sydney suggesting the need of having the power to extend the evacuation period and of securing the consent of the court of Madrid for that purpose. Zespedes ruled that after March 19, which was the final date of the eighteen-months period, no lumber could be cut by British subjects. Tonyn, writing on April 4, said that he had been inclined to object to this ruling, but did not because no British planters then remained in the country. As the Spanish government declined to purchase the pews and bells of the church in St. Augustine, and also a fire engine, the English governor shipped them to the Bahamas for the use of a new town that was being built by the loyal emigrants.[224]

In his letter of April 4, which was addressed to Lord Sydney, Tonyn said that, with the exception of a few Minorcans professing the Roman

---

[223] C. O. 5/561, f. 423, f. 427.

[224] C. O. 23/25, June 5, 1784; C. O. 5/561, December 6, 1784; C. O. 5/561, f. 353, April 4, 1785; C. O. 23/26. In regard to the fire engine, see Additional Notes, in Volume II. of this work, p. 379.

Catholic faith, not more than three or four British subjects would remain as residents of East Florida. This was an exaggerated statement, as will appear from figures to be given later. These Minorcans had belonged to Dr. Turnbull's colony at New Smyrna, which had been founded in 1767, when it comprised about fifteen hundred people, including some Greeks and south Italians. Hundreds of the colonists had died of malaria in a few years. After deserting the colony and going to St. Augustine, several scores had lost their lives from exposure during the first rainy season after their arrival there. Governor Tonyn assigned lots to the survivors north of the town, where they built their huts. The men engaged in fishing and other occupations, but some of them joined the militia or served on board the provincial galleys. Having been brought to East Florida in "extremest poverty," they prospered through their industry and frugality. They maintained a small decorated chapel in St. Augustine, which was under the charge of a priest from Minorca. In March, 1784, they formed nearly the largest part of the town's population, the rest being a few English, Americans, French, Germans, and Spaniards. The Minorcans intended to emigrate along with the other British subjects, and consulted Governor Tonyn about it. They solicited him to send most of them to Gibraltar and the others to Dominica and the Bahamas. Before April, 1785, a considerable number had already withdrawn to the Bahamas, a few to Dominica, and some to Europe. The Minorcan priest, Pietro Campo, whom Tonyn called "Pedrus Camps," decided to leave the country along with the governor, but the Spanish governor had brought him a promotion in the church of Minorca and detained him for another year, besides bringing three other priests, two of whom were Irishmen. He had also exerted himself to induce persons of the Catholic faith to become Spanish subjects, especially the Minorcans. The decision of Pietro Campo and his followers to remain in East Florida Tonyn regarded as a violation of the treaty of peace, and he so informed Lord Sydney.[225]

Tonyn wrote that according to the entries in the books of the commis-

---

[225] C. O. 5/560, pp. 289-290; C. O. 5/561, f. 353; Carita Doggett, *Dr. Andrew Turnbull and New Smyrna Colony*, pp. 45-46, 163-164, 191; Morrison (ed.), *Schoepf's Travels in the Confederation*, II. 230-231. The old parish registers at St. Augustine have many records by the priest, Pietro Campo, or as he is called in the Spanish documents, Pedro Camps.

sioner of evacuation the emigrants numbered about ten thousand, that it was concluded that more than four thousand had gone into the interior parts of America among the mountains, and that at least three thousand had returned to the American states. This statement is contained in a letter of April 4, 1785, and shows that the previous six months had been a season of great activity for the transports.

The same letter contained the further information that "the notorious" Daniel McGirth, Major William Cunningham, and other British subjects had been recently confined in "filthy dungeons" by the Spanish authorities on criminal charges, and all intercourse with them refused. Zespedes wrote to Tonyn that they would not be tried for want of sufficient evidence, but were destined to be sent to a place where it would be out of their power to give further trouble. This suggested the Spanish mines to Tonyn, who was being incessantly importuned by their friends to intercede in their behalf. Tonyn requested the Spanish governor to ship the culprits to some part of the British dominions, but his suggestion was ignored. Major Cunningham was deported to Cuba as a prisoner on May 1, 1785, for taking an active part in a dispute between some Spaniards and Americans. Probably the others were also sent to Cuba.[226]

Early in April, Tonyn had written to Lord Sydney that the transports were nearly ready to sail from East Florida for the last time with their complements of passengers for their different destinations, and that the return of four ships from the Bahamas was awaited to carry off "the gleanings." He had instructed Robert Leaver, the agent for transports, to receive on board the last division of the vessels from those islands the produce of the loyalists there, so that these transports would not return to England empty. Tonyn now expected that the evacuation would be completed in a few weeks, and wrote that he would then sail for Britain in the armed ship *Cyrus* with the other civil officers and several families of emigrants "of the middle and poorer sort." The king's armed galleys which had been in the service of East Florida, would be sent to the Bahama Islands. The governor boasted that the evacuation had been conducted with such care that not a single accident had happened, notwithstanding the removal of an immense property.[227]

[226] C. O. 5/561, f. 817; C. O. 5/561, f. 353; Sabine, *Loyalists of Am. Rev.*, II. 64-65.
[227] C. O. 5/561, f. 353; C. O. 137/85, Jamaica.

It was not until July 13, 1785, that Governor Zespedes informed Governor Tonyn of the receipt of the orders from his royal master, extending the term of the evacuation by four months. Zespedes added that the prolongation should be reckoned from March 19 and expire on July 19. A fortnight after this communication the Spanish governor wrote again to intimate that the prolongation had elapsed, and that in consequence of new excesses committed by British subjects every one of them who remained without his permission, was to depart or be answerable for his failure to do so. This order applied to the ships and transports of the English king, as well as to his subjects. Nevertheless, the armed ship *Cyrus* and several transports did not leave the waters of East Florida until November 19. Writing to Lord Sydney from the *Cyrus* on August 10, Tonyn said that, the evacuation being now completed, he hoped to pay his respects to his lordship in England.[228]

He took this occasion to remark that the Spaniards suffered Florida to be in the greatest want of money, that some of the British had advanced money to Zespedes's government and might long go without repayment, and that others were involved by debts of the Spanish inhabitants and would probably be losers. No country, he asserted, was ever left in a more deplorable state of desolation than Florida then was. The movable property of the emigrants had been collected at St. Marys to be shipped in small craft, and the people expected all that could not be sold to be removed. In Tonyn's declaration of accounts for contingent expenses from June 24, 1773, to September 1, 1785, are noted certain large sums spent for the benefit of the refugees.[229] These items are:

For tools, provisions, and clothing April 1, 1782, to June 1, 1785	£ 6,575 12s 0d
For the hire of small craft to convey subjects and their property from St. Augustine to St. Marys, March 19, 1784, to September 1, 1785	12,885 3 3
For other expenses of the final evacuation, June 25, 1783, to September 1, 1785	9,379 6 10½
	£28,840 1s 13½d

[228] C. O. 5/561, f. 665, f. 681.   [229] C. O. 5/561, f. 701.

Toward the end of August, Tonyn again wrote to Lord Sydney from the *Cyrus*, saying that he had dismissed the last division of the emigrants and given final orders for the vessels to proceed to their destinations, but they were waiting for a fair wind. They did not get their fair wind, however, until September 4, but the wind failed, and they had to wait a week longer before another favorable opportunity offered. This time it carried them out of the port of St. Marys over the first bar, then shifted to adverse quarters. The *Cyrus* struck on a lost anchor, and was perforated with a hole that let in six inches of water an hour. For twenty-four hours the little fleet was on the bar in a critical situation. Tonyn at once sent an express vessel to New Providence to summon a transport, and, lest it should not be found there, sent letters with the same message to Lieutenant Governor Powell of the Bahamas asking him to transmit them to Admiral Innis at Jamaica. The express vessel was wrecked on the island of Abaco, but the master of it succeeded in reaching New Providence and made known the predicament of the British civil officers and their fellow colonials. Another express vessel was dispatched to Jamaica. At that time the last division of four transports from East Florida, comprising the *Polly*, *William and Mary*, *Ann*, and *Two Sisters*, was disembarking in the Bahamas its complement of loyalists and negroes. Of these four transports the *Two Sisters* and the *Ann* responded to Tonyn's appeal for succor, and returned immediately to Amelia Harbor at the mouth of St. Marys River. Meantime, the marine officers had decided that the *Cyrus* must lie on shore for repairs. These various measures, the hire of small craft to take the passengers off the disabled ship, and the purchase of additional provisions cost another £800, but the *Cyrus* was put in tolerable condition to sail. However, her passengers would not return to what they considered a leaky ship. They preferred to take their chances on board the *Two Sisters*, which arrived at Portsmouth, England, with Tonyn, his secretary, Peter Edwards, Chief Justice James Hume, and probably some of the other civil officers, in January, 1786. On the 11th of that month the governor wrote from Portsmouth to Lord Sydney, telling of his arrival and of being accompanied by the *Ann* transport until they had reached soundings. The two transports were under orders to go to London and discharge their cargoes.[230]

[230] C. O. 5/561, f. 709, f. 777, f. 789, f. 797, f. 801; C. O. 23/25. See also Volume II. of this work, p. 380.

The disastrous effects of the evacuation were experienced throughout the settled region of East Florida, but were most conspicuous in St. Augustine and the town of St. Johns Bluff. The new additions and much of the older portion of the capital had been rapidly vacated. A sudden blight had fallen also on St. Johns in the spring of 1783, with the arrival of the news of the cession. Since the influx of thousands of refugees during the latter half of the preceding year, St. Johns had trebled in size and reached a population of fifteen hundred or more. It had a fine harbor, and was the business and shipping center for the stretch of country along the St. Johns River, which contained many of the best plantations in East Florida and produced quantities of naval stores and lumber for export. Then suddenly the favorable prospects of the flourishing village vanished. Thomas Williamson could sell no more of his town lots, and was left with one hundred and ninety-eight of them on his hands. In some cases he had not received the money for those he had parted with. At length he took down his own dwelling-house and shipped it to Jamaica. Some of his fellow townsmen also dismembered their houses and transported them more than twenty miles to St. Marys beach, with a view of sending them to one of the Bahama Islands, or some other destination. Further disappointment awaited the owners at the beach, either through the loss of some of their property by theft or through their failure to secure space on the crowded transports for their bulky lumber. Occasionally a sale was made of such property on the beach, which was constantly visited by loyalists who were making their arrangements to leave the province. A trader from St. Johns Bluff, who had been denied room on board a transport for the parts of his house, saw the opportunity for business on St. Marys. Accordingly, in the spring of 1784, he built a structure there, and kept a store in it as late as 1785. By that time the village of St. Johns Bluff was a deserted place. On St. Marys beach there was left only a medley of discarded flatboats, frames of dismantled houses, and other unwieldy objects, which the agent for transports had not permitted to be carried on board the vessels. According to Governor Tonyn, the Spaniards laid violent hands on some of the personal property of the emigrants. He stated that he had prevented this seizure of property "in a great measure," but that "otherwise the Spaniards were disposed to have seized the whole." That they did not easily surrender property they had appropriated was shown in the case of some negroes lost by John Fox as he was about to leave the country. At Tonyn's request, David Yeats and James Hume went on board a Spanish *guarda de costa*, or brigantine, at St. Marys in September, 1785, in search of the slaves, but were told they were not there. Later the slaves were produced, but not delivered up. There was much complaint by British subjects during the last year of the evacuation of the theft by Spaniards of negroes, horses, carts, and household furniture.[231]

Acting under instructions, Tonyn had taken pains at the close of his stay to cultivate among the Indians favorable sentiments toward the Spaniards and the necessity of living in friendship with them. This task was the more difficult because during recent years opposite principles had been zealously inculcated among the red men. Governor Zespedes was even more concerned to gain their friendship. He therefore did not spare expense, or neglect the use of other means to win their favor.[232]

Some of the people from East Florida, who had taken refuge in the Bahamas, became so dissatisfied with conditions there that they returned and settled at New Smyrna. However, the Spanish government soon forced them to withdraw to the American states. One of those who returned was William Augustus Bowles, a refugee and notorious adventurer from Maryland, who was sent by Lord Dunmore, then governor of the Bahamas, to open trade with the Indians. Bowles's real object appears to have been to recover possession of East Florida from Spain with the help of the Indians. Bowles brought with him only about sixty men to Mosquito Inlet [now Ponce de Leon Inlet], and proceeded inland to St. Johns River to attack an Indian trading-post near Lake George. Warned in ample time by friendly red men, the traders succeeded in having a company of Spanish soldiers dispatched from St. Augustine to protect them. Thus forestalled, "General" Bowles proceeded northward to the Indian town of Cuscowilla

[231] *Hist. MSS. Comm., Am. MSS. in R. Inst.*, III. 192, 224; T. 77/19, "Report of the Governor, President (and others) of the Bahama Islands"; T. 77/20. See also Volume II. of this work, pp. 13-14, 107, 112, 113, 116, 125, 175, 185, 220, *passim*.

[232] C. O. 5/561, pp. 359-361.

in Alachua, where his men deserted and the Indians would not join him. He was far more successful in gaining influence over the Creeks, to whom he next resorted. He married a Creek woman, was joined by Daniel McGirth, styled himself commander-in-chief of the Creek and Cherokee nations, and claimed to be acting under the authority of the British government. Bowles induced several of the Creek chiefs to seize certain trading-houses for the goods they contained, after which they took up their headquarters at Micosukie Old Town in mid-Florida. The trading firm of John Forbes & Co. persuaded the Seminole Indians to attempt the capture of Bowles. The agent of the firm collected a force of seven hundred braves and led it to Micosukie. Warned by McGirth, Bowles effected his escape to the Oclockony River and went into hiding for a brief time. These incidents took place in 1792. When he emerged from his concealment, Commander-in-Chief Bowles led a large body of Creeks to St. Marks River, at the head of Apalachee Bay, and captured the armed schooner *Sheerwater* with its cargo of drygoods for the traders. He then took the fort and town of St. Marks, as he found the garrison off its guard. This was the port of his own trading vessel from New Providence. However, he remained in possession of the town only a few weeks, being driven out by Governor Arturo O'Neill and a detachment of Spanish troops from Pensacola. The authorities at St. Augustine now offered a reward of six thousand dollars for the arrest of Bowles, who had fled to the Creek nation, and the Indians surrendered him. He was sent as a prisoner to Madrid and thence to Manila. Being permitted to return to Europe, he soon sailed for the Creek country and was operating there once more in 1801. At that time the United States government took measures to thwart his schemes. In 1804 he fell again into the hands of the Spaniards and was sent to Morro Castle at Havana. There he died in December, 1805.[233]

---

[233] T. 77/20, No. 6; White, *Historical Collections*, p. 281; Williams, *The Territory of Florida*, 1837, pp. 191-192; Fairbanks, *Hist. of Florida*, pp. 244-246, 248; Sabine, *Loyalists of the Am. Rev.*, I. 245-246; Brevard, *A History of Florida*, I. 14, 16-23, 188.

Chapter XII.

The refugees from East Florida in the Bahama Islands, and in Jamaica and Dominica, 1783-1810.—In the Bahamas: The first transports with refugees from East Florida to Jamaica and New Providence.—Factors that drew settlers from Florida to the Bahamas.—Lieutenant Wilson's survey of the islands.—His report and the assignment of Brigadier General McArthur to the command of the Bahamas as factors in attracting settlers.—The negotiations for the purchase of land in the islands and estimates of the number of Floridians recently arrived.—Their distribution among the Bahamas.—Schoepf's journey to New Providence late in March, 1784.—John Wells and The Royal Bahama Gazette.—*Governor Maxwell's comments on the evacuation of East Florida.—The loss of the transport* David *at Nassau.—Lands and provisions for the newcomers.—The memorial of the Associated Loyalists at St. Marys to Maxwell.—A new code for slaves and free colored people in the Bahamas.—Efforts in Florida to counteract unfavorable reports concerning the islands.—Tonyn's announcement of the sailing of the last transport.—Lieutenant Governor Powell's statement about the number of whites and blacks from East Florida in the Bahamas.—The retirement of Maxwell from the governorship.—The last division of transports from East Florida lands its passengers in the islands.—The accession of whites and negroes from January, 1786, to January, 1789.—The loyalist party in the Bahamas.—The British government buys out the lords proprietors.—The Bahama Islands in a new era.—The increase in imports and exports.—Other benefits due to the influx of loyalists.—The report of the select committee of the house of assembly in 1789.—Missions in the Bahamas conducted by the Society for the Propagation of the Gospel.—The Refugees in Jamaica: Jamaica as a refuge for loyalists from every quarter.—The enactment of a relief measure.—The protest of the vestry of Kingston.—Employments for the negroes until lands were granted.—Colonel Archibald Campbell becomes governor before the arrival of the fleet from Charleston with troops and refugees.—Brigadier General Alured Clarke is made lieutenant governor.—The arrival of transports with loyalists and slaves from East Florida.—Some notable refugees in Jamaica.—Alexander Aikman and* The Royal Gazette of Jamaica.—*Proprietors from East Florida and other provinces petition for provisions.—The restriction of Jamaica's trade.—The hurricanes of 1784 and the next two years.—The production of sugar, coffee, indigo, and cotton.—Loyalists from East Florida in Dominica: The arrival of transports in June and August, 1785.—Generous treatment of the newcomers by the authorities of the island.—The numbers who emigrated from East Florida during the entire evacuation period.—The numbers who went to Europe and to Nova Scotia.—Those* who remained with the Spaniards.—The return of proscribed South Carolinians and Georgians under the modified banishment acts of 1782.—The emigrants to "other foreign parts."

IN THE BAHAMAS

IN 1781, while the Bahama Islands were still in the possession of Great Britain, John Maxwell being the governor, James Edward Powell was sent thither from England to take the post of lieutenant governor. Powell had been a merchant and member of the council in Georgia for some years up to the capture of Governor Sir James Wright and his official board in 1776. He had then fled to Charleston, and in November, 1777, had arrived in England. Four years later he had been appointed to the lieutenant governorship of the islands by the king and made judge of the admiralty court there by the lords of the admiralty. Arriving at Nassau in the island of New Providence in December, 1781, his term of office was brought to a sudden close on May 8, 1782, when Governor Maxwell, captain general and commander-in-chief of the Bahamas, signed articles of capitulation to Juan Manuel de Cagigal, the captain general and commander-in-chief of the island of Cuba. Thus the Bahamas passed into the hands of Spain until a year later the treaty of peace was signed, and the islands were recovered by England.[284]

Another refugee who witnessed the conquest of the Bahamas by the Spaniards, was Colonel Josiah Tattnall, who had been a fellow-member with Powell in the council of Georgia. Returning from England in March, 1780, to take up his duties as a member of the council and as receiver general of the quit-rents, he was, nevertheless, not content to remain in Savannah. He had tried to reach the Bahamas in 1777, and when in December, 1781, his friend Powell became the lieutenant governor of the islands he had a sufficient inducement for going thither. Shortly after arriving at Nassau, he was appointed judge surrogate of the court of admiralty under Powell and was also made comptroller and deputy auditor. The conquest of the Bahamas by the Spanish force under Cagigal from Cuba turned him adrift once more, but instead of accompanying Lieuten-

---

[284] Egerton (ed.), *R. Comm. on Loyalist Claims, 1783-1785*, p. 201.

Refugees in Nearby Islands

ant Governor Powell and Governor Maxwell back to England, Colonel Tattnall took refuge at St. Augustine. This was probably about the beginning of June, 1782. He remained in East Florida during the time of the great influx of the loyalists from Georgia and South Carolina, but returned to the Bahamas during the evacuation of the province. He was appointed surveyor general of lands in the islands in February, 1784, with a salary of £100 a year.[235]

During the progress of the Revolution both the Bahama and the British West India Islands had been the refuge of loyalists from the revolted provinces, but they had come singly, by families, or in small parties. The successive evacuations of Savannah and Charleston during the latter half of 1782 had brought them in throngs not only to East Florida, but also to the West Indies and Bahamas. When the tidal wave of evacuation struck East Florida it swept it nearly clean of its seventeen thousand British subjects, carrying them in all directions. Most of them were swept to the islands lying to the southward. There were a comparatively few persons who sought to avoid the gathering force of the surge by setting out in the two transports to which they had been assigned late in June, 1783. One of these vessels sailed from St. Augustine on the twenty-fifth of that month for Jamaica, and the other about the same date for New Providence.[236]

Various factors combined during the next few months to impel an increasing number of people to leave East Florida for the Bahamas. At the end of July, General Carleton issued orders from New York by which these islands were included as a part of the Southern District and placed under the command of Brigadier General McArthur at St. Augustine. It soon became known that Carleton had recommended to the British government that the ungranted and escheated lands in the Bahamas be given free of all expenses to those loyalists who had lost their estates through their allegiance, and would settle there. Then came a backset in the form of an unfavorable report of a committee of prospective settlers, who returned from a visit to New Providence and gave out the statement that the soil was rocky and that there were "no tracts contiguous where any considerable

---

[235] Egerton (ed.), *R. Comm. on Loyalist Claims, 1783-1785*, pp. 318-319.
[236] *Hist. MSS. Comm., Am. MSS. in R. Inst.*, IV. 92-93.

number of negroes could be employed." However, Great Abaco Island, the most fertile of the scattered archipelago, gained favor among the Floridians because a body of more than fourteen hundred associated loyalists at New York chose it for their habitation. These associators soon let it be known that they were to be joined in settling that island by fifteen hundred refugees from East Florida. The arrival of a fleet of transports and victualers at St. Augustine on September 12, 1783, stimulated the movement to the Bahamas. Among the number of inhabitants who now applied for conveyance thither were Superintendent Browne and many of his Carolina King's Rangers. By October 1, some of the newcomers were building a town near the south end of Great Abaco, named Carleton Town. From there John Harding, their agent, addressed a memorial requesting provisions for six months, medicines, saws, nails, a supply of coarse linen, etc. Not far away another village was soon to be begun. In the latter part of October, Brook Watson, the commissary general at New York, suggested to Carleton that it would be "seasonable" to send six months' provisions for a thousand men to Abaco and a like quantity to New Providence for the new settlers. Accordingly, a supply of provisions was sent from New York, and a supplementary quantity for two thousand people was requested from Major General Edward Mathew, the commanding officer of the British West Indies. Both supplies were consigned to General McArthur at Nassau, the capital of the Bahamas, in New Providence.[237]

Meantime, Lieutenant John Wilson, the acting engineer at St. Augustine, had gone to the Bahamas to make his general survey of the islands under Carleton's orders of July 14, 1783. He had arrived at Nassau on August 7, where he found Colonel Andrew Deveaux living in the government house with his negro servants. At the fort a white man was in charge of the stores, and attended to firing the morning and evening gun. Wilson found that the islands were little known to the inhabitants, that only seven of them had been hitherto occupied, namely, New Providence, Eleuthera, Harbor Island, Cat Island, Exuma, Long Island, and Turks Island. Their total population in May, 1782, was about four thousand, but Wilson's

---

[237] *Hist. MSS. Comm., Am. MSS. in R. Inst.*, IV. 158, 203, 224, 233, 247, 248, 340, 351, 420, 421, 422. Concerning General McIntyre, see Additional Notes, in Volume II. of this series, p. 335.

classification does not enable one to tell how many whites there were. Basing his figures on taxation, the results were as follows:[238]

    464 white taxables
    103 free born mulattoes, etc.
                      Total, taxables, 1,380
    16 manumitted slaves
    800 slaves
    Non-taxable inhabitants   2,619
    Total, inhabitants   4,002
    Capable of carrying arms   523

However, Northcroft says that before the immigration there were seventeen hundred and fifty white people in the colony and twenty-three hundred colored, giving a total of four thousand and fifty, which is very close to the total given above. Northcroft's figures represent the population as estimated from reliable sources at the beginning of 1784. Wilson reported that the white inhabitants had never been remarkable for their loyalty, but that the blacks had always shown themselves to be good friends of government, particularly those who were free.[239]

When Lieutenant Wilson returned to St. Augustine, he made on the whole a reassuring report concerning the agricultural conditions in the Bahamas, attributing their uncultivated state to the indolence of the old inhabitants, who contented themselves with whatever nature produced without improving their land. They raised guinea corn, sugar cane, a few yams, and cassava without taking the trouble to clear the land, but all the fruits common in the West Indies would grow in the Bahamas with very little cultivation. He thought that settlers from the continent, being more accustomed to industry, would subject the soil to a fairer test than it had had before. This favorable report, together with the successive letters from General Carleton stating that numbers of loyalists had gone, or were going, from New York to the Bahamas, undoubtedly inclined many of the British

[238] Manuscript copy of Lieut. Wilson's report in Boston Public Library; J. H. Stark, *Hist. and Guide to the Bahama Islands*, pp. 172-173.

[239] Manuscript copy of Lt. Wilson's report; J. H. Stark, *Hist. and Guide to Bahama Islands*, pp. 172-173; *Nassau Guardian and Bahama Islands' Advocate and Intelligencer*, Sat. Supplement, October 18, 1913.

subjects in East Florida to make their new homes in those islands. This inclination was turned into decision in the case of numbers when it became known that Brigadier General McArthur was to assume command of the islands as soon as the troops should leave the province. As noted in an earlier chapter there was much friendly feeling for McArthur among the leading inhabitants, and probably among the people generally. During the last three months of 1783 the commanding officer of the garrison was occupied with closing up the affairs of his command in East Florida and embarking the provincial regiments for their respective destinations. Hence he did not arrive at Nassau with a detachment of one subaltern and a score of privates of the 37th Regiment until in January, 1784. As the troops had been embarked on November 1, those going to the Bahamas may have reached there much sooner than McArthur.[240] It may have been at this time that Dr. Thomas Cobham, formerly a prominent "practitioner in physics" in Wilmington, North Carolina, but later assigned as surgeon to the naval hospital at St. Augustine by Admiral Digby, was removed with the hospital to New Providence.[241] With McArthur had come also a number of transports and ordnance vessels with military stores from St. Augustine. These were followed within the same week by seven ships and two brigs crowded with refugees.[242]

Already in December, official information had been received by Governor Tonyn that negotiations had been undertaken for the purchase of land in the Bahamas, so that tracts could be granted to refugee settlers, and that land would also be appropriated to their use in the West Indies. Late in January, 1784, one William Walker wrote from Nassau that since his former letter nearly a thousand loyalists, including their families, had come from East Florida to the Bahamas and that double that number was still to come. He estimated that there were then three thousand in the islands.

[240] Stark, *Hist. and Guide to the Bahama Islands*, pp. 172-173; *Hist. MSS. Comm., Am. MSS. in R. Inst.*, IV. 351, 356.

[241] Evangeline W. Andrews and C. M. Andrews, *Journal of a Lady of Quality*, Yale Hist. Publications, VI. 321.

[242] Northcroft in his *Sketches of Summerland*, p. 281, says that McArthur and his fleet arrived at Nassau on September 25, 1784. Both the direct and cumulative evidence show that he is mistaken in the date. For some of the loyalist settlers, see Volume II. of this work, pp. 263-284, 361-362.

Refugees in Nearby Islands 187

Few of those already arrived seemed to be content, and "several" were trying to make their peace with America and return thither. Others thought of "going to West Florida and turning Spaniards." They had very little money, but many of them possessed from ten to one hundred negroes each. If they could obtain grants of land of from fifty to one hundred and fifty acres in the island of St. Vincent he would come and bring others with him.[243] On March 1, McArthur wrote from New Providence to Lord Sydney that six hundred loyalists had been brought there at the government's expense and about fifty at their own. He added that two settlements had been formed near the south end of Great Abaco Island, and that a considerable number was going to Exuma Island. As he was short of provisions he had promised rations only to discharged soldiers and very needy refugees. A few days before, however, a brig had arrived with eleven hundred barrels of provisions from the Barbadoes, but evidently these had not yet been landed. He had brought with him a small detachment of the 37th Regiment lest the colony of loyalists from New York, which had settled on Great Abaco, should prove refractory. He employed this squad of soldiers not only to support the police but also to guard the provisions. He came with orders to do all in his power to accommodate the refugees and to persuade the people in the islands to form themselves into a militia for their own security. He made necessary repairs on old Fort Nassau, which he found in a ruinous state, and built structures near it to receive the supply of powder and the ordnance stores which he had brought with him.[244]

It may have been after the arrival of the January fleet that a return, or list, of the refugees in the Bahamas was compiled.[245] This return gives the names of the settlers, the number of slaves belonging to each of them, the names of the provinces from which they emigrated, and of the islands in which they located. The date of this list is unknown, but its figures fall so far short of the total number of immigrants from East Florida as derived from other sources that one must assume it to be of early date, or very

---

[243] C. O. 5/561, f. 329.

[244] *Nassau Guardian and Bahama Islands' Advocate and Intelligencer*, Sat. Supplement, October 18, 1913; *Hist. MSS. Comm., Am. MSS. in R. Inst.*, IV. 348.

[245] C. O. 23/25.

incomplete. The following summary shows the distribution of the Floridians:

Name of Island	Whites	Blacks
New Providence:		
1. Nassau	21	33
2. Western District	14	214
Great Abaco	31	359
Exuma	13	206
Cat Island	2	52
Eleuthera	1	4
Total	82	868

At the end of March, 1784, Governor John Maxwell wrote from Nassau that a number of refugees from New York and St. Augustine had settled in several of the principal islands of the Bahama group, and that in Great Abaco they had laid out a town called Carleton. Almost at the time of his writing, Johann David Schoepf, the traveler, left the harbor of St. Augustine on a sloop for New Providence. It was "crammed with people and cattle, luggage and household furniture," and carried a number of black women and children who were being sent to the island for sale. Along the coast Schoepf noticed at frequent intervals the skeleton, or wreckage, of a foundered ship. On board one of the Africans entertained his fellows by playing on a rude "gambee" and singing in the Guinea tongue. The negro's *viol da gamba* was only a notched bar of wood with one end resting against an empty cask and the other against his breast. Over the notches he rubbed in time with his rhythmic song a stick, while shaking the clappers of another stick split lengthwise. The sloop passed Great Abaco, recently settled, Schoepf tells us, by many families of American refugees who had made a beginning of two little towns, Carleton and Marsh's Harbor. They had been given provisions and other necessaries to supply them at first, and could catch plenty of fish in the adjacent waters. Entering the harbor of New Providence on April 6, the passengers landed at Nassau, the small capital of the Bahamas, whose single street with its row of houses and gardens hugged the hilly shore. The place was filled with refugees from the mainland, and many other loyalists who had been banished from

Georgia and South Carolina, and were awaiting the outcome of their trials or permission to return. During the following months the Bahamas fleet made other voyages to New Providence from St. Marys River with its complement of loyalists and negroes, while small groups of emigrants sailed for the same destination in vessels which they bought, or hired, for the purpose.[246] One of the refugees who settled in the town of Nassau at that time was John Wells, the elder brother of Dr. William Charles Wells, publisher of *The East Florida Gazette*. As Dr. Wells had gone to Great Britain in May, 1784, John probably brought his brother's printing press from St. Augustine, for he soon established *The Royal Bahama Gazette*.

Governor Maxwell's comments on the evacuation of East Florida contained in a letter of June 9, 1784, to General McArthur, who was then absent from New Providence, illustrates the character of the man who was already in difficulties with the refugee settlers under his care through his oppressive measures. Maxwell said that he understood from Governor Tonyn that there was no telling when St. Augustine would be evacuated, and that in some measure it would depend on the supply of provisions Maxwell could send him. The governor of the Bahamas declared that the transports had been at St. Marys River for three months past, with some of the loyalists on board consuming provisions that would have sufficed for their voyage to the Bahamas, or anywhere else. He regretted McArthur's temporary absence, fearing a revolt, and enclosed a proclamation he had published on account of the riotous conduct of some refugees who had been the last to arrive from St. Augustine, when they had seen the American flag flying in Nassau Harbor. The Americans with that flag, he asserted, had brought them bread for their support. Governor Maxwell offered Tonyn one hundred barrels of provisions, which was all he could spare, especially as Tonyn estimated that five thousand more emigrants from his province would remove to the Bahamas.[247]

Maxwell had replied to Tonyn's letter of May 10 on June 5, saying that the transport *David* had been wrecked on the bar at Nassau on May 1

---

[246] Morrison (ed.), *Schoepf's Travels in the Confederation*, II. 248-249, 251, 259, 264; Sabine, *Loyalists of the Am. Rev.*, II. 407.

[247] C. O. 23/25.

and that only fifteen hundred barrels of its cargo, much damaged, had been salvaged. However, he had six months' supply of provisions in store for four thousand people, including their negroes. He could spare a few hundred barrels, if Tonyn would send a transport and bear the expense.[248]

By September, 1784, the negotiations between the British government and the lords proprietors of the Bahamas had reached such a stage that instructions were issued to Lieutenant Governor James Powell to grant unoccupied lands in the islands to the refugees in the proportion of forty acres to every head of a family and twenty acres to every white or black person in a family. Provisions also continued to be needed. On October 4, William Gamble, the commissary for the islands, certified that he had received two hundred and forty-eight orders from Governor Maxwell from the 29th of the preceding May for victualing three hundred and eighty-seven loyalists, including sixty-four women, in addition to twenty-three hundred negroes, all from East Florida.[249]

Late in October, the board of associated loyalists at St. Marys River in that province addressed a memorial to Maxwell praying for a quantity of provisions and declaring that they would rather die with their swords in their hands than go to the inhospitable regions of Nova Scotia, or to the Bahamas, or deny their religion and become Spanish subjects, or return to the states at the risk of insult and assassination, even though they had lost all, been abandoned by their sovereign, and deserted by their country. This memorial was signed by John Cruden as president of the associators. In his reply Maxwell resented the bitter aspersions of the memorialists upon their king and country, and told them plainly that everything possible was being done for them. He also said that such provisions as he had were for the loyalists who came to the Bahamas, and that Cruden would do his associates a particular favor by advising them to embark immediately. When they should arrive they would receive a six months' supply and land to cultivate for their immediate needs until permanent grants could be issued to them.

The rapid increase in the number of negroes in the Bahamas, partly by

[248] C. O. 23/25.
[249] Shattuck (ed.), *The Bahama Islands*, Geographical Soc. of Baltimore Publication, 1905, p. 424; Siebert, *Legacy of Am. Rev. to British West Indies and Bahamas*, p. 20.

the accession of those brought in by the loyalists and partly by purchase from African slave ships, excited fears among the whites and, in 1784, the general assembly enacted a new and severe code for the regulation of slaves and free colored people. Death was made the penalty for assault on a white person by a slave; any one who manumitted a bondman could be fined £90; both slaves and free negroes found at large with firearms could be disarmed by white persons, and the testimony of slaves against freedmen was to be regarded as valid in all trials for capital, or criminal, offenses.[250]

In a letter of early December, 1784, to Lord Sydney, Tonyn remarked that great pains had been taken to stem the current of unfavorable reports concerning the Bahama Islands, but that such reports had produced a bad effect, especially among those people who had nothing to be confiscated by the American states, or any debts to recover on their return thither. Emissaries from the states were in East Florida, and persuaded some of the refugees to go back. Many more, however, had gone to the interior parts of America, among the mountains.

In East Florida, Governor Tonyn published the announcement that the last transport would leave St. Marys River on February 20, 1785, "with all the refugees who had not yet availed themselves of his Majesty's bounty." This notice was intended to hasten the evacuation, the term of which as defined in the treaty of peace was rapidly expiring. However, the term was lengthened by four months, and emigrants continued to take passage for the Bahamas and other destinations.[251]

The population of old inhabitants was soon outnumbered by the newcomers, who threw the Bahamas into a turmoil of activity. Early in March, Lieutenant Governor Powell wrote from New Providence that about twenty-seven hundred whites and blacks had emigrated from East Florida to the islands, and that word had been received from Governor Tonyn that many more might be expected, in part, from New York. Many of the refugees were dissatisfied with conditions as they found them in the Bahamas, and were treated with little consideration by Governor Maxwell and the old inhabitants. There was no regret on the part of the loyalists when Maxwell retired from office and left for England in the summer of 1785.

[250] C. O. 23/25 and 23/26.   [251] See *ante*, pp. 170, 172.

They had accused him of trying to withhold the right of trial by jury and of acting in a tyrannical manner; they alleged that some of the laws were repugnant to those of the mother country, and they demanded reform. Although the loyalists gained some seats in the commons house of assembly in 1785, the old settlers remained in control, and declared ineligible several members who favored the new party for absenting themselves contrary to the house's orders. By its orders also a petition from the loyalists for the dissolution of the assembly was burnt by the common hangman. A memorial of seventy-two officers from North Carolina, dated February 9, 1785, which was presented to Lord Sydney, strongly recommended Lieutenant Colonel John Hamilton of the late Royal North Carolina Regiment for the governorship of the islands when that dignified office should become vacant. The petitioners stated that they had forfeited their estates, that those who had gone to Nova Scotia were unable in their present state of finances to clear the ground and raise the necessaries of life in a climate so severe and inhospitable to southern constitutions, and that the Bahamas were the only place in the British dominions suitable for them.[252]

In September, 1785, the last division of transports from East Florida landed its passengers in the Bahamas. Of these one hundred and fourteen were loyalists and two hundred and forty-nine negroes. In a short time they were experiencing the greatest want, according to the commissary, William Gamble. Further light is thrown on their pitiable condition by a letter of March 9, 1786, from the committee of correspondence of the Bahamas to the colony's agent in London. The committee requested immediate relief for these unhappy people. Being the last to arrive, the committee explained, they had not been put on a footing with the former immigrants as regards provisions and plantation tools. Most of these loyalists, who were of "the poorer sort," were in a shocking state, destitute not only of houses but also of the very necessaries of life. The committee declared that they were perishing daily.

From January, 1786, to January, 1789, the accession to the population of the Bahamas from the West Indies, Nova Scotia, and other places, to-

---

[252] Siebert, *Legacy of Am. Rev. to British West Indies and Bahamas*, pp. 25-26; E. A. Jones (ed.), *Journal of Alexander Chesney*, p. 117.

gether with new negroes bought from the slave ships, was four hundred whites and twenty-one hundred blacks. In other words, from January, 1784, to January, 1789, the number of the white inhabitants was doubled and that of the negroes more than trebled in the Bahamas. The wretched condition of some of the American loyalists did not escape the notice of John Cruden, who was at Nassau in the early part of May, 1786, and he proposed a lottery for their benefit. Later in the same year, Cruden, like other refugees in the islands, made the voyage to Nova Scotia for the purpose of submitting his claim for the loss of his American property to the commissioner on loyalists' claims, Colonel Dundas. He soon returned to the Bahamas and died there on September 18, 1787, at the age of thirty-three years. The demise of his uncle, John Cruden, the elder, had occurred in the island of Exuma, in the preceding year.[253]

By the latter part of 1786, the American loyalists had become the stronger political party in the Bahama Islands. In October, 1787, Lord Dunmore became governor and was soon asked to dissolve the general assembly in petitions from New Providence, Great Abaco, Exuma, and Cat islands, but would not consent. Accordingly, the assembly continued until the end of his administration eight years later. An act was then passed limiting the life of a legislature to seven years.[254]

Meantime, the negotiations between the British government and the lords proprietors of the Bahamas were brought to a conclusion in March, 1787. On the 19th of that month an indenture was signed by the duke of Beaufort, Lord Craven, Sir John Wodehouse and his lady, Mary and Elizabeth Tyrell, the earl of Coventry, Lord Viscount Weymouth, Lord Carteret, and Louisa Carolina Colleton, by which they sold to the crown their proprietary rights in all manors, lands, tenements, and other real estate, and surrendered all rents, profits, titles, use, and claims derived therefrom to the sole and proper use of the king, his heirs, and successors forever, and for no other use, intent, or purpose whatsoever, for the sum

---

[253] *Nassau Guardian and Bahama Islands' Advocate and Intelligencer*, Sat. Supplement, October 18, 1913; E. A. Jones (ed.), *Journal of Alexander Chesney*, p. 93.

[254] Siebert, *Legacy of Am. Rev. to British West Indies and Bahamas*, p. 26; Morrison (ed.), *Schoepf's Travels in the Confederation*, II. 263 n.

of £12,000. These proprietary rights had been granted to their predecessors by letters patent from Charles II. Under the transfer the government was enabled to issue to the refugee and other settlers in the Bahamas clear and valid titles for the plots of land that had been, or should be, granted to them.[255]

In various ways the evacuation of East Florida and the other southern provinces marked a new era in the history of the Bahama Islands. Besides greatly increasing the white and black populations and leading to the settlement of other islands in the group, it promoted ship building, imports and exports, and cotton raising. Previous to the year 1784, the inhabitants had paid little attention to planting. In 1785, the year of the great hurricane, twenty-four hundred and seventy acres were planted. Both Persian and Anguilla cotton were grown. In 1786, twenty-nine hundred acres were under cultivation, and the crop of cotton exported amounted to one hundred and fifty tons. In 1787, forty-three hundred acres were cultivated and should have produced, according to the average yield of previous years, three hundred and ninety-four tons of clean cotton, but more than two-thirds of the crop were destroyed by the ravages of an insect that did as much damage as the hurricanes that occasionally swept through the islands. Scarcely more than one hundred and twelve tons of cotton were harvested in 1788, the loss being estimated at two hundred and eighty-two tons of clean cotton.[256]

During these years Nassau enjoyed an increasing commerce. New vessels were needed and were built in the islands, some as large as three hundred tons. It has been recorded that six square-rigged ships could occasionally be seen at once in Nassau Harbor. Back in 1773 and 1774 the exports had amounted only to £5,216 and the imports to £3,592. In 1786 and 1787 the latter increased to £136,359 and the former to £58,707.[257]

The influx of the loyalists, many of them planters but others from vari-

[255] Malcolm, *Hist. Documents relating to Bahama Islands*, No. 16; Fiske, *The West Indies*, p. 125; Shattuck (ed.), *The Bahama Islands*, Geographical Soc. of Baltimore Publication, p. 426.

[256] *Nassau Guardian and Bahama Islands' Advocate and Intelligencer*, Sat. Supplement, October 18, 1913.

[257] McKinnen, *Tour of the British West Indies in the Years 1802 and 1803*, pp. 218-219.

ous walks of life, and not a few who were men of energy and resource, manifested itself in a general awakening. The refugees from the mainland were not only accountable for the introduction of superior varieties of cotton and better methods of tillage, but also for the building of new towns, the enactment of new laws, the purchase of the Bahamas by the crown, and the formation of a loyalist party which took part in island politics and sought the share in the government that its numbers entitled it to. In 1789, a select committee of eight members of the house of assembly, of whom at least four were refugees from East Florida, Superintendent Thomas Browne being the chairman, made a report on the state of the Bahama Islands. The committee pointed out the advantages of location of the islands for trade and the serviceableness of the soil for the increase and improvement in the culture of cotton; it suggested the production of coffee, cocoa, the Madeira grape, and the reed cane, as also the breeding of cattle and sheep; it called attention to the numerous salt ponds on certain islands as sources of immense quantities of salt; it dealt with the recent increase in the population and the rising production and export of cotton, and closed its report with a strong plea for new public buildings. It complained that under the same roof and on the same floor in Nassau were to be found the court, the house of assembly, and the jail. The assembly had found it necessary to remove to a private house, rented for the purpose; the court room was ruinous and unsafe, while the jail was insecure for the confinement of debtors and criminals. As there were no public buildings for the assembly, the council, or any of the public offices, these were so widely separated as to be highly inconvenient. The out-islands had neither churches, workhouses, nor any other public buildings required by their populations. The recent loss of crops had rendered it impossible for the inhabitants of the colony to raise the funds necessary for the erection of a two-story building at a cost of £6,000 to accommodate the courts of justice, the assembly, the council, and the public offices, besides another at a cost of £2,000 for a jail.

When Brigadier General McArthur had arrived in the Bahamas, he and Lieutenant Wilson, the engineer, had done what they could to put Fort Nassau, then almost a ruin, into a tenable state. They had also constructed a magazine for the powder and ordnance stores, and other structures near the fort, which were surrounded with strong picketing. After the great hurricane of 1785, substantial abutments were built to support the ramparts from falling into the sea. Lord Dunmore, realizing the weakness of Fort Nassau, caused Fort Charlotte to be erected on a commanding height near the town, which served as a defense not only for Nassau and its western approaches, but also for the bar in the harbor. Inasmuch as Fort Nassau, with its ordnance and barrack yards, was near the center of the town, and enclosed buildings that might be fitted for the use of the different civil departments with ample space for the erection of other public edifices later, the committee recommended that application be made for the grant of the site of Fort Nassau and the ordnance and barrack yards, or of a sum to defray the expense of the public buildings immediately wanted, and that the council in its legislative capacity be requested to concur in the application.[258]

In the early part of the Revolution, the Society for the Propagation of the Gospel had maintained two missionaries in the Bahamas, one for Harbor Island and Eleuthera and one for New Providence. It had also supported a schoolmaster in Harbor Island, who received £10 a year while the missionaries received £50 each. Books were sent out for the mission libraries and catechisms, prayerbooks, and tracts for distribution among the parishioners. Later a missionary was stationed on Exuma Island. This was scanty provision for the religious needs of a population now greatly increased by the multitude of refugees from the southern provinces and from New York. The missionaries visited the various settlements two or three times a year to conduct worship and perform baptismal, marriage, and funeral ceremonies, and in some instances appointed a capable person in each settlement to read the service every Sunday and hear the children repeat the catechism.

The Exuma mission included Long and Cat islands. There had been but two settlements of old inhabitants on Long Island, but when the Rev. William Gordon visited it in February, 1790, he found it settled from one end to the other, the plantations numbering sixteen and the population three

---

[258] *Nassau Guardian and Bahama Islands' Advocate and Intelligencer*, Sat. Supplement, October 18, 1913.

Refugees in Nearby Islands

thousand whites and blacks. A minister was needed to take charge of several little congregations. Exuma had thirty-eight plantations with one hundred and sixty-five whites and thirteen hundred and twenty negroes. Cat Island contained about six hundred inhabitants. The total population of this mission, including the three islands, was fifty-one hundred.

Nassau on New Providence was a town of about twenty-five hundred people, most of the whites being of Scotch extraction, "many of them Dissenters, but moderate and conformable to the Church." The edifice was too small for half of the congregation. A chapel was needed in the eastern part of the town, where a large room was being used for services on Sunday afternoons. The missionary, John Richards, then preached to the negroes. He discovered that some four hundred of the latter were Anabaptists from the Carolinas, who had their own black preachers from the states. He complained of the lack of a parsonage and a glebe and of the failure of the missionaries to receive their salaries during most of 1791 from the Bahamas government. Mr. Richards reported one hundred and sixty-three baptisms since his arrival at Nassau on November 5, 1790. He had made visits to Long and Cat islands, and said that Andros and other islands contained many settlers and should have ministers. He estimated the population as follows:

Islands	*Population*	*Length in miles*	*Width in miles*
New Providence	5,000	30	6 or 7
Long	2,200	70	7
Exuma	1,200	40	5
Caicos	900	60	
Crooked	700	40	
Cat	600	60	10 or 12
Turks	800	7	1½
Watlings	100	25	
Harbor, Eleuthera	1,500		
Andros Islands, Abaco	220		
Total	13,220		

One wonders how Mr. Richards missed it so widely on the population of

Great Abaco Island, which was the choice of nearly three thousand refugees, fifteen hundred from New York and about fourteen hundred from East Florida. It is possible, of course, that a typographical error in the printed report of the Society for the Propagation of the Gospel accounts for the discrepancy.

The winter of 1790-1791 caused much sickness in the Bahamas and "proved fatal to many poor families," according to the Rev. Thomas Robertson, the missionary for Harbor and Eleuthera islands. During 1791, he visited the distant islands, maintained his church on Harbor Island, and conducted a school of "thirty scholars." The Rev. William Gordon reported from Exuma in a letter of May 13, 1791, that Long Island had four hundred and thirty-five whites and fifteen hundred and five blacks. In 1773, it was without "a single inhabitant," but began to be settled by a few poor families from New Providence at that time. These settlers established two small villages, one of ninety free inhabitants and the other of seventy. A few loyal refugees came in 1782. Gradually it became known that the land there was well adapted for raising cotton, and from 1785 to 1791 a great many more refugees immigrated, besides some natives from New Providence. At first these settlers lived in huts, ate "salt provisions in general," paid a double price for what they imported from Providence, and exhausted their means in developing their plantations and buying negroes to cultivate them. The slaves were ignorant and dishonest and the old settlers given to "all the vices of the seafaring life." Many of them could scarcely read, but the gentry "acquired a great tincture of infidelity" by perusing the works of Mandeville, Gibbon, Hume, Voltaire, and Rousseau. Hence a "conversible Clergyman" was necessary, or at least a schoolmaster or catechist, and modern books of divinity by "writers of character and rank."

Mr. Gordon ministered to a good many loyalists in Great Exuma, officiating on Sunday mornings in a large room which they hired for use as a chapel and in the afternoons at his own lodgings. Each third Sunday he preached at a village eight miles distant. He wished that he might conduct family worship among a few scattered inhabitants at the west end of Great Exuma and visit occasionally Little Exuma, where he had once preached to

Refugees in Nearby Islands 199

about twenty whites. He could do these things and go once a year to several islands where there was no public worship if released from his duties on Long Island. As the three islands under his care were a day's sail apart he bought a vessel for his voyages. He received £30 currency from the Bahamas government for his ministrations on Long and Cat islands, besides the £50 paid him by the society. The latter added a gratuity of £10 in appreciation of his faithful services, and on his advice employed Mr. Cruden as schoolmaster at a salary of £15.

On Mr. Gordon's recommendation and after investigating conditions in the Bahamas, the society sent a missionary to Long Island, namely, the Rev. Patrick Fraser, who soon died and was succeeded by the Rev. Daniel Warner Rose. Mr. Rose had been stationed in Dominica until August, 1795. The society secured a promise of aid from the secretary of state and on this assurance sent instructions to the governor of the islands. About the same time Mr. Gordon was transferred from Exuma to the mission of Harbor Island and Eleuthera, and two bills were passed by the assembly to provide a fund for the erection and repair of churches, the better support of ministers and schoolmasters, and the procuring of parsonages and glebes. Three new parishes were added to the existing ones. In 1796, there were only four missions in the islands, of which two were vacant. These were to be filled and a fifth one added. Caicos Island was chosen for the new mission.

However, by December, 1799, two were again vacant. On Long Island, the vestry decided to complete the parish church and so put an end to worship in "old uninhabitable houses." In 1800, the assembly voted £1,000 for this purpose, but the sum was insufficient on account of "the high price of lumber and materials." The negroes on the island had become Baptists, and their black preachers made a practice of immersing them in the sea, extorting "a dollar or stolen goods." One of the preachers harangued hundreds of them on Saturday nights, which the missionary thought might lead to "dreadful consequences if it was not stopped by authority." He hoped to win them back by more psalm-singing when the new church should be finished. At Exuma he found the planters and four hundred of their slaves engaged in making salt from a pond. He preached to the gentlemen and ladies under a canopy and officiated in four different parts of the island. He planned to visit these people several times a year until a minister should be appointed, for which they had made liberal provision.

The new missionary sent to Exuma, the Rev. Henry Groombridge, died at the end of six months and was followed by Daniel Warner Rose in December, 1802, from Long Island. On Christmas, Mr. Rose dedicated the new church, but reported that the fluctuating state of the island rendered it inadvisable to send another clergyman there. As the governor and council had opened the port, he hoped that the inhabitants would not be forced to emigrate to other countries. By the help of a free mulatto woman who could read, he formed some of the best negroes into a society in the hope of inculcating Christian morals. Many of the blacks were Baptists, thirty-five were free, and ten hundred and seventy-eight slaves. The white population numbered only one hundred and forty.

The provision for the building of new churches and the more liberal support of ministers and schoolmasters under the laws enacted by the general assembly of the Bahamas in 1795 seems to have led the Society for the Propagation of the Gospel to withdraw its support from the missions in those islands from 1803 onward. Besides the new edifices mentioned above one was erected at that time in the eastern district of Nassau on New Providence. The society was also influenced by the advice received from Governor John Halkett in 1803. He wrote that, "considering the late great migrations and other circumstances," he could not recommend that another missionary be sent out. By 1810, there were only two missions in the Bahamas, one in New Providence, namely, St. Matthews parish, and the other in Eleuthera, and both were vacant. By 1814, if not earlier, the society no longer included the islands among its mission fields.[258a]

IN JAMAICA

Jamaica received loyalists and their slaves from Connecticut, Massa-

---

[258a] *Sermon preached before Incorporated Soc. for the Propagation of the Gospel in Foreign Parts* [with Abstract of Proceedings of the Soc.], 1779, pp. 41, 60, 61; 1780, pp. 41, 42, 55; 1791, pp. 25, 38-40; 1792, pp. 35, 56-65; 1796, pp. 55-57; 1800, pp. 29, 42-46; 1802, pp. 33, 48-50; 1804, pp. 31, 48-51; 1810, p. 33; 1814, pp. 28-34.

Refugees in Nearby Islands

chusetts, New York, Philadelphia, Maryland, Virginia, the Carolinas, Georgia, East Florida, the Bay of Honduras, and the Mosquito Shore. They came in large numbers especially from Georgia and South Carolina. After the evacuation of Savannah in July, 1782, four hundred families from Georgia with nearly five thousand slaves went to Jamaica, besides a number from Honduras. The great convoy from Charleston arrived at Kingston on January 13, 1783, with twelve hundred and seventy-eight white people—men, women, and children—and twenty-six hundred and thirteen negroes, or a total of nearly thirty-nine hundred. East Florida did not furnish more than one-fifth of this total to the population of Jamaica. Rations were distributed to the newcomers, and as soon as possible the loyalists hired out their slaves to labor on the public works and on sugar and other plantations. The cultivation of indigo seems to have received a decided impetus from the influx of the loyalists.[259]

Late in February, 1783, the general assembly of Jamaica passed an act to relieve and assist the refugees who had, or should, come to settle. They were exempted for seven years after their arrival from the payment of taxes on their slaves or any other taxes, except quit-rents on such lands as they might purchase or patent. They were also released from all services, offices, or duties, except the obligation to serve in the militia. They were required, however, to take out certificates on affidavit before the magistrate of the parish, or precinct, where they intended to settle within three months after the passage of the act, or after their arrival, and these certificates were recorded in the office of the secretary of the island. Loyalists who received patents for land must settle and plant at least a part of it and make other improvements within two years from the date of their patent, under penalty of losing the land for failure to comply with the conditions.[260]

While approving the general purposes of this act, the vestry of Kingston protested in a petition to the general assembly at the end of November, 1784, against the burdens which it imposed on their parish. Kingston had

---

[259] Siebert, *Legacy of Am. Rev. to British West Indies and Bahamas*, pp. 38-39; *South Carolina Hist. and Genealogical Magazine*, January, 1910, p. 26; Rev. G. W. Bridges, *The Annals of Jamaica*, p. 190.

[260] *Journals* of Assembly of Jamaica, VIII (1784-1791), 32-33; Siebert, *Legacy of Am. Rev. to British West Indies and Bahamas*, pp. 35-37.

a larger number of refugees than all the other parishes combined. Seventy loyalist householders in Kingston were exempt from parochial taxes, though many of them were "opulent" and engaged in commerce, while others were tradesmen or mechanics with lucrative employments. There were also many poor refugees, who crowded the parish house at public expense, or received a weekly allowance of money for outside support, not to speak of considerable sums expended to pay the passage of some of these people to other countries. These items amounted to not less than £3,172 up to the end of November, 1784, the sum being made up by public and private contributions in the parish of Kingston. This petition was referred by action of the commons house of assembly to the committee of the whole for inquiry into the state of the island, for the refugees were distributed in a number of other parishes, including Port Royal, St. Andrew, St. Catherine, St. George, St. Elizabeth, St. Thomas-in-the-Vale, and Trewlawney. Many of these loyalists had brought slaves with them, either few or many as the case might be. One was in charge of about two hundred negroes, less than half being his own property. For some time they were employed on the public works, afterward in "jobbing." Another loyalist was accompanied by more than four hundred blacks, of whom over two hundred belonged to Sir James Wright, the former governor of Georgia. Still another had about one hundred and eighty, nearly two-thirds of these being the property of William Bull, who had recently been the lieutenant governor of South Carolina. That many of the refugees procured patents for land under the terms of the act of 1783, goes without saying. For example, in the parish of St. Elizabeth tracts of land were granted to one hundred and eighty-three newcomers. The claim for payment by the surveyors of these lands led to an inquiry by the commons house of assembly, during which it was "stated in evidence that none but amphibious creatures" could live there, the region being little better than a swamp.[261]

In July, 1782, Colonel Archibald Campbell, who with a force from New York had captured Savannah at the end of December, 1779, was lieutenant governor of Jamaica. In December, 1782, he was promoted to the

---

[261] Siebert, *Legacy of the Am. Rev. to the British West Indies and Bahamas*, p. 39; Eaton (ed.), *Recollections of a Georgia Loyalist*, p. 218; Gardner, *Hist. of Jamaica*, pp. 211-212.

governorship. On the 13th of the following month, a convoy arrived from Charleston with sixteen hundred troops, including the 63d, 64th, and 71st regiments, together with a detachment of the 84th. More than four hundred white families, who brought with them forty-five hundred negroes, arrived in this fleet to settle in Jamaica. Fearing an attack on the island by the French, who had already captured five of the West India Islands, Governor Campbell raised two battalions of black troops in Jamaica, the Windward Islands, and America during the winter of 1782. The governor's vigilance in defensive measures convinced the French that, until they could obtain reinforcements, they would not dare to attack the island.[262]

It will be recalled that the evacuation of Savannah in July, 1782, had been conducted by Brigadier General Alured Clarke. During that ordeal he had won the regard of the Americans by his courtesy and his protection of property. After sending many of the Georgians to East Florida, Jamaica, and other destinations, he served as muster master general of the Hessian troops. During May, 1783, he had been at Philadelphia, arranging for the march of the prisoners-of-war to Elizabethtown, New Jersey. Later in this year he was made lieutenant governor of Jamaica, where he had unlimited opportunities to show kindness and give assistance to the numbers of refugees still arriving in the island. He saw to it that the provisions intended for the loyalists from East Florida went to nobody else. The first shipload from that province had arrived at Kingston in the summer of 1783, a six weeks' supply of provisions having been sent for them by Brigadier General McArthur from St. Augustine. In the spring and summer of 1784 transports brought more refugees with their slaves from East Florida to Jamaica. Early in December, the transports were back again in St. Marys River and once more filled with emigrants and their effects for another voyage to Jamaica and the West Indies. In the latter part of July, 1785, a transport arrived at Kingston with loyalists and their families and negroes from the Florida peninsula. This vessel was bound for the Mosquito Coast, but Lieutenant Governor Alured Clarke exerted his influence to keep them from going thither for the present, as he had been instructed to do. Accord-

---

[262] *Hist. MSS. Comm., Am. MSS. in R. Inst.*, III. 18, 32, 102, 251, 273, IV. 71, 77, 80, 101, 106, 109, 239, 259; C. O. 5/561, f. 353; Cundall, *Biog. Annals of Jamaica*, p. 20.

ing to the records of William Brown, the commissioner for evacuation in East Florida, only one hundred and ninety-six loyalists and seven hundred and fourteen negroes went to Jamaica and the small islands of the Spanish Main. Most of these settled undoubtedly in Jamaica. In comparison with the multitudes of whites and blacks who emigrated from Savannah and Charleston at the close of the Revolution, they formed an insignificant proportion, the loyalists from East Florida being only about one-tenth of those from Georgia and about one-sixth of those from South Carolina.[263]

Since the evacuation of Savannah, Captain Moses Kirkland had been a resident of Jamaica, settling in St. George's Parish; and since May, 1783, John Lothion, a refugee from Amelia Island to the Florida mainland after suffering losses at the hands of the Americans, had lived in Kingston, Jamaica. In the spring of 1784, Lieutenant Colonel Joseph Robinson of the South Carolina Royalists and his wife went to Jamaica, probably because a part of his regiment "continued in service in the West Indies." As Colonel and Mrs. Robinson found the climate of the island unhealthy, they remained only about a year and then departed for New Brunswick. In the autumn of 1785, Dr. William Martin Johnston, the son of Dr. Lewis Johnston, formerly president and treasurer of the council of Georgia, settled at Kingston, being joined there in the following December by his family. Most of the members of the two Johnston families had been refugees at St. Augustine for sixteen months, during which time, according to the younger Mrs. Johnston, they ate fish as their "chief dependence and ration." When Dr. Lewis Johnston was ready to leave East Florida, he was granted a transport to "go wherever he wished in the British Dominion." He chose to return to Scotland, which was his native country. His son had already crossed the Atlantic to pursue his medical studies in Edinburgh and London. Late in May, 1784, the elder Johnston embarked for Greenoch with the two families. Later Dr. William Martin Johnston sailed for Jamaica, and was there joined by his wife and children, as mentioned above. He was well received by Lieutenant Governor Clarke, and was nominally assigned to a regiment in order that he might draw island

---

[263] *Hist. MSS. Comm., Am. MSS. in R. Inst.*, IV. 170, 203, 233, 247, 248, 294, 339, 340; C. O. 5/561, f. 353. For some of the settlers of Jamaica, see Volume II. of this work, p. 362.

pay at the rate of twenty shillings a week for himself, ten shillings for his wife, and five shillings for each of his children. Before long he was engaged in combating yellow fever, which "made great havoc among all newcomers and sailors," although it seems not to have attacked the old inhabitants. Later Dr. Johnston became the attending physician on the estates of James Wildman, one of the members of the Jamaica council, in St. Andrew's Parish, near Kingston, and lived at Liguana.[264]

The newspaper of the colony was *The Jamaica Mercury*, as it was first named, which had been founded by Alexander Aikman in 1778. Aikman was a refugee from Charleston, South Carolina, where he had been an apprentice to Robert Wells, the leading bookseller and printer of the town, and the publisher of a newspaper. In January, 1782, Mr. Aikman married Louisa Susannah Wells, the second daughter of his former master, who had worked with him during four years in her father's establishment. She bore him eight daughters and two sons. For some years, the older son, Alexander, was in charge of the printing and newspaper publishing business. On becoming printer to the king and the colony, in 1780, Mr. Aikman, Sr., changed the title of his paper to *The Royal Gazette*. It was a small double sheet, ten and a half inches long by eight and a half wide. It was still being published by its founder in May, 1787, when it had reached the twenty-first number of its ninth volume. For many years Mr. Aikman was a member of the house of assembly in Jamaica.[265]

Already before the first transport from East Florida had carried its quota of loyalists to the island, the supplies of provisions sent thither for the great number of refugees from Georgia and South Carolina were becoming exhausted. On April 8, 1783, a score of "loyal subjects formerly of the

---

[264] Sabine, *Loyalists of the Am. Rev.*, I. 603-604; E. A. Jones, *Journal of Alexander Chesney*, pp. 105-108; *Hist. MSS. Comm., Stopford-Sackville MSS.*, II. 69-70; *South Carolina Hist. and Genealogical Magazine*, XVIII. 69-71; A. O. 13/36; A. O. 12/92; Eaton (ed.), *Recollections of a Georgia Loyalist*, pp. 11-12, 24, 29, 64, 73-74, *passim*; Siebert, *Legacy of Am. Rev. to British West Indies and Bahamas*, pp. 39-41.

[265] Sabine, *Loyalists of the Am. Rev.*, I. 155-156; R. *Gazette*, Jamaica, May 19-26, 1787, in Library of Am. Antiquarian Society at Worcester, Mass.; Louisa S. Wells, *Journal of a Voyage from Charleston, S. C., to London, 1778*, pp. 111-113; *Gentleman's Magazine*, X., new ser., p. 556; CI., pt. ii, p. 571.

Southern provinces" addressed a memorial to General Carleton requesting a further allowance until they could find "lands or employment, especially for their negroes." Among the signatures to this memorial were those of Charles Ogilvie, Alexander Wright, William Knox, and Greenwood & Higginson, all of them proprietors of lands and slaves in East Florida. Some of these loyalists were able to hire out their negroes to labor on the public works, or to send them out "jobbing," that is, to do the planting and other heavy work on sugar and other plantations.[266]

Early in July, 1783, an order in council was promulgated restricting the shipment of live stock, grain, lumber, and other American products to the West Indies to British vessels, and prohibiting the importation from the states into those islands of salt beef, pork, and fish. Most of the West Indies sent remonstrances and petitions to parliament against this policy in 1784, on the ground that they were largely dependent upon America for their supplies. The general assembly of Jamaica took a definite stand in favor of free trade with the United States as being essential to the successful management of the island estates, getting bread for the inhabitants, and averting impending ruin. What seemed like ruin came at the end of July, in the form of a hurricane that sunk, drove ashore, or dismasted all the vessels in Kingston Harbor, wrecked the public buildings, and caused the loss of many lives. Early in August, Lieutenant Governor Clarke saw fit to use his discretionary power for the purpose of suspending the embargo on the importation of provisions in foreign bottoms for the next six months. At the same time, the planters increased their acreage in corn and other agricultural produce. Scarcely had they harvested their crops in 1785 when another hurricane swept over Jamaica. This time the governor prohibited the exportation of provisions to other suffering colonies in place of opening the ports again to American ships. However, this measure did not prevent a scarcity of food during the remainder of the year. Late in October, 1786, a third storm brought fresh disaster upon the people of Jamaica. The important lesson learned by the islanders from these storms and the restriction on importations was the necessity of growing a much larger proportion of

[266] *Hist. MSS. Comm., Am. MSS. in R. Inst.*, IV. 19; Gardner, *Hist. of Jamaica*, p. 158.

the provisions they needed. The navigation laws were not enforced after 1792, and were repealed by parliament a few years later.[267]

However, the increased production of foodstuffs did not reduce the size of the sugar and coffee crops in Jamaica. On the contrary, in 1787, these crops exceeded those of any former year. The cultivation of coffee was coming rapidly into favor during the years 1782 and 1783, when the loyalists were arriving in great numbers. Some of them also raised considerable quantities of indigo, which had been much cultivated in East Florida. The growing of cotton, to which many of the planters of South Carolina and Georgia had been accustomed, was more or less interfered with by the variable climate of the West Indies.[268]

IN DOMINICA

On June 18 or 19, 1785, a transport arrived at Dominica, one of the Lesser Antilles, from East Florida with about one hundred and fifty loyalists, who had come to settle. From Governor Tonyn came a message that two more ships with upward of four hundred on board would follow in a few days. As there was not a house or a shed for their shelter, Governor J. Orde was at a loss what to do with them. Every place was full. His only resource seemed to be the transports in which they came. By detaining these their passengers could be protected from the rainy season, which was just beginning. The governor could furnish provisions, and at the proper time plots of ground for the immigrants to cultivate and build on. His council was in full accord with these arrangements, and the general assembly voted a bonus of £16 10s to each loyalist, besides passing an act exempting them from taxes for fifteen years. On August 5, the *Elizabeth* transport brought one hundred and forty more refugees from East Florida, and again it was reported that two additional transports were to be expected. Late in August, while Governor Tonyn was wearily waiting on board the *Cyrus* in Amelia Harbor for good sailing weather, between two hundred and three hundred loyalists and their negroes arrived from that port, among them being the slaves of Lord Hawke and the governor himself.

---

[267] Gardner, *Hist. of Jamaica*, pp. 212-213; Edwards, *Hist. of the West Indies*, III. 284.
[268] Gardner, *Hist. of Jamaica*, pp. 159, 241-242.

Tonyn had failed to sell his negroes to the Spaniards in Florida. No doubt he found a market for them in Dominica. Governor Orde was instructed to distribute provisions among the immigrants according to their necessities. A supply of tools was late in arriving, but was looked for in February, 1786. Sickness had broken out among the slaves of the loyalists, and on account of the large expense for medicines Mr. Orde directed the surgeon to the garrison to supply a part of them from the king's stores.[269]

SUMMARY OF EMIGRANTS FROM EAST FLORIDA

The summary of the numbers of British subjects who emigrated from East Florida to the Bahamas, West Indies, and elsewhere during the evacuation period of two years and five months, is given in a tabulation, or return, made by William Brown, the commissioner for evacuation, substantially as follows:

Destinations	Whites	Blacks	Totals
To Europe	246	35	281
To Nova Scotia	725	155	880
To Jamaica and the Spanish Main	196	714	910
To Dominica	225	444	669
To the Bahama Islands	1,033	2,214	3,247
To the States of America	462	2,561	3,023
To other Foreign Parts	61	217	278
With the Spaniards	450	200	650
Total	3,398	6,540	9,938

Commissioner Brown adds that at the time of the peace it was supposed that about five thousand people, mostly of the back country, went over the mountains to the states and other places.[270] This statement is somewhat different from that of Governor Tonyn, who testified, after his return to London, that in February, 1784, on the receipt of the news of the peace, four thousand of the inhabitants started for the settlements on the lower

[269] C. O. 71/9, June 20, August 4, 5, 24, September 28, October 7, 1785, February 20, 25-27, 1786; C. O. 23/26. For some of the settlers in Dominica, see Volume II. of this work, p. 362.

[270] C. O. 5/561, f. 817. I have taken the liberty of adding the third column of figures to show the totals.

Mississippi. In several of his letters, Tonyn refers to some of these people as having gone to settle in the mountains to the westward.

A few words of comment may be appropriate concerning some of the figures and phrases given in Commissioner Brown's interesting table. The expression "To Europe" seems to be used here as it often was in the letters of civil and military officers writing from St. Augustine to mean "to England," or "to Great Britain." Several vessels during the evacuation took a number of persons who had been resident in East Florida back to the mother country before the *Two Sisters* and the *Ann* sailed for London on November 19, 1785, with Governor Tonyn, other civil officers, and some families of the middle and lower classes. As one would expect these persons returning to Britain took but few negroes with them. The number of white people listed as having emigrated to Nova Scotia is surprisingly large in view of the references in the letters of Tonyn and other persons in East Florida to the inhospitable climate of that remote region. It should be remembered, however, that General Carleton made it clear that generous grants of land were to be provided in Nova Scotia for the troops that went thither for their discharge. It is safe to say that most of those who embarked for Nova Scotia were members of the provincial regiments and their families. Nearly a third of all the white residents of East Florida who registered and obtained passes to leave the province in the regular way proceeded to the Bahamas, and their slaves formed about one-third of the total number of negroes deported during the evacuation.

Almost as many whites remained with the Spaniards as returned to the states, but most of the former were undoubtedly Minorcans. Only two hundred negroes stayed in East Florida. Some of these may have been slaves who had been with the Minorcans in Dr. Andrew Turnbull's colony at New Smyrna. Others had probably been acquired in one way or another by the Spaniards. In view of the dispute between Tonyn and Zespedes about the negroes and the opposition which Tonyn said the Spaniards showed to the removal of those for whom no title of ownership could be produced, it is surprising that only two hundred remained in the province.

One would like to know more about the group of British subjects that returned to the States. Both William Drayton, the former chief justice, and his friend Dr. Turnbull, the former secretary of East Florida and clerk of its council, were permitted to return to South Carolina and live out their lives there; but both these gentlemen had been personal enemies of Governor Tonyn, and Drayton was closely related to William Henry Drayton, who had become a member of the committee of safety of South Carolina after being suspended from its council. But apart from these considerations the relaxing of the law of confiscation, banishment, and amercement in South Carolina in 1783, by which seventy-seven persons were permitted to return conditionally and the sale of their estates was stopped, and the increasing lenity shown by the legislatures during the next few years, enabled the proscribed South Carolinians and other loyalists who had lived in East Florida to become residents in that state. Among these were James Penman, Spencer Man, the former's attorney, and Andrew Turnbull, Jr. The legislatures in Georgia followed the example of those in Carolina, beginning in 1784, when an act was passed relieving certain groups from banishment and transferring names from the confiscation to the amercement lists. During each of the next five years measures were adopted to soften the severe law of 1782, and admit to residence and the rights of property those who had been in enforced exile. Many of the persons who took advantage of these modifications of the banishment acts, owned considerable numbers of slaves who, like their masters, much preferred going back to the old plantation to venturing into unknown British colonies. The number of these negroes who were taken back to the states was more than one-third of the total number in East Florida.[271]

Those British subjects who emigrated to "other Foreign Parts," as mentioned in Commissioner Brown's table, were probably Minorcans for the most part who chose to embark for Gibraltar. One suspects that they were attracted by that British possession not chiefly because it was in British hands, but because it was not too far away from the island from which they had first gone to East Florida. A number of the Minorcans, however, seem to have preferred settling in Jamaica or Dominica.

[271] Nevins, *The Am. States during and after the Rev., 1775-1789*, pp. 393, 417; Treasury Solicitor's Papers, miscellaneous; Andrews, *Guide to Materials for Am. Hist., to 1783, in Public Record Office of Great Britain*, II. 269, where Spencer Man's name is wrongly printed Spencer Mason. On refugees from East Florida in England, see Volume II. of this work, p. 363.

BIBLIOGRAPHICAL LIST OF MANUSCRIPT AND PRINTED MATERIALS USED IN THE PREPARATION OF THIS WORK

MANUSCRIPT MATERIALS

Act for the better Government and Regulation of Negroes and other Slaves in this Province [East Florida]. London, Colonial Office Papers, 5/624.

Audit Office Papers (London), 12/92, 12/109, 13/36. Also, No. 3. Examinations in London: Memorials, Schedules of Losses and Evidences, East Florida Claimants.

> Vol. LX. of the "Loyalist Series," in the New York Public Library, which was utilized in the present work, is a transcript of No. 3.

Colonial Office Papers (London): 5/540, fols. 119, 234, 357, 358, 393, 397-400, 407-410, 479; 5/541, fols. 225, 261; 5/546, fol. 71; 5/547, fols. 23, 47, 135; 5/548, fol. 243; 5/549, fols. 9, 73-75, 265, 273, 280; 5/550, fols. 167-174, 209, 213, 217, 225; 5/557, fols. 43-49; 5/559, fols. 125-128, 461-469, 529-614; 5/560, No. 6, fols. 477, 481, 507, 717, 721, 741, 751, 757, 761, 765, 781, 789-791, 797, 805-810, 835, and folder at end of volume; 5/561, fols. 229, 317, 329, 337, 353, 371, 423, 427, 665, 681, 701, 709, 777, 789, 797, 801, 817; 5/562 (1787-1789); 5/563, fols. 151-154, 492-512; 5/564; 5/567, fols. 139-140; 5/572 (Journals of the Commons House of Assembly, East Florida; Journals of the Upper House of Assembly, East Florida, March 27 to November 12, 1781); 23/26; 71/9; 137/85.

Manuscripts of the Marquis of Lansdowne: Vol. LII. 307; Vol. LXVI. 685-688.

Massachusetts Historical Society. Miscellaneous Papers, 1769-1793. Vol. V.: Reports of Col. Nisbet Balfour and John Spranger, Commissioners on East Florida Claims. Transmitted from the East Florida Claims Office, Southampton Buildings, Chancery Lane, by H. C. Litchfield, the Secretary of the Commission, to Lord Sydney. C.O. 5/562. 1787-1789. One Vol. containing—

> I. Report with preliminary Schedule, transmitted February 5, 1787.
> II. Report, with Schedules of Claims and Amounts allowed and Observations, transmitted March 13, 1787.
> III. Report, with similar Schedules, transmitted May 12, 1787.
> IV. *Idem*, transmitted November 3, 1787.
> V. *Idem*, transmitted March 14, 1788.
> VI. Report, with Abstract, transmitted June 12, 1788.
> VII. *Idem*, transmitted December 22, 1788.
> VIII. Report, containing a general Summary of Claims and Amounts allowed, transmitted June 6, 1789.

Privy Council Papers (London): 1/50 (May 8, 1764); 1/52 (October 30, 1766); 1/57 (October 24, November 11, 1783).

Privy Council Register (London): Vol. C. 441; CX. 437, 459-460; Vol. CXII. 125.

Raymond, Rev. William Odber: Notes from the Muster Rolls of the Provincial Regiments.

<small>Made from Manuscript Notes in possession of Mr. Raymond, St. Johns, New Brunswick.</small>

Records of Loyalist Immigrants and Certificates of Loyalty.

<small>Copies from the original records at Saint Jago de la Veyga, Jamaica, in the possession of the author.</small>

Report of the Governor, President, Commander-in-Chief, and Council of the Bahama Islands upon the following Claims: Treasury Papers, 77/19.

Treasury Papers: 77/15; 77/20; Vol. XXX. 1789-1795.

Treasury Solicitor Papers: 3362, 3366. East Florida claims for Losses on the Mosquito Shore, 1780, 1780-1820.

PRINTED MATERIALS

I

BOOKS AND PAMPHLETS

Aikman, Mrs. Louisa Susannah (Wells): The Journal of a Voyage from Charleston, S. C., to London, undertaken during the American Revolution by a daughter of an eminent American Loyalist in the Year 1778, and written from Memory only in 1779. New York, Printed for the New York Historical Society, 1906. Pp. 5, [2], 121. Frontispiece (portrait); facsimile. [Half title: The New York Historical Society. The John Divine Jones fund series of Histories and Memoirs. II.]

<small>Only 200 copies of this work were printed for sale.</small>

Alvord, Clarence Walworth: The Mississippi Valley in British Politics. A Study of the Trade, Land Speculation, and Experiments in Imperialism culminating in the American Revolution. 2 vols. Cleveland, The Arthur H. Clark Company, 1917.

<small>See Volume I.</small>

American Antiquarian Society: Proceedings. Worcester, Mass., 1843 to date (*continued*). Old series, 75 vols., and to 1926 (inclusive), the new series, 36 vols. The first series runs from May 31, 1843, to April 28, 1880, when the new series begins.

<small>See the *Proceedings* for October, 1909; October, 1913; October, 1927.</small>

Andrews, Charles McLean: Guide to the Materials for American History, to 1783, in the Public Record Office of Great Britain. 2 vols. Washington, D. C., The Carnegie Institution of Washington, 1912-1914.

Bibliography

Ashe, Samuel A'Court: History of North Carolina. 2 vols, Volume I. from 1584 to 1785. Greenboro, Charles L. Van Nappen, Publisher, 1908; Volume II. from 1783 to 1925. Raleigh, Presses of Edwards & Broughton Printing Co., 1925.
>See Volume I.

Bacot, John Thomas Watson: The Bahamas: a Sketch. London, Belfast, 1869.
────── The same. London, Longmans, 1871.

Bartram, William: Travels through North and South Carolina, Georgia, East and West Florida, the Cherokee Country, the extensive Territories of the Muscogulges, or Creek Confederacy, and the Country of the Choctaws; containing an Account of the Soil and natural Productions of those Regions; together with Observations on the Manners of the Indians. Embellished with Copper Plates. Philadelphia, Printed by James and Johnson, 1791. Pp. xxxiv, 522.
>Other editions were issued as follows: London, 1792; Dublin, 1793; Berlin (German transl.), 1793; London, 1794; Haarlem (Dutch transl.), 1794; Paris (French transl.), 1799 and 1801.

Brevard, Caroline Mays: A History of Florida from the Treaty of 1763 to our own Times (edited by James Alexander Robertson). A posthumous work published in Memoriam of the Author. 2 vols. DeLand, Florida, The Florida State Historical Society, 1924-1925.

Bridges, Rev. George Wilson: The Annals of Jamaica. 2 vols. London, John Murray, 1827-1828.
>See Volume II.

Butler, Captain Lewis: The Annals of the King's Royal Rifle Corps. 3 vols. London, Smith, Elder & Co., 1913-1926.
>See Volume I.

Campbell, Richard L.: Historical Sketches of Colonial Florida. Cleveland, Ohio, The Williams Publishing Co., 1892. Pp. 284.

Canada. Archives: Report of the Public Archives for the year 1921. Arthur G. Doughty, Keeper of Public Archives. Ottawa, F. A. Acland, 1922. Pp. 1-12.
>This is Appendix E of the volume and is separately paged. It is entitled "Letters from Governor Parr to Lord Shelburne describing the arrival and settlement of the United Empire Loyalists in Nova Scotia, 1783-1784."

Caruthers, Rev. Eli Washington: Interesting Revolutionary Incidents; and Sketches of Character, Chiefly in the "Old North State." 2 series. Philadelphia, Hayes & Zell, 1854.
>See the second series.

Champneys, John: An Account of the Sufferings and Persecution of John Champneys, a Native of Charlestown, South Carolina; inflicted by Order of Congress, for his Refusal to take up Arms in Defence of the Arbitrary Proceedings carried on by the Rulers of said Place Together with his protest, &c. London, Printed in the year 1778.

Chesney, Charles Cornwallis (ed.): "Autobiography of a Carolina Loyalist." In *Military Biography* (New York), pp. 323-341.

First issued in London in 1874.

Cundall, Frank: Biographical Annals of Jamaica. A brief History of the Colony, arranged as a Guide to the Jamaica Portrait Gallery; with chronological Outlines of Jamaica History. Kingston, Published for the Institute of Jamaica by the Educational Supply Co., 1904. Pp. 56.

Curwen, Samuel: Journal and Letters of an American Refugee in England from 1775 to 1784, comprising Remarks on the prominent Men and Manners of that Period, to which are added many biographical Notices of many American Loyalists and other prominent Persons, by G. A. Ward. New York, C. S. Francis & Co., 1842. Pp. xii, 9-578.

Other editions of this work were published in 1844, 1845, and 1864. G. A. Ward was the editor.

Dewhurst, William Whitewell: The History of Saint Augustine, Florida, with an introductory Account of the early Spanish and French Attempts at Exploration and Settlement in the Territory of Florida; together with Sketches of Events and Objects of Interest connected with the oldest Town in the United States; to which is added a short Description of the Climate and Advantages of St. Augustine as a health Resort. New York, G. P. Putnam's Sons, 1881. Pp. viii, 182.

A second edition was issued in 1885.

Dexter, Franklin Bowditch (ed.): The Literary Diary of Ezra Stiles. 3 vols. New York, Charles Scribner's Sons, 1901.

See Volume III.

Dictionary of National Biography. 66 vols. Ed. by Leslie Stephens [and Sidney Lee]. London, Smith, Elder & Son, 1885-1901.

Doggett, Carita: Dr. Andrew Turnbull and the New Smyrna Colony of Florida. [Florida, The Drew Press, 1919.] Pp. viii, [11]-211.

Drake, Francis Samuel: Dictionary of American Biography, including Men of the Time . . . giving also the Pronunciation of many of the foreign and peculiar American Names, a Key to the assumed Names of Writers, and a Supplement. Boston, J. R. Osgood & Co., 1872. Pp. vii-xiv, 1019.

A second edition was published in 1876.

Draper, Lyman Copeland: King's Mountain and its Heroes; History of the Battle of King's Mountain, October 7th, 1780, and the Events which led to it. Cincinnati, P. G. Thomson, 1887. Pp. xv, 17-612.

Drayton, John: Memoirs of the American Revolution, from its Commencement to the Year 1776, inclusive; as relating to the State of South-Carolina; and occa-

sionally refering [*sic*] to the States of North-Carolina and Georgia. 2 vols. Charleston, A. E. Miller, printers, 1821.
: The materials for the work had been collected by the author's father, William Henry Drayton.

Eaton, Rev. Arthur Wentworth Hamilton (ed.): Recollections of a Georgian Loyalist. New York, M. F. Mansfield & Co., 1901. Pp. 224.
: The Georgian Loyalist was Elizabeth Lichtenstein Johnston.

Edwards, Bryan: The History, civil and commercial of the British Colonies in the West Indies. 2 vols. London, printed for J. Stockdale, 1793.
: *See* Volume II. There were many editions of this work, the second being published in London, 1794. There is also a four-volume edition of Philadelphia, 1806, to which is added a general description of the Bahama Islands by Daniel McKinnen.

Egerton, Hugh Edward (ed.): The royal Commission on the Losses and Services of American Loyalists, 1783 to 1785; being the Notes of Mr. Parker Coke, M. P., one of the Commissioners during that Period. Oxford [H. Hart], at the University Press, 1915. Pp. lv, 422.
: Printed for presentation to the members of the Roxburghe Club.

Ellis, George Edward: Memoir of Sir Benjamin Thompson, Count Rumford, with Notice of his Daughter. Boston [1871]. Pp. xvi, 680.
: Published in connection with an edition of Rumford's complete works, by the American Academy of Fine Arts and Sciences.

Fairbanks, George Rainsford: The History of Florida; from its Discovery by Ponce de Leon, in 1512, to the Close of the Florida War, in 1842. Philadelphia, J. A. Lippincott & Co., 1871. Pp. [4], vii-xii, 13-350.

Fanning's Narrative, Col. David. *See* Savary, Alfred William (ed.).

Forbes, James Grant: Sketches, historical and topographical, of the Floridas; more especially of East Florida. New York, C. S. Van Winkle, 1821. Pp. viii, 9-226.

Force, Peter: American Archives: consisting of a Collection of authentic Records, State Papers, Debates, and Letters and other Notices of publick Affairs, the Whole forming a documentary History of the Origin and Progress of the North American Colonies: of the Causes and Accomplishment of the American Revolution; and of the Constitution of Government for the United States, to the final Ratification thereof. In six Series. Prepared and published under Authority of an Act of Congress. 9 vols. [Washington, 1837-1853.]
: The first, second, and third series have never appeared. The fifth series, left unfinished, ends with the year 1776. *See* the fifth series, Vols. I., II., III., and IV.

Garden, Alexander: Anecdotes of the revolutionary War in America, with Sketches of Character of Persons distinguished in the Southern States, for civil and military Services. Charleston, S. C., The Author, 1822. Pp. vi, ix-xi, 459.

Gardner, William James: A History of Jamaica from its Discovery by Christopher Columbus to the present Time; including an Account of its Trade and Agriculture; Sketches of the Manners, Habits, and Customs of all Classes of its Inhabitants; and a Narrative of the Progress of Religion and Education in the Island. London, E. Stock, 1873. Pp. viii, 512.

> There is an edition of 1909 published in London by J. Fisher Unwin.

Georgia Historical Society: Collections. — vols. Savannah, printed for the Society, 1840-19—.

> Published as follows: Vols. I. and II., 1840-1842; Vol. III., part I, 1848; Vols. III., part II, IX., 1873-1916.
>
> Vol. V. was published by the Savannah chapter of the D.A.R.
>
> See Vol. III., part II (1873), and Vol. V., part II (Order Book of Samuel Elbert, 1902).

Gibbes, Robert Wilson: Documentary History of the American Revolution, consisting of Letters and Papers relating to the Contest for Liberty, chiefly in South Carolina, from Originals, 1764-1776. New York, D. Appleton & Co., 1855. Pp. xi, 292.

Gilman, Caroline: Letters of Eliza Wilkinson, during the Invasion and Possession of Charleston, S. C., by the British in the Revolutionary War. Arranged from the original Manuscripts by Caroline Gilman, New York: Published by Samuel Colman, No. 8 Astor House, Broadway, 1839. Pp. [i-viii], 9-108.

Great Britain: The Journals of the House of Commons.

> See the following volumes:
> XLII.: From Jan. the 23d, 1787 to Oct. the 16th, 1787.
> XLIII.: From Nov. the 15th, 1787 to September the 25th, 1788.
> XLV.: From Jan. the 21st, 1790 to June the 10th, 1790.

Great Britain: The Statutes at Large, from Magna Carta to the End of the Eleventh Parliament of Great Britain, Anno 1761. Continued. By Denby Pickering.

> See Vol. XXXV. (26 Geo. III. Cambridge, Printed by John Archdeacon, 1786), Cap. LXXV., pp. 748-751: An Act for appointing Commissioners to enquire into the Losses of all such Persons who have suffered in their Properties, in consequence of the Cession of the Province of East Florida to the King of Spain.

Gregg, Alexander: History of the Old Cheraws containing an Account of the Aborigines of the Pedie, the first white Settlements, their subsequent Progress, civil Changes, the Struggle of the Revolution, and Growth of the Country afterward; extending from about A.D. 1730 to 1810, with Notices of Families and Sketches of Individuals. New York, Richardson & Co., 1867. Pp. viii, 546.

> Another edition of this work was published by the State Company, Columbia, South Carolina, in 1905.

Bibliography

Historical Manuscripts Commission [British]: Reports on American Manuscripts in the Royal Institution of Great Britain. 4 vols. London, printed for his Majesty's Stationery Office, by Mackie & Co., Ld., 1904-1909.

——— Report of Manuscripts in various Collections. Vol. VI.—The Manuscripts of Miss M. Eyre Matcham; Captain H. V. Knox; Cornwallis Wykeham-Martin, Esq.; &c. Dublin, Printed for his Majesty's Stationery Office by John Falconer, 1909.

See the Manuscripts of Captain H. V. Knox, pp. 81-296.

——— Report of the Manuscripts of Mrs. Stopford-Sackville of Drayton House, Northamptonshire. 2 vols. London, Printed for his Majesty's Stationery Office by Mackie & Co., Ld., 1904, 1910.

See Vol. II.

[Hough, Benjamin Franklin]: Siege of Charleston by the British Fleet and Army under the Command of Admiral Arbuthnot and Sir Henry Clinton, which terminated with the surrender of that place on the 12th of May, 1780. Albany, J. Munsell, 1867. Pp. 224.

Hunt, Gaillard (ed.): Fragments of Revolutionary History: hitherto unpublished Writings of the Men of the American Revolution. Collected and edited under Authority of the District of Columbia Society, Sons of the Revolution. Brooklyn, Historical Print Club, 1892. Pp. xii, 188.

Jamaica: Acts of Assembly passed in the Island of Jamaica. From 1778 to 1783, inclusive. Kingston, Jamaica, 1786.

See pp. 32-33, Act 107 (passed 1st March, 1783): An Act to exempt from Taxes for a limited Time such of his Majesty's Subjects of North-America, Bay of Honduras, and Mosquito Shore, as from Motives of Loyalty have been, or shall be obliged to relinquish or abandon their Possessions in that Country, and take Refuge in this Island, with Intent to settle here.

See also pp. 36-37, the account of Donald Campbell.

Johnson, Joseph: Traditions and Reminiscences chiefly of the American Revolution in the South: including biographical Sketches, Incidents, and anecdotes, few of which have been published, particularly of Residents in the Upper Country. By Joseph Johnson, M.D. Charleston, S. C., Walker & James, 1851. Pp. viii, 592. Folding plates and maps; facsimiles; index.

Johnson, William: Sketches of the Life and Correspondence of Nathaniel Greene, Major General of the Armies of the United States, in the War of the Revolution. Compiled chiefly from original Materials. 2 vols. Charleston, The Author, 1822.

These volumes were "edited" considerably, as is proven by the original Greene Papers which have been acquired by the William L. Clements Library of American History of the University of Michigan.

Johnston, Henry Phelps: The Yorktown Campaign and the Surrender of Cornwallis, 1781. New York, Harper & Bros., 1881. Pp. 206.

Jones, Charles Colcock, Jr.: The History of Georgia. 2 vols. Boston, Houghton, Mifflin & Co., 1883.

  See Vol. II., Revolutionary Epoch.

Jones, Edward Alfred (ed.): The Journal of Alexander Chesney, a South Carolina Loyalist in the Revolution and after. . . . With an Introduction by Wilbur H. Siebert. [Columbus, The University], 1921. Pp. xvi, 166.

  In The Ohio State University *Bulletin*, being Vol. XXVI., No. 4, October 30, 1921; No. 7 of The Ohio State University Studies, Contributions in History and Political Science.

Journals of the Assembly of Jamaica, 1663-1826. 15 vols. Jamaica, 1811-1829.

  See Vol. VIII., October 19, 1784 to March 5, 1791.

Journal (The) of the Lower House of Assembly of the Bahama Islands from the 19th November, 1770 to the 21st December, 1776. Printed by Order of the House, Nassau, The Nassau Guardian, Printers to the Legislature, 1911.

Journal (The) of the General Assembly of the Bahama Islands from the 21st December, 1779 to the 13th February, 1786. Nassau, The Nassau Guardian, 1912.

────── Same. From the 8th January, 1787 to the 23d July, 1790. Nassau, The Nassau Guardian, 1913.

────── Same. From the 7th June, 1791 to the 29th September, 1794. Nassau, The Nassau Guardian, 1913.

Lanier, Sidney: Florida: its Scenery, Climate and History. With an Account of Charleston, Savannah, Augusta, and Athens, and a Chapter for Consumptives; being a complete Handbook and Guide. Philadelphia, J. B. Lippincott [c1875]. Pp. 7-266.

  There was also an edition in 1876.

Lee, F. D.; and J. L. Agnew: Historical Record of the City of Savannah. Savannah, J. H. Estill, 1869. Pp. xii, 200.

Lee, Henry: Memoirs of the War in the Southern Department of the United States. 2 vols. Philadelphia, Bradford & Inskeep, 1812.

  Also edited by Peter Force, Washington, 1827.

Letters of Joseph Clay, Merchant of Savannah 1776-1793 and a List of Ships and Vessels entered at the Port of Savannah for May 1765, 1766 and 1767. Savannah [The *Morning News* Printery and Bindery], 1913. Georgia Historical Society *Collections*, VIII.

List (A) of the General and Staff Officers, and of the Officers in the several British, Foreign, and Provincial Regiments, serving in North-America, under the Command of his Excellency, General Sir Henry Clinton, K.B., with the States of their Commissions as they rank in each Corps and in the Army. New York, Printed by Macdonald & Cameron, 1779. Pp. 65.

[Published by the Great Britain War Office.]

McCall, Hugh: The History of Georgia containing brief Sketches of the most remarkable Events, up to the present Day. 2 vols. Savannah, Printed and published by Seymour & Williams, 1811-1816.

Vol. I. was printed and published by William T. Williams.

McCrady, Edward: The History of South Carolina in the Revolution, 1775-1780. New York, The Macmillan Co., 1901. Pp. xxxii, 899.

——— Same. 1780-1783. New York, The Macmillan Co., 1912. Pp. xxvii, 787.

——— The History of South Carolina under the royal Government, 1719-1776. New York, The Macmillan Co., 1899. Pp. xviii, 847.

Mackenzie, Roderick: Strictures on Lt. Col. Tarleton's History "Of the Campaigns of 1780 and 1781, in the Southern Provinces of North America." . . . Wherein military Characters and Corps are vindicated from injurious Aspersions and several important Transactions placed in their proper Point of View. In a Series of Letters to a Friend, by Roderick Mackenzie. . . . To which is added, A Detail of the Siege of Ninety-Six, and the Re-capture of the Island of New-Providence. London, Printed for the Author; and sold by R. Jameson, . . . 1787. Pp. vi, 186.

McKinnen, Daniel: A Tour through the British West Indies in the Years 1802 and 1803, giving a particular Account of the Bahama Islands. London, J. White, 1804. Pp. viii, 272.

Malcolm, Harcourt Gladstone (compiler): Bahamas. Historical Memorandum relating to the Forts in New Providence, Nassau, Montague, Charlotte, Fincastle. Nassau, New Providence, The Nassau Guardian, 1913. Pp. 46.

Malcolm was deputy speaker of the house of assembly.

——— Historical Documents relating to the Bahama Islands. Compiled by . . . Deputy Speaker of the House of Assembly. Printed by Order of the House of Assembly. Nassau, The Nassau Guardian, Printers to the Legislature, 1910. Pp. [231].

Each document (23 in all) has half title and separate pagination. "The Texts of these documents are derived from the archives of the Colonial Office, the Record Office, and the British Museum, London, and the governor's office and the Record office, Nassau, Bahamas" (prefatory note).

——— A History of the Bahama House of Assembly. Nassau, The Nassau Guardian. Pp. viii, 83, (1), x.

Moore, John W.: History of North Carolina. 2 vols. Raleigh, Alfred Williams & Co., 1880.
See Volume I.

Morrison, Alfred J. (ed.). *See* Schoepf, Johann David.

Moultrie, William: Memoirs of the American Revolution, so far as it related to the States of North and South Carolina, and Georgia. Compiled from the most authentic Materials, the Author's personal Knowledge of the various Events, and including an epistolary Correspondence on Public Affairs with civil and military Officers at that Period. 2 vols. New-York, Printed by D. Longworth, 1802.

Narrative (A) of the official Conduct of Anthony Stokes. *See* [Stokes, Anthony].

Nevins, Allan: The American States during and after the Revolution, 1775-1789. New York, The Macmillan Co., 1924. Pp. xviii, 728.

North Carolina: The Colonial Records of North Carolina. Published under the Supervision of the Trustees of the Public Libraries by Order of the General Assembly. Collected and edited by William L. Saunders, Secretary of State. 10 vols. Raleigh, P. M. Hale, 1886-1890.
Vol. IX., 1771-1775; vol. X., 1775-1776. *See* especially, Volume X.

North Carolina: The State Records of North Carolina. Published under the Supervision of the Trustees of the Public Libraries by Order of the General Assembly. . . . 26 vols. Goldsboro, N. C., Nash Bros., Printers . . . 1886-1907.
Title and imprint vary. *See* Vols. XIII., XIV., XV., XVI., XXIII., and XXIV.

Northcroft, G. J. H.: Sketches of Summerland, giving some Account of Nassau and the Bahama Islands. Nassau, Office of the "Nassau Guardian," 1900. Pp. 6, 309.
Another edition was published in 1912.

Nova Scotia Historical Society: Reports and Collections. Halifax. 1878 to date.

Phillips, Philip Lee: Notes on the Life and Works of Bernard Romans. DeLand, Florida, The Florida State Historical Society, 1924. Pp. 128 and accompanying reproduction of the Map of Florida by Romans, 1774, in 13 sections.

Ramsay, David: The History of the Revolution of South-Carolina, from a British Province to an independent State. 2 vols. Trenton, Printed by Isaac Collins, 1785.

Raymond, Rev. William Odber (ed.): Roll of Officers of the British American or Loyalist Corps, compiled from the original Muster Rolls and arranged alphabetically by W. O. Raymond, LL.D.
Vol. II. of New Brunswick Historical Society *Collections*.

——— Winslow Papers, A.D. 1776-1826. St. Johns, N. B., Printed under the

Auspices of the New Brunswick Historical Society, The Sun Printing Co., 1901. Pp. 3, 5-732.

Reynolds, Charles Bingham: Old Saint Augustine; a Story of three Centuries. St. Augustine, Florida, E. H. Reynolds, 1885. Pp. x, 11-144.

<small>Another edition was printed in 1886.</small>

Sabine, Lorenzo: Biographical Sketches of Loyalists of the American Revolution, with an historical Essay. 2 vols. Boston, Little, Brown & Co., 1864.

<small>This work was first issued in a single volume in 1847, by C. C. Little and J. Brown of Boston.</small>

Saunders, William Lawrence (ed.). *See* North Carolina.

Savary, Alfred William (ed.): Col. David Fanning's Narrative of his Exploits and Adventures as a Loyalist of North Carolina in the American Revolution . . . With an Introduction and Notes by A. W. Savary. Toronto, 1908. Pp. 3, 55.

<small>A reprint from *The Canadian Magazine*. This narrative was first published privately in 1861 in Richmond with an introduction by J. H. Wheeler and notes by J. T. H. Wynne and D. L. Swain. This edition was reissued in New York by Joseph Sabin, in 1865 (pp. xxvi, 86).</small>

Schenck, David: North Carolina, 1780-'81; being a History of the Invasion of the Carolinas by the British Army under Lord Cornwallis in 1780-'81; with the . . . Design of showing the Part borne by North Carolina in that Struggle . . . and to correct some . . . Errors of History. Raleigh, N. C., Edwards & Broughton, 1889. Pp. [4], 11-498.

Schoepf, Johann David: Travels in the Confederation 1783-1784. From the German. Translated and edited by Alfred J. Morrison. 2 vols. Philadelphia, W. J. Campbell, 1911.

<small>This is a translation of *Reise durch einige der mittlern und südlichen vereinigten nordamerikanischen Staaten nach Ost-Florida and den Bahama-Inseln unternommen in den Jahren 1783 und 1784 von Johann David Schöpf* (Erlangen, Bey Johann Jacob Palm, 1788, 2 vols.).</small>

Sermon (A) preached before the Incorporated Society for the Propagation of the Gospel in Foreign Parts; at their anniversary Meeting in the Parish Church of St. Mary-le-Bow, on Friday, February 19, 1779. By the honorable and right reverend Father in God, James Lord Bishop of Saint David's. London, Printed by T. Harrison and S. Brooke, in Warwick-Lane, 1779.

<small>This contains an abstract of the Proceedings of the Society.

The abstracts of the Proceedings consulted includes, besides the one just mentioned, those printed with sermons of the bishop of Rochester (February 18, 1780), the bishop of Oxford (February 18, 1791), the bishop of Lincoln (February 17, 1792), the bishop of Gloucester (February 19, 1796), the bishop of Exeter (February 21, 1800), the bishop of Chichester (February 17, 1804), the bishop of Norwich (February 16, 1810), and the bishop of Ely (February 18, 1814). The sermons and abstracts of 1791, 1792, 1796, and 1800 were printed in Warwick-Lane by S. Brooke, who had removed to Pater Noster Row before printing the later anniversary numbers.</small>

Shattuck, George Burbank (ed.): The Bahama Islands. New York and London, The Macmillan Co., 1905. Pp. xxxii, 630.

> A report of the Bahaman expedition dispatched by the Geographical Society of Baltimore, June, 1903.

Shortt, Adam; and Arthur G. Doughty: Canadian Archives. Documents relating to the constitutional History of Canada 1759-1791. Ottawa, S. E. Dawson, Printer, 1907.

Siebert, Wilbur Henry: East Florida as a Refuge of Southern Loyalists, 1774-1785. Worcester, Massachusetts, American Antiquarian Society, 1928. Pp. 23.

> Reprinted from the *Proceedings* of the American Antiquarian Society for October, 1927.

———— The Flight of American Loyalists to the British Isles. Columbus, Ohio, The F. J. Heer Printing Co., 1911. Pp. 20.

———— The Legacy of the American Revolution to the British West Indies and Bahamas: a Chapter out of the History of the American Loyalists. Columbus, The Ohio State University, 1913. Pp. 50.

> In The Ohio State University *Bulletin*, XVII. No. 27, being No. 1 of the Ohio State University Studies, Contribution in History and Political Science.

———— "The Loyalists in West Florida and the Natchez District." [Cedar Rapids, Iowa, 1916.]

> Pp. 465-483 of *Mississippi Valley Historical Review*, II. March, 1916.

———— "The Tories of the Upper Ohio." Charleston, West Virginia, 1914.

> Reprint from West Virginia, Department of Archives and History of the State, *Biennial Report*, 1911-1912, 1913-1914.

———— The Tory Proprietors of Kentucky Lands. Columbus, Ohio, The F. J. Heer Printing Co., 1919. Pp. 26.

> Reprinted from *Ohio Archaeological and Historical Quarterly*, XXVIII, No. 1, January, 1919.

Siege of Charleston. *See* [Hough, Franklin Benjamin].

Smyth, John Ferdinand Dalziel: A Tour in the United States of America; containing an Account of the present Situation of that Country; the Population, Agriculture, Commerce, Customs, and Manners of the Inhabitants; Anecdotes of several Members of Congress, and general Officers in the American Army; and many other singular and interesting Occurrences. With a Description of the Indian Nations, the general Face of the Country . . . Likewise Improvements in Husbandry that may be adopted with great Advantage in Europe. 2 vols. London, Printed for G. Robinson, J. Robson, and J. Sewell, 1784.

> The author of this work adopted the name of Stuart in 1793.

South Carolina: Statutes at Large of South Carolina edited, under Authority of the

Legislature, by David J. McCord. 10 vols. Columbia, S. C., Printed by A. S. Johnston, 1841.

See Volume IV.

The Public Law of the State of South Carolina, from its first Establishment as a British Province down to the Year 1790. . . . By John Faucherand Grimke. Philadelphia. Aitkin & Son, 1790.

See under years 1776, 1782, 1783, 1784.

Southey, Captain Thomas: Chronological History of the West Indies, by . . . Commander, Royal Navy. 3 vols. London, Longmans, Rees, 1827.

Stark, James Henry: Stark's History and Guide to the Bahama Islands . . . including their History, Inhabitants, Climate, Agriculture, Geology, Government, . . . Boston, J. H. Stark [c1891]. Pp. x, 243.

Stedman, Charles: The History of the Origin, Progress, and Termination of the American War. 2 vols. Dublin, Printed for Messrs. P. Wogan, P. Byrne, J. Moore, and W. Jones, 1794.

Stevens, Benjamin Franklin: The Campaign in Virginia, 1781. An exact Reprint of six rare Pamphlets on the Clinton-Cornwallis Controversy, with very numerous important unpublished Manuscript Notes by Sir Henry Clinton, K.B., and the omitted and hitherto unpublished Portions of the Letters in their Appendixes added from the original Manuscripts. With a Supplement containing Extracts from the Journals of the House of Lords, a French Translation of Papers laid before the House, and a Catalogue of the additional Correspondence of Clinton and Cornwallis, in 1780-'81. 2 vols. London, 1888.

Stevens, Rev. William Bacon: A History of Georgia from its first Discovery by Europeans to the Adoption of the present Constitution in MDCCXCVIII. 2 vols. Vol. I.: New York, D. Appleton & Co., 1847. Vol. II.: Philadelphia, E. H. Butler & Co., 1859.

See especially Vol. II.

[Stokes, Anthony]: A Narrative of the official conduct of Anthony Stokes, of the Inner Temple, London . . . His Majesty's Chief Justice, and one of his Council of Georgia; and of the Dangers and Distresses he underwent in the Cause of Government: some Copies of which are printed for the Information of his Friends. [London, 1784.] Pp. 112.

Apparently written by Stokes, although the third person is used throughout.

Tarleton, Sir Banastre: A History of the Campaigns of 1780 and 1781, in the southern Provinces of North America. Dublin, Printed for Colles, Exshaw, White [and others], 1787. Pp. vii, 533.

Another edition was published in London in 1787.

Van Tyne, Claude Halsted: The Loyalists in the American Revolution. New York, The Macmillan Co., 1902. Pp. xii, 360.

Verrill, Addison E.: "Relations between Bermuda and the American Colonies during the Revolutionary War." In *Transactions* of the Connecticut Academy of Arts and Sciences, XVIII. pp. 47-64. New Haven, Yale University, July, 1907.

Watkins, Robert and George: A Digest of the Laws of the State of Georgia. From its first Establishment as a British Province down to the Year, 1798, inclusive, and the principal Acts of 1799; in which is comprehended the Declaration of Independence; State Constitutions of 1777 and 1789, with Alterations and Amendments in 1794. Also the Constitution of 1798. Philadelphia, Printed by R. Aitkin, 1800. Pp. vi, 837, 28.

Wells, Louisa S. *See* Aikman, Mrs. Louisa Susannah (Wells).

White, George: Historical Collections of Georgia; containing the most interesting Facts, Traditions, biographical Sketches, Anecdotes, etc., relating to its History and Antiquities, from its first Settlement to the present Time. Compiled from original Records and official Documents. New York, Pudney & Russell, 1855. 3d ed. Pp. 2,688.

Williams, John Lee: The Territory of Florida: or, Sketches of the Topography, civil and natural History of the Country, the Climate, and the Indian Tribes from the first Discovery to the present Time, with a Map. New-York, A. T. Goodrich, 1837. Pp. vi, [1], 8-300.

Winslow, William Odber. *See* Raymond, W. O.

Wright, J. M.: History of the Bahama Islands with a special Study of the Abolition of Slavery in the Colony. New York, The Macmillan Co., 1905. Pp. 3, 419-584.

<small>A reprint of *Bahama Islands*, a dissertation in the Johns Hopkins University.</small>

II

PERIODICALS AND NEWSPAPERS

Acadiensis. St. Johns, New Brunswick. Quarterly devoted to the interests of the maritime provinces of Canada. 8 vols. 1901-1908.

<small>*See* Vol. VII., January, 1907.</small>

American Historical Review. Quarterly. Published by the American Historical Association. 1894 to date. Vols. I.-XXXIV.

<small>*See* XXVIII. 13-23.</small>

Annual Register: A review of public events at home and abroad. London. 1758—.

<small>*See* 1783.</small>

Bibliography

City Gazette & Daily Advertiser. Charleston, S. C. Daily, 1787-1820+.

> This paper was published under a variety of titles: namely, *The South Carolina Weekly Gazette; The South-Carolina Gazette, & Public Advertiser; The Charleston Morning Post, and Daily Advertiser,* 1786-1787; *The City Gazette, and the Daily Advertiser,* which name with minor changes, it retained until 1820 and after.
> *See* issue for March 14, 1792.

East Florida Gazette. St. Augustine. Weekly. 1782-1784[?]

> Vol I. seems to have covered the period of January 25, 1782-February 1, 1783. The succeeding numbers probably continued to be issued regularly during 1783 and to May, 1784, when Dr. William Charles Wells, the publisher of the paper, sailed for England. His elder brother, John Wells, may have continued to publish the *Gazette* until he left for the Bahamas.
> In the summer of 1927, Mr. Worthington C. Ford, then secretary of the Massachusetts Historical Society, found three issues of this paper in England.
> *See* issue covering the period Saturday, February 22 to March 1, 1782.

Florida Historical Society Quarterly. Ed. by Julien C. Yonge, Pensacola. July, 1922 to date.

> *See* Volumes IV., No. 1 (July, 1925), V., No. 4 (April, 1927), VI., No. 1 (July, 1927), VII., No. 2 (October, 1928) and No. 3 (January, 1929).

Gazette of the State of Georgia. Savannah. Weekly. January 30, 1783-October 16, 1788. After the latter date the title was changed to *Georgia Gazette.*

> *See* issues for October 9, and Nos. 570, 573, 591.

Gentleman's Magazine; or Monthly Intelligencer. Ed. by Sylvanus Urban, Gentleman. January 1731-September, 1907. Vols. 1-302, 303, Nos. 1-3.

> The volume numbering is irregular and the name changes slightly.
> *See* new series X., 1838.

Jamaica Mercury. Kingston. Weekly. Established in 1778.

> The name was changed later to *The Royal Gazette.*

London Chronicle; or, Universal Evening Post (continued as *London Chronicle* after July 2, 1765). Founded 1757.

> *See* issues for July 22-24, 1783.

Mississippi Valley Historical Review. Published quarterly by the Mississippi Valley Historical Society. Cedar Rapids, Iowa, June, 1914, to date.

> *See* Vols. I., II., and IV.

Morning Chronicle, and London Advertiser (continued as *Morning Chronicle* from about 1789). Daily. Founded 1769.

> *See* issue for July 30, 1783.

Nassau Guardian and Bahama Islands Advocate and Intelligencer. Daily.

> *See* the Saturday Supplement, October 11, 1913.

North Carolina Booklet. Published by the North Carolina Society, Daughters of the Revolution.

See Volume V., No. 3, 1905-6.

Pennsylvania Magazine of History and Biography. Published quarterly by The Historical Society of Pennsylvania. Philadelphia, 1877 to date, 52 vols.

See issue for January, 1889.

Rivington's Gazette. New York. Weekly and semi-weekly. 1777-1783.

This paper had a number of names: namely, *Rivington's New-York Gazeteer; Rivington's New-York Gazette; Rivington's New York Loyal Gazette; Royal Gazette; Rivington's New-York Gazette, and Universal Advertiser.* It was finally discontinued December 31, 1783.

Royal Gazette. Kingston, Jamaica. Weekly. May 26, 1787-November 26, 1836. Formerly the *Jamaica Mercury (q.v. ante).*

See issues for May 19 and 26, 1787.

Royal Gazette. Charleston, S. C. Semi-Weekly. March 3, 1781-September 28, 1782 (last issue located).

See issues for September 12, November 18 and 21, December 8, 1781, and June 19 and 22, 1782.

South Carolina Historical and Genealogical Magazine. Published quarterly by the South Carolina Historical Society, Charleston, S. C. 29 vols. January 1, 1900 to date. Imprint changes.

See issues for January and July, 1910, January, 1913, January, 1915, and October, 1916.

South-Carolina and American General Gazette. Charleston, S. C. Weekly and semi-weekly. April 4, 1764-February 28, 1781.

This was a continuation of *The South-Carolina Weekly Gazette.*
See issue for February 14, 1779.

III

[SCIENTIFIC WORKS BY WILLIAM CHARLES WELLS, M.D.]

The most important of these are as follows:

An Essay on single Vision with two Eyes, together with Experiments and Observations on several other Subjects in Optics (London, 1792).

"Observations on the Influence which incites the Muscles of Animals to contract in galvanic Experiments." In *Philosophical Transactions*, 1795, XVII., 548.

"Observations and Experiments on the Colour of the Blood." In *Philosophical Transactions*, 1797, XVIII., 228.

"Observations on Erysipelas." In *Transactions Med. and Chir.*, 1800, II., 213.

"Observations and Experiments on Vision." In *Philosophical Transactions*, 1811, 579; and in *Nicholson's Journal*, 1812, XXXI., 321.

An Essay on Dew, with several Appearances connected with it (London, 1814, 1815).

An Account of a Female of the White Race of Mankind, part of whose Skin resembles that of a Negro (London, 1820).

    This, his last work, contains a memoir of the author's life written by himself.

Index

ABACO ISLAND, Bahamas: vessel wrecked on, 176; pop., 197. *See also* Great Abaco Island.
Abbott, Capt. Henry: appointment, 156.
Acts: of parliament, relating to Amer. Affairs, 18; of Amer. Colonies, their effect, 61; of first general assembly (E. Fla.), 93; to encourage settlement, 95; for better governing of negroes, 96-99; commended by Tonyn, 98; negro bill passed, 100; to control drinking and gaming places, 132, 133; of general assembly (Bahamas), limiting life of legislature, 193; for erection and repair of churches, 199; of general assembly (Jamaica), to assist refugees, 201, 202; of general assembly (Dominica), to benefit refugees, 207; of banishment in S. C. and Ga. softened, 210.
Adams, Samuel: burned in effigy, 35.
Addresses: of loyalty, 34; to Tonyn, 64, 65; from general assembly (Ga.), against evacuation, 103; from general assembly (E. Fla.), about evacuation, 103; of thanks from general assembly (E. Fla.), to McArthur, 152; on services of John Cruden, 167; from Brit. subjects to Zespedes, on extension of time, 171.
Africans: *See* Negroes; *and* Slaves.
Agriculture: Indian, 10.
Aikman, Alexander (refugee): founds newspaper in Jamaica, 205.
Aikman, Alexander, Jr.: in charge of publishing business, 205.
Alachua, Fla.: 10; operations of Bowles in, 178.
Alachua Tribe: lower Creeks, 10.
Allatchaway (Alachua) Indians: in St. Augustine, 28.
Allen, Col. Isaac: in expedition to Savannah, 73.
Alligator Creek Bridge: skirmish at, 58, 59.
Alvord, Clarence W.: cited, 4 n., 212.
Amelia Harbor, Fla.: loyalists embark in, 156; transports return from Bahamas to, 176; Tonyn writes from, 175, 176; Tonyn on board of *Cyrus* in, 207.

Amelia Island, Fla.: removal to, 37; negroes carried to mainland from, 40; Elbert's expedition at, 46; Lothian from, 204.
Amelia Narrows, Fla.: part of R. Howe's force at, 58.
America: loyalists try to make peace with, 187; refugees go from E. Fla. to interior, 191; black troops raised in, 203.
American Antiquarian Society: *Proc.*, cited, 29 n., 136 n., 212.
American States: Tonyn fears return of refugees to, 140; pass resolutions against return of loyalists, 143; Tonyn on number of emigrants to, 174, 208, 209; Span. gov't. forces withdrawal to, 178; emissaries in E. Fla. persuade refugees to return to, 191.
Americans: few in St. Augustine, 173; in dispute with Span., 174; Clarke wins respect of, 203; Lothian suffers losses from, 204.
Anabaptists: black, in Nassau, 197.
Andrews, Charles M.: cited, 8 n., 186 n., 210 n., 212.
Andrews, Evangeline W.: cited, 186 n.
Andros Islands, Bahamas: settlers in, 197.
Annual Register: cited, 4 n., 224.
Apalachee Bay, Fla.: Bowles captures the *Sheerwater* near, 179.
Apalachee Old Fields, Fla.: 3, 14.
Apalachee River, Fla.: western boundary of J. Bryan's lease, 14.
Appleton, ———: *Cyclopaedia*, cited, 3 n.
Appraisal: of property in E. Fla., 147.
Archives: MSS. in, cited, 3 n., 8 n., 14 n., 15 n., 17 n., 18 n., 22 n., 23 n., 24 n., 31 n., 32 n., 33 n., 34 n., 35 n., 37 n., 39 n., 40 n., 44 n., 46 n., 50 n., 65 n., 66 n., 67 n., 69 n., 89 n., 91 n., 92 n., 97 n., 99 n., 100 n., 104 n., 106 n., 124 n., 125 n., 128 n., 129 n., 130 n., 132 n., 135 n., 138 n., 141 n., 145 n., 150 n., 153 n., 155 n., 156 n., 159 n., 162 n., 163 n., 164 n., 165 n., 166 n., 168 n., 169 n., 170 n., 171 n., 172 n., 173 n., 174 n., 175 n., 176 n.

178 n., 185 n., 187 n., 189 n., 190 n., 191 n., 203 n., 204 n., 205 n., 208 n.

Armstrong, Fla.: R. Howe's expedition at, 58.

Ashe, Gen. John: operates in Ga., 75.

Ashley Ferry, S. C.: Brit. troops cross, 77.

"Assize of bread": law for, 133.

Attorney general: orders *re* shipment of negroes from E. Fla., 122.

Augusta, Ga.: 24; Moore attacked near, 59; occupied by Hamilton, 74; Browne advances to, 83, 84; capitulation of Browne at, 86; Seymour at, 118.

Awards (for losses): to Graham, 111; to Ball, 126.

Bachop, Capt. Adam: commands sloop, 53.

Bacot, John Thomas Watson: cited, 147 n., 213.

Bahama Islands: pop., 184, 185, 192, 193, 209; effect of acquisition, 148; property in E. Fla. said to have been exchanged for, 138; in turmoil of activity, 191; new era in, 194; Wilson's mission to, 150; McArthur in command of, 152; gov., 159, 182; lords proprietors, 190, 193; gen'l. assembly, 191, 199, 200; articles sent to, from E. Fla., 172; vessels at, 170, 174, 176; houses may not be sent to, 177; gov't. pays salary of clergyman, 199; gospel society withdraws from, 200; letters regarding emigrants to, cited, 185; reports on, cited, 151, 185.

Refugees and loyalists go to, ix, 101, 118, 125, 126, 135, 143, 145, 150, 157, 167, 170, 173, 174, 176, 183, 184, 187, 190, 191, 192, 208, 209; various persons go to, 118, 125, 126, 135, 145, 150, 152, 157; Creeks wish to go to, 139; not suitable for refugees, 140; selected by old settlers, 143; many prefer, 150; troops may go to, 143; Minorcans go to, 173; slaves go to, 187; factors impelling people to go to, 183, 184; loyalists unwilling to go to, 190; suitable for N. Carolinians, 192; conveyance to, asked, 152; land promised to refugees, 145, 149; proposed purchase of land, 186.

Bailey, G. T.: thanked, viii.

Baillie, Robert: member of commons house, 91; chairman of committee, 94.

Baker, Capt. John: attacks Wright's fort, 26.

Baker, Col. ———: crosses St. Marys, 46.

Balfour, Col. Nisbet: at Charleston, 81.

Ball, Col. Elias, Jr. (refugee): threatened with deprivation of rations, 122.

Ball, Col. Elias, Sr.: member of committee of refugees, 124; sketch, 126.

"Banditti": in E. Fla., 141, 144, 153, 161, 164-167.

Baptists: negroes in Bahamas become, 199, 200.

Barbadoes Islands: provisions sent to New Providence from, 187.

Barracks: at St. Augustine, 18-19; at Fort Tonyn, 59.

Bars: at St. Augustine, 116, 117, 129; at mouth of St. Marys, 116; at Nassau, the *David* wrecked on, 189, 190.

Barter: with Indians, 11, 67.

Bartram, William: cited, 8-12, 12 n., 213.

Beaufort, ———, duke of: sells proprietary rights, 193.

Beaufort, S. C.: troops removed from, 77; Prevost at, 78; the *Eliza* lost near, 143; Deveaux at, 145.

Bellew, ———: steals stallion, 167.

Bell's Mill, N. C.: troops at, 87.

Bernardo de Gálvez (Span. gov. of La.): information of plans sought, 81; at Pensacola, 89.

Bibliographical list: MSS. and printed material, 211-226.

Bisset, Capt. Robert: attends meetings, 34, 45; criticises Tonyn, 37; affidavit, 64; letter to, cited, 144.

Blackburn, Levett: his land grant, 110.

Blankets: Indians trade for, 11.

Blockhouses: near bar of St. Johns River, 121; at Mosquito Inlet, 121; deserters from latter, 144.

"Bloody Bill" Cunningham: *See* Cunningham, Maj. William.

Boards: Associated Loyalists — at St. Marys, 190. Police — at Charlestown, 113. Trade and Plantations — make provision for missionaries, 5; charges filed with, 36; its committee reports on land grants, 49, 50; Tonyn writes about general assembly to, 99, 100; its reply on negro bill, 100.

Boca Chica, Fla.: Col. Fanning returns to, 157.

Bowles, William Augustus (refugee): tries to recover E. Fla., 178-179.

Brevard, Caroline Mays: cited, 179 n., 213.

Briar Creek, Ga.: Prevost on, 75.

Bridges, George Wilson: cited, 201 n., 213.

Britain: *See* England; *and* Gt. Britain.

Britigny, Chevalier ——— de: prisoner at St. Augustine, 56.

British: sequester property in S. C., 123; merchants remain in Charlestown, 129. Dominions — refugees to seek new homes in, 140; N. Carolinians prefer Bahamas, 192. Government — to provide "commodious residence," 140; to appropriate land in W. Indies, 159; loyalists must depend on justice of, 169; acquires lands in Bahamas, 190. Crown — Indians regard highly, 120; D. McGirth said to have negroes of, 165. Troops — barracks for, 19 (*see also* Troops). Officers — unwilling to relinquish negroes, 115, 122; Subjects — Zespedes allows to withdraw, 161, 162; still in E. Fla., 167; Span. confine in dungeons, 174; advance money to Span. gov't., 175; complain of Span., 177-178; in E. Fla., prefer Bahamas, 185, 186; numbers and destinations of, 208, 209; *see also* English; *and* Loyalists. Commissioners on Loyalist Claims — mentioned, 111; testimony of loyalists before, 158; Cruden submits claim to, in Nova Scotia, 193.

Broad River, S. C.: Robinson on, 52.

Brown, William: member of commons house, 91; speaker of commons house, 92; appeals for Indians to be kept quiet, 138; commissioner of evacuation, 155, 174; his estimate of whites and blacks in E. Fla., 168; Cruden disapproves conduct of, 169; gives summary of Brit. subjects and negroes emigrated from E. Fla., 204, 208; comments on summary, 209.

Browne, Lt. Col. (*or* Superintendent) Thomas (refugee): hostile to committee of safety, 24; tarred and feathered, 25-26; commissioned, 26, 38; in Fuser's expedition, 44; routs Baker's detachment, 46; at Fort Tonyn, 50; his right to command Brit. officers disputed, 57; at Fort McIntosh, 58; sends message from Alligator Creek Bridge, 59; retreats with rangers, 60; affidavit, 64; succeeds Stuart, 76; at Savannah, 78; movements, 83, 84; attacked, 85; capitulates, 86; on St. Johns River, 109; accompanied by Indians, 111; subsists conclave of northern Indians, 120; estimates number of Creeks visiting St. Augustine, 121; asked to keep Indians quiet, 138; asked to provide security, 139; writes for vessels to remove Creeks, 139; recalls officers and traders, 139; holds conference with Indian delegations, 143, 144; to remain at St. Augustine, 151; applies for conveyance to Bahamas, 152, 184; to distribute presents to Indians, 155, 184; chairman, committee of commons house (Bahamas), 195; letters to and by, cited, 139, 142, 151.

Bryan, Jonathan: leases Indian lands, 3, 14; Tonyn charges association of Drayton with, 34.

Bull, Col. ———: threatened with withholding of rations, 122.

Bull, Gen. Stephen: his plantation pillaged, 145.

Bull, William: slaves of, in Jamaica, 202.

Butler, Capt. Lewis: cited, 43 n., 44 n., 53 n., 56 n., 57 n., 73 n., 74 n., 213.

Butler, Capt. William: overtakes W. Cunningham, 128.

Butler, Mrs. ———: writes to Carleton regarding slaves, 115.

CABBAGE SWAMP, Fla.: troops escape into, 58.

Cagigal, Juan Manuel de (capt. gen. of Cuba): Maxwell capitulates to, 182.

Caicos Island, Bahamas: pop., 197; chosen for new mission, 199.

Caloosahatche, Fla.: Indian town, 8.

Calos (Bay), Fla.: Span. from Cuba fish in, 11.

Camden, S. C.: battle near, 55; occupied by Lord Rawdon, 84.

Cameron, Allan (refugee): at St. Augustine, 24; mission and capture, 28-30; agent to Cherokees, 50; succeeds Stuart, 76.

Campbell, Capt. Alexander: on Cooper River, 87, 88.

Campbell, Col. Archibald: leads expedition to Savannah, 52, 71, 73, 74; preparing for departure, 75; receives letter from Carleton, 114; lt. gov. and gov. of Jamaica, 202, 203; raises black troops, 203.

Campbell, Lord William: gov. of S. C., 52.

Campo (Camps), Pietro (Pedro, Pedrus): Minorcan priest in St. Augustine, 173.

Camwood: exported, 67.

Capitulation: urged, 45, 46; affidavits concerning, 63; of J. Maxwell, 182.

Capoy, Fla.: Indian town, 8.

Cargill, Daniel: apprehended by W. Young, 167.

Carleton, Gen. Sir Guy: evacuation under orders from, 101, 102; Tonyn asked to apply for force to, 103; resolutions sent to, 104; dispatches forwarded to, 105; sends order announcing transports for Savannah, 105; Wright protests to him against surrender of Ga., 107; Graham asks instructions from, 107; approves delay in evacuating E. Fla., 108; approves sending troops to St. Augustine, 114; threatens removal of troops and stores, 122; Tonyn regards himself independent of, 123; sends proclamation for cessation of hostilities, 138; suggests granting lands to refugees in E. Fla., 141; promises replacement of *Eliza's* cargo, 143; Cruden's papers sent to, 148; gives people of E. Fla. free choice of destination, 148; suggests sending Wilson to New Providence, 149; orders inclusion of Bahamas in Southern District, 183; promises grants of land in Nova Scotia, 209; memorials to, cited, 108, 113, 120, 149, 150, 158; letters to, cited, 115, 116, 142, 152.

Carleton Town, Bahamas: built by refugees in Great Abaco Island, 184, 188.

Carolina: loyalists convey intelligence to E. Fla., 50. See also North Carolina; *and* South Carolina.

Carolina King's Rangers: See Troops: Provincial regiments and forces.

Carolinas: loyalists from, 4; loyalists and slaves go to Jamaica from, 201. See also North Carolina; *and* South Carolina.

Carolinians: help defeat Cherokees, 47, 48; provisions for, 120.

Carter, ———: cited, 4 n.

Carteret, Lord ———: sells proprietary rights in Bahamas, 193.

Casanovas ——— (Friar): minister to Minorcans, 6.

Case of the Inhabitants of East Florida (The): cited, 135.

Cassels, Col. James: member of committee of refugees, 124; sketch, 126.

Caswell, Richard: gov. of N. C., 55.

Cat Island, Bahamas: occupied, 184; whites and blacks from E. Fla. in, 188; petition from, 193; included in Exuma mission, 196; pop., 197; visited by Richards, 197; ministrations of Gordon in, 199.

Catherwood, Dr. Robert: member of council, 4; suspended, 131, 132.

Catholics: Greek, highly regarded by Anglican Church, 6.

Cattle: near St. Marys, 39; taken from Ga., 44, 45, 51; carried off by scouts and Indians, 50; taken to Charleston by Thompson, 88; stolen on news of cessation, 140, 141; sloop for New Providence crowded with, 157; carried to New Providence, 188.

Census: of refugees and negroes sent from Savannah to E. Fla., 105; of *id.* in E. Fla., 124; at Charleston of people who sailed for E. Fla., 129, 130; by W. Brown of emigrants from E. Fla. and their destinations, 208.

Cession (E. Fla. to Spain): loss of property through, 8; Tonyn to publish notice of, 138; effect, 140, 141, 144, 177.

Champneys, John (refugee): to conduct public sales, 147; "friendly sale" of land of, 147.

Chapman, William: raid on tract of, 37.

Charles II (Eng. king): grants proprietary rights, 194.

Charleston, S. C.: proclamation in, 24; Brit. expedition to, desired, 29; Prevost's expedition to, 76-78; refugees and loyalists in, and leave, 87,

103, 126, 127, 128, 129, 156, 201, 203, 204, 205; various persons in, 87, 107, 110, 126, 127, 128, 156, 182, 205; number of emigrants in Jamaica from, 201, 204; ships at, 107, 126, 170, 203; Brit. operations from, 88; the evacuation, 102, 105, 113, 114; troops leave, 105, 114; provisions sent from, 119, 120, 170.

Charlottetown, N. C.: Cornwallis and army move to, 86.

Chedabucto (*or* Guysborough), Nova Scotia: *Argo* transport on way to, 158.

Cherokees: hold talk with Cameron, 27; on western frontier of Ga., 41; Tonyn requests their dispatch into S. C. or Ga., 47; Prevost asks protection for, 47; Cameron agent to, 50; accompany Browne to Augusta, 84; party of, joins Browne, 85; delegation at St. Augustine, 120; capture of ammunition for, 127; fear resentment of, 138; ready to depart, 139; Bowles calls himself commander-in-chief of, 179.

Chester, Peter (gov. of W. Fla.): Kirkland bears despatches to, 50.

Chickasaws: well disposed, 50; send delegation to St. Augustine, 120.

Choctaw Nation: Seminoles hostile to, 11; habitat, 41; well disposed, 50; party of, embarked for St. Augustine, 107; returns, 111; sends delegation to St. Augustine, 120.

Christians: among Indians, 10.

Christie, James (refugee): attends meeting, 48.

Church of England: site of Span. bishop's house in St. Augustine transferred to, 5.

Churches: 5; included in barracks of St. Augustine, 19; powder removed to Indian church, 122; bills passed in Bahamas for erection and repair of, 199.

Citron trees: planted, 80.

Claraco y Sanz ——— (gov. of Bahamas): capitulates to Deveaux, 146, 147.

Clark, Angus: commands troops during Indian disturbance, 13.

Clarke, Col. (*or* Gen.) Alured: at Savannah, 81; attacks Musgrove's mills, 85; goes to New York, 107; lt. gov. of Jamaica, 203; receives Dr. Johnston, 204, 205; suspends embargo on importations, 206.

Clarke, Col. Elijah: attacks Augusta, 85; Browne capitulates to, 86.

Clay, Joseph: cited, 53, 54.

Clerk: of market, 5.

Clinton, Gen. Sir Henry: Kirkland submits plan to, 52; appoints Cameron successor to Stuart, 76; leads expedition to Charleston, 83; leaves Charleston, 84; sends message to Tonyn, 101; captures Charleston, 127; letters to, cited, 55, 59, 60, 77, 87.

Clinton-Cornwallis Controversy: cited, 56 n.

Clitherall, Dr. James (refugee): tries to recover slaves, 123.

Coats, James: deposition, 63.

Cobham, Dr. Thomas (refugee): removed to New Providence, 186.

Cockspur Island, Ga.: loyalists at, 106.

Cocoa: exported, 68; will grow in Bahamas, 151.

Coffee: Indians trade for, 11; exported, 68; in Jamaica, 207.

Colleton, Louisa Carolina: sells proprietary rights, 193.

Colonel's Island (*or* Bluff), Ga.: troops in, 72, 73.

Colonel Hay's Station, S. C.: captured, 128.

Commerce and Trade: Indian trade, 11; exports from E. Fla., 67-69; exportation of provisions prohibited, 93.

Commissioners: empowered to issue licenses, 133; of evacuation (*see* Brown, William); of loyalist claims (*see* British); of trade and plantations (*see* Boards).

Committees: of safety (Ga.), denounced, 125; of correspondence (Bahamas), requests relief, 192.

Commons House of Assembly: in E. Fla. — election of members to, 91; officers chosen for, 92; address to and from Tonyn, 93; passes negro bill, 96; report on slow progress in E. Fla., by committee of, 94, 95; inquiries about signing of bills, 95, 96; appeals to Browne, 138. In Bahamas — loyalists gain seats in, 192; report on Bahamas by committee of, 195. In Jamaica — acts on petition, 202; A. Aikman, member of, 205.

Confiscations: acts (laws), various considerations regarding, 123, 126; of property of N. C. loyalists, 56; *id.*, of various persons, 111, 126; relaxation of laws, 210.

Congress, Provincial (S. C.): activities, 25, 127.

Connecticut: loyalists go to Jamaica from, 201.

Connolly, Dr. John: his schemes, 28, 29.

Constables: act for electing, 93.

Continental Congress: Kirkland in custody of, 29; summons Lee, 43.

Continentals: Lee collects, 43; decimated by death, 59.

Convent: in barracks, 19.

Copper: exported, 69.

Cork, Ireland: transport in cove of, 159.

Cornwallis, Lord Charles: at Charleston, S. C., 84; orders deserters hanged, 85; his movements in N. C., 86; commissions Ball and Cassels, 126; letters, 55, 87.

Corradine's Fort, S. C.: W. Cunningham attacked near, 128.

Cotton: exported, 69; in Bahamas, 194; in Jamaica, 207.

Councils: Privy: suspension reported to, 131, 132. E. Fla. — instituted, 4; Forbes member of, 6; meetings, 4, 5, 12, 13, 14, 15, 17, 18, 22, 23, 32, 33, 34, 35, 39; revives trade with Creeks, 13, 14; acts against Jonathan Bryan, 14; Drayton before, 15; Gordon admitted and suspended, 15-17; offers rewards, 21, 39; acts on troops for Lord Dunmore, 22; finds fault with Drayton, 31; charges against Drayton submitted to, 33, 34; as upper house of assembly, 91, 92; opposes recovery of slaves, 123; suspends Catherwood, 131, 132; Bahamas — members of, 182; asked to concur in application, 196. Georgia — of safety, Browne antagonizes, 24.

County Harbor, Nova Scotia: S. C. Royalists receive lands at, 152.

Courts: Admiralty — Tonyn refuses to surrender negroes not condemned by, 123; in Bahamas, judges for, 182. Vice admiralty — Catherwood suspended from, 131, 132. Common law — Catherwood suspended from, 131, 132. Common pleas — jurisdiction, 93. General — negroes tried before, 97.

Coventry ———, earl of: sells proprietary rights, 193.

Cowdriver (Cherokee chief): at St. Augustine, 10, 144, cited, 139.

Cowford (Jacksonville), Fla.: detachment at, 30; Prevost at, 59.

Craig, Maj. James Henry: occupies Wilmington, 87; driven into Charleston, 87.

Craven, Lord ———: sells proprietary rights, 193.

Creeks (Indians): habitat, 8-12, 41; trade with, 3, 13; lease lands, 14; communication with, important, 23; aid sought, 40, 57; imprisoned, 47; favor Americans, 48; Tonyn entertains, 51; at St. Augustine, 60, 120, 148; embark for *id.*, 107; expected at *id.*, 153; to join Prevost, 75; lower, suffer famine, 80; in reinforcement for Charleston, 83; return to their nation, 111; resentment feared, 138; wish to go to Bahamas, 139; Bowles gains influence over, 179; they surrender him, 179.

Crooked Island, Bahamas: pop., 197.

Crucifixes: Indians wear, 10.

Cruden, James (refugee): in New York, 148.

Cruden, John (refugee): in Tortola, 122; in St. Augustine, 123; in New York, 148; praised, 167; at St. Marys River, 169; president of associated loyalists, 190; proposes lottery, 193; schoolmaster, 199; sketch, 169, 170.

Cruden, John (uncle of preceding and refugee): head of company, 170; in Exuma Island, 170; death, 193.

Cruden, John, & Co.: merchants in N. C., 169, 170.

Cuba: bishop, 6, 11; Span. from trade at St. Marks, 11; W. Cunningham deported to, 174; Maxwell capitulates to capt. gen. of, 182.

Cumberland Island, Ga.: expeditionary force in, 73.

Cuming, Witter: member of council, 4.

Cundall, Frank: cited, 203 n.

Cunningham, John: killed, 128.
Cunningham, Col. Patrick (brother of following and refugee): goes to St. Augustine, 126; sketch, 127.
Cunningham, Col. (*or* Gen.) Robert (refugee): plans capture of Augusta, 26; commands militia, 84; goes to St. Augustine, 126; goes to Nova Scotia, 154; sketch, 127.
Cunningham, Maj. William (refugee): goes to St. Augustine, 126; imprisoned by Span., 173; sketch, 128.
Curwen, Samuel: cited, 128 n., 214.
Cuscowilla, Fla.: name for Alachua, 10; location, 8; capital, 10; Talahasochte compared to, 11; McLatchie in, 10.
Cypress Trees: canoes made from, 11; plantation of James Hume, 81; location, 81.
Cyrus (ship): Tonyn to sail for England in, 174; leaves E. Fla., 175; Tonyn writes from, 175, 176; disabled, 176; Tonyn on, 207.

D ANIEL'S ISLAND, S. C.: mil. force sent from, 88.
Darien, Ga.: American galleys at, 59.
Dartmouth, ——— earl of: mentioned, 7, 12, 15, 17; letters, cited, 18, 23, 24; Cruden writes, 169.
Davis, T. Frederick: cited, 117 n.
De Brahm, William Gerard: surveyor general, 19.
Debts: act for recovery, 93; owing to loyalists, 113; Brit. merchants to recover, 129.
Declaration of Independence: effect, 35, 36.
Delawares (Indians): send chiefs to St. Augustine, 120.
Deserters: reward offered for, 39; bring information to St. Augustine, 66; ordered hanged by Cornwallis, 85; from Royal North Carolina Regiment, 153.
Detroit, Mich.: Connolly and Cameron start for, 28, 29; Indians from, 120.
Deveaux, Maj. (*or* Lt. Col.) Andrew: leads expedition, 145-147; at Nassau, 184; sketch, 145.
Dewhurst, William Whitewell: cited, 36 n., 214.
Digby, Rear Admiral Robert: orders evacuation, 102; sends vessels to E. Fla., 108; assigns Cobham to hospital, 186; Tonyn writes, 150.

Dissenters: in Nassau, 197.
Dobbins, ———: ships mahogany, 169, 170.
Docherty, Bryan: reward offered for arrest, 39.
Doctor's Lake, Fla: Georgians settle on, 109.
Dodd, Capt. Benjamin: appointed to council, 35; buys plantation, 38.
Doggett, Carita: cited, 8 n., 34 n., 35 n., 36 n., 37 n., 59 n., 60 n., 173 n., 214.
Dominica (island): refugees go to, ix, 101, 207, 208; emigrants intend settling in, 170; Minorcans wish to go to, 173; Rose in, 199; Minorcans go to, 210.
Douglas, Lt. Col. John (refugee): Graham employs, 110; deputy sec'y. of Indian affairs, 120; on refugee committee, 124.
Dowd, Capt. ———: with Deveaux's expedition, 146.
Draper, Lyman Copeland: cited, 129 n., 214.
Drayton, John: cited, 43 n., 128 n., 214.
Drayton, William (chief justice of E. Fla.): mentioned, 3; member of council, 4; involved in Bryan's lease, 14, 15; interrogated by council, 17, 18; charges against, 33, 34; trial, 64; suspended, 33, 64; goes to England, 35; reinstated, 43; criticises Tonyn's administration, 45; orders publication of grievance, 31, 34; renews strife with Tonyn, 63; removes to S. C., 65, 80, 209, 210, 128 n.
Drayton, William Henry: activities on lower Enoree River, 127; member of committee of safety, 210; letter, cited, 17, 18, 24, 27.
Drayton Hall: location, 65; Drayton removes to, 65.
Dry goods: exported, 68, 69.
Dundas, Col. ———: commissioner on loyalist claims, 193.
Dunmore, Lord, John Murray: gov. of Va., 17; gov. of Bahamas, 178; troops for, 18, 22, 23; Kirkland visits, 28; Cameron visits, 28; sends Kirkland to Gage, 29; sends Bowles to E. Fla., 178; petitioned, 193.
Dupont, Gideon, Jr. (refugee): his mission to New York, 113, 114.

E AST FLORIDA (Brit. prov.): sources of material on, ix-x; exports, 67-69; negroes shipped to, 78; reasons alleged for slow progress, 94, 95; condition, 144, 175; provisions asked for, 159; indigo in, 207; loyalty, 4; hears of Revolution, 18; correspondence with rebels forbidden, 33; cut off from provisions, 22; danger of invasion, 47; plan to attack, 23; expeditions and attacks against, 37, 45-47, 51, 52, 76; rumored Span. exped. against, 89.

Distribution of troops in, 30; Prevost brings troops to, 38; S. C. Royalists formed in, 52, 53; Schopholites arrive in, 54; armed vessels of, 56; Americans learn of troops in, 57; aid asked for defense, 81; loyalist regiments leave, 83; prov'l regiments sent to, 105, 114.

King favors as asylum for refugees, 23, 24; refugees in, 106, 109, 115, 158, 183; refugees talk of leaving, 142; sent to Eng., 145; go to Bahamas from, 186; return from Bahamas to, 178; go to Jamaica from, 201, 203; *see also, below*, through Evacuation.

Negroes in, 106, 126; not to be shipped from, 122; negroes go to islands from, 201, 203, 204; pop., before and after arrival of loyalists, 115; settlers talk of leaving, 142; loyalists plan and go to various destinations, 149, 151, 156, 186, 201, 203, 204, 209.

Tonyn hopes for Brit. retention, 109, 141; his attitude on cession, 139; preparations for transfer, 157; residents unwilling to remain under Span., 158; Brit. subjects still in, 167.

Evacuation: process and events, etc., of, 101, 102, 114, 138, 142, 145, 152-157, 167, 168, 170-177, 189, 191, 204, 208-210; addresses and resolutions on, 108, 109; last transports from, 174, 176, 192; number to emigrate from, 150, 183; number in islands from, 186, 204; proportion of pop. in Bahamas from, 209; loyalists in Bahamas victualled from, 190.

Gov't.: Council — instituted, 4; members, 6, 15-17, 131, 132; members suspended, 15-17, 131, 132 (*see also* Drayton, William; *and* Turnbull, Andrew); meetings, 4, 5, 12, 13, 14, 15, 17, 18, 22, 23, 32, 33, 35, 39; various activities, 13, 14, 21, 22, 31, 93, 96-99, 123, 131, 132; becomes upper house of assembly, 91-92; members, 91-92; contest with lower house, 96-99. General assembly (two houses)— provided for, 4; petitioned for, 65; election provided for, 88; election and business of first, 91-100; legislation recommended, 89; contest over negro bill, 96-99; dissolved, 98-99; date of election for second, 99; other activities, 103, 109, 114, 115, 132, 133, 152. Commons House—election for, 91; officers, 92; various activities, 93, 96-99, 138. Indian Dept.—duties, 151.

Miscellaneous: Graham's losses in, 111; Cunninghams go to and leave, 126, 127, 128; malefactors on borders of, 141; wild rumors in, 142; Cruden retires to, 169; priests in, 173; Tattnall in, 183; Johnston leaves, 204. *See also* Tonyn, Patrick.

East Florida Rangers (*see* Troops: Provincial regiments and forces): Browne commissioned to raise, 26, 38; in retaliatory expedition, 44.

East Indies (islands): rumors of provincial regiments being sent to, 142.

Eaton, Arthur Wentworth Hamilton: cited, 202 n., 205 n., 215.

Ebenezer, Ga.: Prevost at, 175; sickness among Brit. troops at, 78; loyalists resort to, 105.

Eden, William: status, 30.

Edinburgh, Scotland: William Charles Wells in, 134; Dr. William Martin Johnston in, 204.

Edwards, Capt. Peter (refugee): joins in address, 48; member of assembly, 91; clerk of chancery, 92; clerk of public accounts, 155; horse stolen from, 167; goes to England, 176.

Egan, Mr.: persons on estates of, 168.

Egan, Stephen: member of assembly, 91.

Egerton, Hugh Edward (ed.): cited, 39 n., 53 n., 56 n., 58 n., 75 n., 80 n., 126 n., 128 n., 158 n., 182 n., 183 n., 215.

Egmont, Lady ———: protection asked for her plantation, 43; W. Cunningham buys land claimed by, 128; persons on estates of, 168.

Elbert, Col. Samuel: leads expedition against E. Fla., 45-47; proposed capitulation to, 45, 46, 63; collects troops, 50; operations in Ga., 51; captures the *Hinchenbrook* and *Rebecca*, 56.

Index 237

Elections: commanded by royal writ, 91.
Electors: of commons house, 91.
Elephants' teeth: exported, 68.
Eleuthera Island, Bahamas: occupied, 184; whites and blacks from E. Fla. in, 188; missionary for, 196; pop., 197; Robertson goes to, 198; Gordon transferred to, 199.
Elizabethtown, N. J.: prisoners-of-war in, 203.
Ellis, George Edward: cited, 88 n., 215.
Elphinstone, Capt. Keith: urges post at St. Marys Harbor, 60; advises postponement of evacuation, 102.
England: King, relinquishes right of taxation, 92, 93; petition to, 103; protection promised to loyalists, 107; continuance of sovereignty in E. Fla. hoped, 109; chiefs swear vengeance against, 144; breaks promise, 157; aspersions against, 190; proprietary rights sold to, 193.
  War Office, promotes Tonyn, 99.
  Wright sails for, 39; Turnbull in, 62; Graham in, 110; Tattnall goes to, 125; *id.* returns from, 182; objection to cession in, 137, 138; news of evacuation received from, 141; old settlers and refugees choose to go to, 143; Manson and Wylley plan to go to, 144; transports to return to, 174; Powell goes to, 182, 183; Maxwell goes to, 183, 191; emigrants from E. Fla., in, 209. *See also* Great Britain.
English: noblemen, agents act for, 138, 139; few in St. Augustine, 173. *See also* British.
Estaing, Charles Hector, Comte d': invited to besiege Savannah, 78; fails in siege, 79; captures Tattnall, 125.
Europe: selected for settlement, 159; Bowles returns to, 179; Brit. subjects emigrate to, 208, 209.
Eustace, Col. John Skey: makes charges against Catherwood, 132, 133.
Evacuation: remonstrances against, 102-104; a measure of necessity, 114; instructions regarding, 154-155; retarded, 170, 172; time set for completion, 174; conducted with great care, 174, 175; expenses of, 175; disastrous effects, 177; Tonyn attempts to hasten, 191; of southern states, 101, 102, 183; of Ga., 105-107; of Charleston, 113, 114, 129, 131; of E. Fla., 138, 142, 145, 152, 153-157, 167, 168, 170-177, 189, 191, 204, 208-210; to lower Mississippi region, 156, 157; to Jamaica and Bahamas, 156; to W. Indies and Nova Scotia, 157, 167, 168; to various islands, 170, 171; Maxwell comments on, 189. *See also* Charleston; East Florida; Georgia; North Carolina; Savannah; *and* South Carolina.
Exports: of E. Fla., 67-69.
Exuma Island, Bahamas: Cruden in, 170; he dies in, 193; occupied, 184; number going to, 187; whites and blacks from E. Fla. in, 188; petition from, 193; missionary in, 196; plantations and pop. of, 197; Gordon reports from, 198; is transferred from, 199; salt made on, 199; Groombridge and Rose sent to, 200. *See also* Great Exuma Island.

FACTIONS: in E. Fla., 15, 17, 34, 35.
Fairbanks, George Rainsford: cited, 36 n., 147 n., 162 n., 167 n., 171 n., 215.
Fanning, Col. David: plans to raise recruits, 54, 87; agrees to join Deveaux, 145; raises men for him, 146; goes to Mississippi country, 156, 157; Mosquito Inlet, 157; sketch, 156.
Farley, Samuel: special duties, 133; negroes of, 165.
Fatio, Francis Philip: appointed justice of peace, 162; stops suit for stolen slaves, 165; persons under care of, 168; buys land in "friendly sale," 171.
Fennell, Capt.: with Deveaux expedition, 146.
Ferguson, Col. Patrick: defeated, 86.
Fernández, Lt. Col. Antonio: operations by, 165.
Fiske, ———: cited, 194 n.
Flag: American causes riot, 189.
Fletchall, Col. Thomas: leader of loyalists in S. C., 127.
Florida: student of history of, ix. *See* East Florida; *and* West Florida.
Florida Brigade: Prevost commands, 74; reaches Savannah, 75.
Florida Historical Society: *Quar.*, cited, 8 n., 19 n.

Florida State Historical Society: official thanked, ix.

Floridas: rumored exchange of, 143; retention by Eng. expected, 157. *See also* Evacuation.

Flour: exported, 68.

Forbes, ———: sent to Havana, 81.

Forbes, Rev. John: rector in St. Augustine, 3; member of council, 4, 6, 7; appointed chief justice, 34; goes to Europe for health, 118.

Forbes, John, & Co.: hostile to Bowles, 179.

Forbes, Thomas: member of commons house, 91.

Force, Peter: cited, 22 n., 23 n., 25 n., 29 n., 30 n., 31 n., 32 n., 42 n., 43 n., 50 n., 51 n., 128 n., 215.

Ford, Worthington C.: thanked, x.

Forks, Fla.: Indian town, 8.

Forts and Fortifications: negroes employed on, 58, 63, 79, 88; Tonyn sends plans of, 115; on New Providence Island, 146.

    Barrington: surrender demanded; captured, 51; Howe's camp near, 59.

    Charlotte: capture planned, 24; captured, 27; reduced in Ga., 74.

    Charlotte, Nassau: location, 196.

    Cornwallis: location, 86; attempted escape from, 86.

    Conradine's: location, 128.

    Cumberland: strong post planned for, 28.

    Galphin: location, 86; loyalist troops captured at, 86.

    George: location, 57; detachment protects, 57; condition, 62.

    George: location and name, 72, 73-74 (*see also, below*, Morris).

    Howe: location, 54; Elbert at, 47, 54; Amer. forces at, 57; Brit. forces at, 72.

    McIntosh: garrisoned, 44; Prevost at, 58.

    Morris: location, 72; former name, 73-74 (*see also, above*, George).

    Nassau: repaired, 187-195; weak, 196.

    Natchez: location, 157; Fanning plans to go to, 157.

    Picolata: location, 37; Indian towns near, 8; garrison ordered for, 32.

    Pitt: plans regarding, 28.

    Prince's: location, 84; royalist troops at, 84.

    St. Mark: garrison for, 32.

    Tonyn: location, 50, 51; royalists at, 50, 53; scouting party at, 51; loyalists at, 52; burned, 59; council of war at, 66.

    Wright's: location, 26, 38, 42; attacked, 26, 42.

Fothergill, Dr. ———: Bartram gathers specimens for, 9.

Fox, John: property stolen, 167, 178.

Fraser, Rev. Patrick: sent to Long Island, 199; death of, 199.

Fraser, Maj. Thomas: commands S. C. Royalists, 87, 88, 142; asks discharge of men, 142.

Frazer, Rev. John: second missionary to E. Fla., 6; sketch, 6.

Frederick the Great: Tonyn serves under, 3.

French: few at St. Augustine, 173; capture some of W. Indies, 203; Consul, invites d'Estaing to besiege Charleston, 78.

Furlong, Maj. Jonathan: Kirkland carries letters from, 28; commands garrison, 30; asks permission to take command to Va., 32; instructions given to, 32, 33.

Fuser, Col. Lewis V.: leads expedition from E. Fla., 44; fortifies St. Johns Bluff, 58; commands garrison, 60; endorses Drayton, 63; at Sunbury, 71; at Fort Morris, 72; joins Prevost, 73; assumes command in St. Augustine, 74; takes measures for defense, 79; death of, 80.

GAGE, Gen. Thomas: issues orders, 18, 23; Cameron and Kirkland go to see, 28, 29; letters to and by, 18, 22, 23, 27.

Gale, Samuel: book, cited, 135.

Galleys: *See* Ships.

Gamble, William (commissary): victuals loyalists, 190; reports condition of loyalists, 192.

Gardner, William James: cited, 202 n., 206, 207 n.

Garrisons: Span.: in E. Fla., 3, 161.

    Brit.: at St. Augustine, 28, 30, 35, 79, 103, 122, 144, 152; of Fort Morris, 73; at Stono Ferry, 77; on Port Royal and Lady's islands,

Index 239

78; at Augusta, 85; of Fort Cornwallis, 86; of New Providence, 146, 147; of St. Marks, 179. Amer.: at Col. Hay's Station, 128.

Subsistence, 49, 122; cattle for, 50; strength and position, 57, 81; in Prevost's command, 73; called to defense of Savannah, 78; surrender, 86; Choctaws in, 107; executions in, 128; allowed to march out, 146, 147; removal feared and protested, 152, 153. *See also* Militia; *and* Troops.

Gates, Gen. Horation: defeated, 84.

General Assembly: *See* Bahamas; Dominica; East Florida; Georgia; *and* Jamaica.

George III: his brother, 13; gov't. characterized, 48.

Georgia: royal gov't. in, 75; officials in, 80, 182, 204; gen'l. assembly, 103. Mil. operations in, 39, 51, 74, 75; invasion proposed, 51; invasion feared, 99; frontiers protected, 84; invasion of, prohibited, 110; plan to attack St. Augustine from, 165. Refugees from, 4, 108, 124, 153, 158; members of committee of refugees, 124; loyalists leave, 23, 188, 189, 201; they convey intelligence, 50; laws against loyalists, 60, 61; some remain in, 106; negroes sent to, 37, 78; slaves plundered from, 141, 144; confiscation of property in, 111; malefactors commit depredations in, 141; fear of banishment removed, 210; evacuation of, 101, 102, 105-108. Wright from, 38; Tattnall returns to, 125; Amer. commissioner from, 131; Powell flees from, 182.

Georgia Historical Society: *Collections*, cited, 43 n., 45 n., 54 n., 57 n., 76 n., 126 n., 216.

Georgians: confer with Lee, 41; help defeat Cherokees, 47, 48; fear invasion, 50; leave Georgia, 108, 109, 203 (*see also*, Georgia); number capable of bearing arms, 115; bring their own provisions, 119; express preference for W. Indies, 158.

Germain, Lord George: activities against colonists, 30; complaints made to, 35, 39, 46, 66; appointments by, 76, 125; promise to loyalists, 105; letters to and by, cited, 30, 35, 36, 39, 46, 55, 66; Tonyn sends address to, 49.

Germans: few at St. Augustine, 173.

Germany: paymaster of army in, 17; *see also* Frederick the Great.

Gibbes, Robert Wilson: cited, 128 n., 216.

Gibbon, Edward: read in Bahamas, 198.

Gibraltar: exchange rumored, 143; Minorcans go to, 210.

Ginger: exported, 69.

Glazier, Maj. (*or* Lt. Col.) Beamsley: succeeds Fuser, 80; requests negroes, 88; has charge of provisions and military stores, 103; replaced by McArthur, 114; appointment by, 124.

Gordon, Arthur: member of council, 3; seeks admission to council, 15-17; advocate general, 13.

Gordon, John: a Catholic, 5; buys property, 5; property conveyed to, 19.

Gordon, Rev. William: visits Long Island, Bahamas, 196; reports its pop., 198.

Graham, Capt. ———: retires before enemy, 40.

Graham, Maj. ———: relieves Browne, 58.

Graham, Lt. Gov. John: at Tybee Island, 107; in E. Fla., 110; Indians accompany from Savannah, 111; embarkation of negroes of, 168.

Graham's Redoubt: Prevost at, 47.

Granary: Indian public, 10.

Grant, Gov. James: gift to church, 5; recommends Gordon for Council, 16; letters to, cited, 27, 30.

Grant, Lt. ———: sent to guard St. Marys, 39.

Grants of Land: *See* Landgrants.

Graves, Vice-Admiral Thomas: Tonyn writes, 30.

Gray, Alexander: builds stone wall, 19; affidavit of, 64.

Great Abaco Island, Bahamas: refugees go to, 149, 150, 184; new towns founded in, 184; provisions for, 184; McArthur writes of new settlements in, 187; whites and blacks from E. Fla. in, 188; petition from, 193; pop., 197, 198. *See also* Abaco Island.

Great Britain: mentioned, 204; R. and W. C. Wells go to, 134; men of Royal North Carolina Regiment (*or* Volunteers) go to, 142, 153; expected to retain the Floridas, 157; sale of lands on condition of restoration of E. Fla.

to, 171. *See also* British; England; *and* English.
Great Exuma Island, Bahamas: loyalists in, 198. *See also* Exuma Island.
Great Hammock, Fla.: Indian town, 8.
Great Island, Fla.: Indian town, 8.
Greaves, Capt. ———: orders to, 32.
Greek Catholics: favorably regarded by Anglican Church, 32.
Greeks: at New Smyrna, 6, 173; theft attributed to, 140, 141, 167; some likely to stay in E. Fla., 158.
Greene, Gen. Nathaniel: invests Ninety Six, 86; pursued by Cornwallis, 87; drives Craig's command into Charleston, 87.
Greenoch, Scotland: transport at, 159, 204.
Greenwood & Higginson: sign memorial, 206.
Gregg, Alexander: cited, 84 n., 216.
Grenada Island, W. Indies: Jollie arrives from, 32.
Grierson, Col. ———: attempts escape from Fort Cornwallis, 86.
Grimké, John Faucheraud: cited, 59.
Groombridge, Rev. Henry: sent to Exuma Island, 200.
Guilford Court House: battle at, 87.
Gulf of Mexico: small boats unable to cross, 157.
Guysborough: *See* Chedabucto.
Gwinnett, Button: plans expedition, 45.

Hager's Town, Md.: loyalists arrested at, 29.
Halifax, Nova Scotia: loyalists plan to go to, 142; vessels to convey troops to, 151; the *Argo* and other transports at, 158.
Halifax Inlet, Fla.: Fanning at, 146.
Halifax River, Fla.: Fanning removes to, 156.
Halkett, John (gov. of Bahamas): advises against sending another clergyman, 200.
Hamilton, Archibald (brother of following refugee): in New York, 55; property confiscated, 56.
Hamilton, Lt. Col. John (merchant): imprisoned, 54; in New York, 55; wounded, 55; property confiscated, 56; in expedition to Savannah, 74; his operations in Ga., 74, 75; in S. C., 77; in defense of Savannah, 78; in advance to Charleston, 83; with Cornwallis and army, 86, 87; reports resolution, 142; recommended for governorship, 192.
Hampton, Col. Richard: attacked at Orangeburgh, 128.
Hancock, John: burned in effigy, 35, 36.
Hanging Rock, Ga: Carolina King's Rangers at, 84.
Harbor Island, Bahamas: Deveaux in, 146; occupied, 184; missionary and schoolmaster for, 196; pop., 197; Robertson sent to, 198; Gordon transferred to, 199.
Harding, John: petition by, 184.
Harris, Lt. Col. ———: on St. Marys, 47.
Havana, Cuba: Forbes sent to, 81; Span. garrison sent to, 147; Bowles imprisoned in, 179. *See also* Cuba.
Haven, Stephen: acts as deputy clerk, 92.
Hawke, Lord ———: chairman of meeting, 137; Tonyn writes, 168; his slaves in Dominica, 207.
Hay's Station, S. C.: captured, 128.
Henderson, E. F.: cited, 3 n.
Hessians: officer of troops, 203.
Hester, William: sells land, 117.
Hesters Bluff, E. Fla.: fortified, 45, 46; loyalists at, 117 (*see also* St. Johns Bluff).
Hewitt, John: completes state house, 19.
Hewitt, William: completes state house, 19.
Hides: exported, 67, 68.
Higginson: *See* Greenwood & Higginson.
Highlanders: of N. C. among loyalists, 55.
Hist. MSS. Comm.: cited, 3 n., 38 n., 39 n., 48 n., 51 n., 53 n., 56 n., 57 n., 58 n., 60 n., 71 n., 74 n., 75 n., 76 n., 77 n., 78 n., 79 n., 80 n., 84 n., 85 n., 88 n., 89 n., 99 n., 102 n., 104 n., 105 n., 107 n., 108 n., 109 n., 110 n., 111 n., 114 n., 115 n., 116 n., 118 n., 120 n., 121 n., 122 n., 124 n., 125 n., 128 n., 129 n., 131 n., 138 n., 139 n., 141 n., 142 n., 143 n., 144 n., 147 n., 148 n., 149 n., 150 n., 151 n., 152 n., 153 n., 156 n., 170 n., 178 n., 183 n., 184 n., 187 n., 203 n., 204 n., 205 n., 206 n., 217.

Index

Holland, Wells in, 134.
Holmes, John: member of council, 4.
Honduras: settlement on bay proposed, 159; loyalists and slaves leave 201.
Honey: Indians trade for, 11; exported, 68.
Horses: stolen, 44, 66, 140, 141, 166, 167, 178.
Howard, Capt. Carlos: secretary to Zespedes, 161; aids Tonyn, 162, 171, 172.
Howe, Gen. Robert: leads expedition, 51, 52, 56-60; fears invasion of Ga., 66, 67.
Howe, Gen. Sir William: approves employment of Indians, 38; Kirkland submits plan to, 52; letters to, cited, 27, 38; dispatches from, 50.
Hume, David: works read in Long Island, 198.
Hume, James (refugee): chief justice of E. Fla., 80; presents resolutions, 97; presents memorial, 152; gives opinion, 162; horses stolen from, 166; goes to England, 176; sent in search of stolen negroes, 198.
Hutchinson's Island, Ga.: location, 145.
Hutson's Ferry, Ga.: Prevost at, 75.

IMRIE, JOHN (refugee): in East Florida, 61 n.
Indians: contact with whites, 8-16; towns, 8, 10-11; pop., 8-9, 10, 11; trade, 10-11; presents given to, 12; sign lease, 14; to coöperate with Brit., 25; Stuart's messages to, 27; in congress with Tonyn, 32; dep't. for in E. Fla., 151; at New Smyrna, 36; sent to St. Marys, 38; accompany parties of loyalists, 39; Tonyn suggests employment of, 39; on western frontier of Ga., 41, 42; communicate with E. Fla., 42; steal horses and cattle, 44, 50; massacres by, 42, 157; claim lands near Alachua, 48; at Fort McIntosh, 58; an annoyance in Ga., 66; barter with, 11, 67; in expedition to Sunbury, 72; in operations against Charleston, 83; at Augusta, 85; capture of supplies for, 86; at Savannah, 106; Graham asks instructions regarding, 107; frequent St. Augustine in delegations, 132; to remain, 148; to be kept in good temper, 153; Tonyn encourages friendliness for Span., among, 178; Bowles sent to open trade with, 178; in Alachua, refuse to join him, 179. *See also*, the several Indian Tribes.
Indigo: exported, 67, 68; large crops in Jamaica reported, 156; loyalists cultivate, 201, 207.
Innes, Col. Alexander: his rank, 52; accompanies Campbell, 71; at Savannah, 74; in advance to Charleston, 83; at Prince's Fort, 84; at Musgrove's mills, 85; goes to New York, 87.
Island Ford, S. C.: plantation at, 127.
Italians: at New Smyrna, 6, 173.
Ivory: exported, 68.

JACKSON'S CREEK, S. C.: Phillips from, 31.
Jamaica: Gov., 113; lt. gov., 203. General Assembly — act by, 201; favors free trade with U.S., 206. French attack on, feared, 203. Indigo raised in, 156; hurricanes in, 206; restricted shipments to, 206. Refugees (and loyalists) go to, ix, 101, 107, 108, 143, 156, 158, 167, 201, 202, 203; people of E. Fla. plan to go to, 105; slaves go to, 107, 201, 202, 204; 208; projected arrival of loyalists announced, 113, 114; old settlers go to, 143; passage to, offered, 146; preferred by slave owners, 150; transports to and from, 148, 154, 170, 171; house shipped to, 177; Minorcans go to, 210; *journals*, cited, 201 n.
Jameson, Dr. J. Franklin: thanked, x.
Jericho, Fla.: location, 79; Penman in, 79.
John's Island, S. C.: Prevost occupies, 77; Craig driven from, 87.
Johnson, ———: trades stolen horses, 166.
Johnson, Joseph: cited, 129 n., 217.
Johnson, William: cited, 116 n., 129 n., 217.
Johnston, Andrew (son of following refugee): signs petition, 48.
Johnston, Mrs. Elizabeth Lichtenstein (refugee): cited, 129, 129 n., 136 n., 154 n., 156, 156 n., 157, 158 n., 159 n.
Johnston, Dr. Lewis (refugee): offices held by, 48; transported free, 156; sails from St. Marys, 159; goes to Scotland, 204.
Johnston, Capt. Lewis, Jr. (son of preceding refugee): signs petition, 48; at Alligator Creek

bridge, 58, 59; at Midway meetinghouse, 72; at Augusta, 85.

Johnston, Dr. William Martin (refugee): offices held by, 204; in Jamaica, 204.

Jollie, Martin: appointed to council, 32; sides with Turnbull and resigns, 34.

Jolta-noga. *See* Suolanocha.

Jones, Charles Colcock, Jr.: cited, 15 n., 43 n., 44 n., 54 n., 57 n., 73 n., 74 n., 75 n., 80 n., 84 n., 86 n., 105 n., 106 n., 107 n., 126 n., 218.

Jones, Edward Alfred (ed.): cited, 26 n., 29 n., 31 n., 52 n., 53 n., 57 n., 58 n., 71 n., 86 n., 126 n., 128 n., 158 n., 167 n., 170 n., 192 n., 205 n., 218.

Juries: act relating to, 93; for trial of slaves, 97, 100.

    Grand: grievance, 31; favors prov'l. legislature, 92.

Justices of peace: in trial of slaves, 97, 100; to certify applicants for license, 132; appointed by Zespedes, 162.

K

KELSALL: *See* Spalding & Co.

Kemp, George: member of council, 91.

Kennedy, Rev. John: appointed vicar, 7; returns to Scotland, 7.

Key West, Fla.: Fanning in, 157.

King: *See* England.

King's Bridge: loyalists at, 127.

Kings Mountain, N. C.: defeat at, 86.

Kingston, Jamaica: convoy at, 201; petition of vestry at, 201, 202; provisions for loyalists at, 203; transports with refugees at, 203; Lothian in, 204; Johnston in, 204.

Kingston Harbor, Jamaica: hurricanes in, 206.

Kip, Jacobus: signs petition, 34; member of assembly, 91.

Kirkland, Capt. (*or* Maj.) Moses (refugee): at St. Augustine, 24, 27; plan frustrated, 24; aids Amer. cause, 27; Brit. desire to win over, 27-28; aids Brit., 28; submits plan for expedition, 52; with expedition to Savannah, 71; movements of, 83, 84; in command of loyal militia, 84; joins Browne at Augusta, 85; in Jamaica, 204.

Knox, Robert: letter, cited, 15, 16.

Knox, William: signs memorial, 206.

L

LADY'S ISLAND, S. C.: Brit. garrison on, 78.

Laidler, Ralph: completes state house in St. Augustine, 19.

Lake George, Fla.: Bowles attempts attack near, 178.

Landgrants: in E. Fla., 4; instructions regarding, 4, 12, 190; execution of, 13; various considerations concerning large grants, 48, 49, 50, 94, 95, 109; acreage and number of, 49; promised to recruits, 87, 145; to refugees, 88, 108, 141; to old settlers, 88; Georgians obtain few, 109; to loyalists, 149, 153, 154; officers recommended for, 151; in Bahamas, 149, 183, 190; in Nova Scotia, 154, 209; in Jamaica, 201, 202.

Lands: *See* Plantations; *and* Property.

Lane, Maj. ————: at Fort Morris, 73.

Lanier, Sidney: cited, 61 n., 218.

Laws: against loyalists, 60, 61.

Leadbeater, Rev. John: mentioned, 3; absentee from St. Marks parish, 5-8.

Lease: Indians sign, 14.

Leather: exported, 67, 68.

Leaver, Robert: manages transports, 155; on board *Two Sisters*, 170; instructions to, 174.

Lee, Gen. Charles: confers with Georgians, 41; expedition against E. Fla., 42, 44; summoned to Philadelphia, 43.

Lee, Col. Henry: Browne capitulates to, 86.

Lee, F. D.; and J. L. Agnew: cited, 73 n., 74 n., 218.

Lee, Henry: cited, 75 n., 84 n., 86 n., 218.

Leeward Islands, W. Indies: transports from, 154.

Lemon trees: Hume plants, 80.

Lemprière, Capt. Clement: complaint against, 21; various activities, 21-22.

Leslie, Gen. Alexander: at St. Augustine and Savannah, 80; sends Thompson against Marion, 88; conducts evacuation, 101, 113; Carleton grants authority to, 102; remonstrances to, 102-104; reports figures of emigrants, 105, 129, 130; Carleton approves action, 108; permits Graham to go to Eng., 110; proposes negotiation, 115; sends provisions from Charleston, 119, 120; warns Tonyn about shipment of plundered slaves, 122; asked to send tools to E. Fla., 124; letters to and by, cited, 116, 122, 145.

Leslie, John: member of commons house, 91; receives appointment, 169.

Leslie, Panton & Co.: member of firm, 169.

Lesser Antilles: refugees in, 207.

Letters of Joseph Clay: cited, 50 n., 53 n., 54 n., 60 n., 218.

Letters of Marque: issued, 43.

Letters Patent: government of E. Fla. erected by, 4.

Levett, Francis: appointed provost marshal general, 13; member of upper house, 91; horses stolen from, 166; thieves apprehended, 167.

"Liberty Boys": their leader, 15.

Library of Congress: material from used, x; officials thanked, ix-x.

Lignum vitae: exported, 69.

Lime trees: planted, 80.

Lincoln, Gen. Benjamin: in Ga., 77; at Sheldon, S. C., 78; coöperates with d'Estaing, 78.

Linder, John: characterized, 164.

Lindsay, Capt. Charles Stewart: his command, 87, 88.

Liquors: Indians trade for, 11.

Little Exuma Island, Bahamas: Gordon visits, 198.

Little St. Johns River, Fla.: location, 11.

Little River Regiment: P. Cunningham commands, 127.

Lofthouse, Capt. Alvara: his vessel boarded and looted, 21, 22.

Logwood: exported, 69.

London, Eng.: Wright in, 26; Tonyn's bills protested in, 62; Wells in, 134; meeting held in, 137, 138; hint of exchange of Floridas in letter from, 143; Bisset in, 144; transports to go to, 176; request for relief made in, 192; Johnston in, 204.

Long Island, Bahamas: occupied, 184; included in Exuma mission, 196; plantations and pop. of, 196, 197, 198; visited, 197; settlers to go to, 198; Gordon desires release from duties on, 199; Fraser and Rose sent to, 199; parish church on, 199; Rose transferred from, 200.

Long Warrior: Seminole chief, 11.

Lookout Tower (Anastasia Island), Fla.: detachment at, 30.

Lord, Benjamin (refugee): and family in East Fla., 61 n.; member of commons house, 91.

Losses: *See* Property.

Lothian, John (refugee): in Jamaica, 204.

Louisians: Span. gov., 81.

Love, John: appointment, 92.

Loyalists: at St. Augustine, 31, 101; at Wright's fort, 42; at Fort Barrington, 44; in Ga., 50, 74, 75, 101, 105, 106; in Carolinas, 50; at Fort Tonyn, 52; on Savannah River, 75; in Great Abaco Island, 149, 150, 151, 187; at St. Marys, 177, 190; in Bahamas, 186, 188, 192; in Jamaica, 200, 201; in Dominica, 207; from Ga., 48, 77, 105, 107; from N. C., 54, 55; leave Charleston, 129; leave Amelia Harbor, 156; from New York, 149, 150, 151; from E. Fla., 149, 150, 151, 207 (*see also* East Florida). Leave Savannah and St. Augustine, 101; go to E. Fla., 105, 107; go to Jamaica, 114, 204; go to U.S., 114; go to Bahamas, 149, 150, 151, 188, 189, 192; go to Nova Scotia, 158; go to small islands, 204. Great numbers, and reasons therefor, 60, 61, 119, 140, 168, 186. Petitions by, 42, 48, 49, 206; property confiscated, 56; plantations plundered, 76; evacuation causes losses, 101; prepare to surrender possessions, 147; property stolen, 164-167; receive landgrants, 75, 141; claims, 141; accompany expedition, 56; join Prevost, 77; cause increase of exports, 67-69; postponement of removal advised, 102; effect of evacuation on E. Fla., 103; transfer allegiance, 106; provisions distributed to, 122; to learn treaty terms, 138; intentions asked, 138; prospect of evacuation agitates, 139; impression given by concentration in E. Fla., 140; U.S. do not wish their return, 143; recommended to Maxwell, 159; must trust to justice of Brit. gov't., 169; little market for their effects, 171; have

244   Loyalists in East Florida

no Anglican clergyman, 171; build new town in Bahamas, 172; gain seats in Bahama commons house, 192; become dominant party, 193; act aiding, passed in Jamaica, 201; benefit by relaxation of confiscation laws, 210.

McARTHUR, ARCHIBALD (Brit. officer): becomes brig. gen., 117; goes to St. Augustine, 114; characterizes St. Johns Bluff, 117; takes defensive measures in E. Fla., 121; threatens to withhold rations, 122; administrative measures by, 124; receives proclamation, 138; transmits letters, 142; promises provisions, 143, 158, 159; rewards refugees, 144; instructions to, 149, 152; general assembly sends address to, 152; assumes command in Bahamas, 155, 183, 186; letters by and to, cited, 117, 139, 145, 147, 148, 151, 170, 189.

McCall, Hugh: cited, 43 n., 57 n., 86 n., 107 n., 219.

McCall, Col. James: in attack on Augusta, 85.

McCrady, Edward: cited, 22 n., 25 n., 29 n., 43 n., 73 n., 74 n., 75 n., 77 n., 78 n., 79 n., 84 n., 85 n., 115 n., 116 n., 126 n., 128 n., 129 n., 145 n., 219.

McGirth, Daniel (refugee): Amer. officers mistreat, 24, 26; on Amer. side, 26; deserts to Brit., 26; recruits rangers, 38; in Fuser's expedition, 44; opposes Baker's detachment, 46; with Graham, 58; in expedition to Sunbury, 72; Tonyn characterizes, 164, 165; Tonyn complains of, 165; arrested by Young, 167; imprisoned by Span., 174; joins Bowles, 179.

McGirth, James (refugee): on Amer. side, 26; deserts to Brit., 26; recruits rangers, 38; Tonyn characterizes, 164.

McIntosh, Col. John: leads expedition to St. Marys, 42.

McKay ———: name of his trading house, 85; Indians driven to it, 85.

Mackinen, Charles William (refugee): planter, 48.

McKinnen, Daniel: cited, 147 n., 194 n., 219.

Maclaine, A.: Cruden's proposal to, 169.

Macleod, Rev. ——— (refugee): in New York, 55.

McLeod, William: member of commons house, 91.

McLatchie, Charles (Indian trader): activities, 9, 10, 11, 12.

McLaurin, Maj. (or Lt. Col.) Evan (refugee): officer of South Carolina Royalists, 53.

Mackie, ———: prosecuted by Drayton, 64.

Madrid, Spain: Tonyn's suggestion to court of, 172; Bowles sent prisoner to, 179. *See also* Spain.

Magnolia Gardens, S. C.: Drayton removes to, 65.

Mahogany: exported, 67, 68, 169, 170.

Maitland, Col. John: evacuates post, 77; protects Beaufort, 78; recalled to Savannah, 78.

Maize (Indian corn): cultivated, 81, 126; not harvested, 107.

Malcolm, Harcourt Gladstone: cited, 147 n., 194 n., 219.

Man, Spencer: joins in address of loyalty, 34; attends conference, 45; volunteer in 60th Regiment, 63; in anti-Tonyn faction, 80; becomes resident in S. C., 210; letter, cited, 30, 31.

Mandeville, John: works read in Bahamas, 198.

Manila, P. I.: Bowles sent prisoner to, 179.

Manin, Capt. Henry (refugee): captain in East Florida Rangers, 38.

Manson, Maj. Daniel: plans to go to England, 144.

Manuscripts: cited, 3 n., 8 n., 14 n., 15 n., 17 n., 18 n., 22 n., 23 n., 24 n., 31 n., 32 n., 33 n., 34 n., 35 n., 37 n., 39 n., 40 n., 44 n., 46 n., 50 n., 65 n., 66 n., 67 n., 69 n., 85 n., 88 n., 89 n., 91 n., 92 n., 97 n., 99 n., 100 n., 104 n., 106 n., 124 n., 125 n., 128 n., 129 n., 130 n., 132 n., 135 n., 138 n., 141 n., 145 n., 150 n., 153 n., 154 n., 155 n., 156 n., 159 n., 162 n., 163 n., 164 n., 165 n., 166 n., 168 n., 169 n., 170 n., 171 n., 172 n., 173 n., 174 n., 175 n., 176 n., 178 n., 185 n., 187 n., 189 n., 190 n., 191 n., 203 n., 204 n., 205 n., 208 n., 211.

Marion, Col. Francis: on Cooper and Santee rivers, 88.

Marsh's Harbor, Bahamas: founded by refugees, 188.
Martin, John: member of commons house, 91.
Martin, John (gov. of Ga.): assures protection to loyalists, 106.
Maryland: Bowles refugee from, 178; loyalists and slaves go to Jamaica from, 200.
Massachusetts: loyalists and slaves go to Jamaica from, 200.
Massachusetts Historical Society: thanked, x.
Master of Chancery: administers oaths, 91; informs commons house of appointment of clerk, 92.
Matanza Inlet, Fla.: Fanning and exiles land at, 156.
Matanza River, Fla.: Graham's lands on, 110.
Matanzas, Fla.: detachment at, 30.
Mathew, Maj. Gen. Edward: provisions requested from, 184.
Mathews, John (gov. of S. C.): negotiates for mutual restitution of property, 115, 116.
Maxwell, John (gov. of Bahamas): Tonyn recommends loyalists to, 159; capitulates, 182; goes to Eng., 183, 191; in difficulties with refugees, 189; issues orders for victualing loyalists, 190; memorial addressed to, 190; his reply, 190; treats refugees badly, 191; letters, cited, 188, 189.
Medicine: exported, 68; supplied to slaves in Dominica, 207.
Melyar, Daniel: bandits at house of, 164.
Memorials: against evacuation, 103; various presented to Carleton, 108, 113, 149, 150, 158, 205, 206; from Dupont and Ogilvie, 114; from Georgians, 120; from London, 137, 138; from Hume and others, 152; from bandits, 164, 165; from Harding, 184; from board of associated loyalists, 190. See also Petitions.
Midway Meeting-House: skirmish at, 72.
Militia: men enlist in, 36, 37; organization ordered, 40, 94; in N. C., 156; strength of Tonyn's, 57; at Augusta, 85; opposes invasions, 93; Tonyn urged to assemble, 121; under R. Cunningham, 127; "Bloody Bill" Cunningham's regiment of mounted, 128; in E. Fla., 148; for Bahamas, 149, 150; refugees in Jamaica serve in, 201. See also Garrisons; and Troops.
Miller, ———: his paper, 135.
Mingoes (Indians): send chiefs to St. Augustine, 120.
Minorca (island): priest from, 173. See also Campo, Pietro.
Minorcans: inclined to remain in E. Fla., 158; Catholics, 158; not included in Brown's estimate, 168; remain, 173, 209; emigrate in part, 172.
Missionaries: in E. Fla., 5-7; in Bahamas, 196-200.
Mississippi River: loyalists go to lower, 156; Tonyn's estimate of number of emigrants to, 156, 208, 209.
Mississippi Valley: refugees go to, 101.
Mobile, Ala.: captured, 81.
Mohawks (Indians): send chiefs to St. Augustine, 120.
Molasses: exported, 68, 69.
Moore, Capt. ———: killed, 59.
Moore, Maj. ———: routed, 127.
Moore, Capt. James: affidavit, 64.
Moore, John: enlists loyalists in N. C., 55.
Moore, John W.: cited, 56 n., 220.
Moore, Philip: member of commons house, 91.
Moore, Roger: heads gang of thieves, 167.
Morrison, Alfred J. (ed.): cited, 110 n., 116 n., 118 n., 119 n., 139 n., 167 n., 173 n., 189 n., 193 n., 220.
Morro Castle, Cuba: Bowles imprisoned in, 179.
Morse, Col. Robert: sends Wilson to Bahamas, 150.
Mosquito [now Ponce de Leon] Inlet, Fla.: privateer enters, 60; blockhouse at, 121; deserters from blockhouse, 144; Fanning presents petition from people near, 156; Bowles at, 178.
Mosquito Shore (or Coast), C. A.: loyalists and slaves go to Jamaica from, 201; transport with families bound for, 203.
Moss, William: member of commons house, 91.
Moultrie, John: lt. gov. of E. Fla., 4; forbids

trade with Creeks, 12; recommends Gordon for council, 16; denies Prevost's authority in E. Fla., 79; president of upper house, 91; letter, cited, 27, 43.

Moultrie, William: cited, 57 n., 128 n., 220.

Moultrie, Col. William (brother of John): commands force, 43.

Mowbray, Lt. John: granted letters of marque, 43; elected member of commons house, 91; regulates small craft, 155.

Mulcaster, Capt. Frederick George (brother of George III): admitted to council, 13, 16, 17; oaths administered to, 21; prepares plans, 28; cited, 30.

Munsell, ———: cited, 84 n.

Murphey, Col. ———: goes to St. Marys, 54.

Murray, Capt. ———: disperses party at Nassau Bluff, 58.

Murray, Maj. Patrick: memoir of Howe's expedition by, 59.

*N*ARRATIVE of . . . *Anthony Stokes*: cited, 106, 106 n., 220.

Nassau, New Providence: Wells goes to, 135; he founds paper there, 189; Deveaux's expedition at, 146; Wilson prepares plan of, 149; provisions sent to, 150, 184; Fanning at, 157; Cruden goes to, 170; Powell at, 182; McArthur and detachment arrive at, 186, 187; whites and blacks from E. Fla. in, 188; Schoepf and refugees land at, 188; effect of Amer. flag at, 189; Cruden at, 193; new church in, 200; increasing commerce of, 194; need of public buildings in, 195, 196; pop. and religious conditions, 197.

Nassau Bluff, Fla.: Amer. at, 58.

Nassau Harbor, Bahamas: effect of Amer. flag in, 189.

Nassau River, Fla.: number able to bear arms on, 33; bandits attacked on, 164, 165.

Negroes: classified, 164; belonging to various persons, 81, 110, 126, 162, 163, 165; in various localities, 66, 78, 105, 106, 113, 115, 129, 130, 156, 162, 163, 167, 168, 187, 190, 191, 193, 196, 197, 199, 201, 207, 209; evacuated, 78, 105, 106, 107, 113, 114, 115, 129, 130, 156, 157, 158, 168, 192, 193, 196, 197, 201, 207, 208; numbers, 130, 187, 190, 191, 193, 196, 197, 199, 208; rapid increase, 190, 191; remain under Span. gov't., 101; few remain in E. Fla., 209; segregated, 78; on ships, 129, 157, 158, 192; stolen, 60, 66, 122, 123, 140, 153, 165, 178; exported, 68; employed on mil. works, 63, 79, 88, 94, 96, 99; requisition for labor of, 96, 99; free must have employment permits, 162, 163; little employment for, in Bahamas, 183; employment in Jamaica for, 206; join Prevost, 77; provisions withheld from masters of, 121; preacher for, 197; laws regarding, 94, 96-99, 100. *See also* Slaves.

Nevins, Allan: cited, 210 n., 220.

New Brunswick, Can.: various persons go to, 157, 203.

New Jersey: volunteers from, 73; prisoners in, 203.

New Jersey Volunteers: *See* Troops: Provincial regiments and forces.

Newport, Ga.: Prevost retires to, 72.

New Providence, Bahamas: Span. expedition against rumored, 89; various persons go to, 119, 125, 126, 149, 152, 157, 158, 182; Seymour dies on voyage to, 119; loyalists and refugees go to, 143, 145, 148, 168, 187, 188, 191, 193; captured, 146; vessels at, 145, 148, 176, 179; committee from reports, 183; provisions for, 184; whites in, 188, 191; blacks in, 188, 191; petition from, 193; missionaries for, 196, 197; Long Island settled from, 198.

New Smyrna, Fla.: Turnbull colonizes, 3, 173, 209; pop., 173; detachment at, 30; *id.*, requested, 44; number able to bear arms at, 33; Tonyn ordered to favor, 35; Indians at, 36, 37; claim of colonists at, 63; depredations at, 60; some buildings unburned at, 156; divided among heirs, 66; refugees return to, 178.

New York (province or state, and city): various persons in, 53, 87, 88, 107, 113, 148, 169, 184; despatches sent to, 105; garrison in, 107; loyalists carry memorial to, 113; loyalists leave, 149, 150, 151, 156, 159, 184, 185, 191, 201; provisions sent from, 122, 184; transports

leave, 156; associators leave, 184; people from, settle in Bahamas, 185; slaves leave, 201.
Ninety-Six Court House, S. C.: location, 127; siege, 31; garrison near, 127.
Ninety-Six District, S. C.: militia stationed in, 74, 84; aid summoned from, 85; Pickens and Lee return to, 86; former resident, 126, 127, 128.
Norfolk, Va.: Cameron and Kirkland at, 28, 29.
North Carolina: loyalists of, 54, 55, 56, 114, 192; property in, confiscated, 56; laws for this, 61; movements of Cornwallis in, 86; Craig leaves, 87; recruits raised in, 87; Fanning former settler of, 156; merchants in, 169; *State Records*, cited, 61 n., 170 n., 220.
North Carolina Highlanders: sent to St. Augustine, 114.
North Carolinians: in E. Fla., 129.
Northcroft, G. J. H.: cited, 185, 186 n., 220.
Nova Scotia: refugees and loyalists go to, 101, 142, 153, 154, 157, 158, 159, 192, 208, 209; loyalists unwilling to go to, 190; unsatisfactory for refugees, 140; troops go to, 142, 152, 153; troops unwilling to go to, 144; information regarding gratuities in, desired, 142; transports in, 154, 157, 158; negroes distributed in, 158; selected for settlement, 159; plight of North Carolinians in, 192; accession to Bahamas from, 192, 193; Cruden submits claim in, 193.
Nova Scotia Hist. Soc.: *Collections*, cited, 154 n., 220.

OAK PARK (villa): Hume buys, 80.
Oaths: of allegiance and supremacy, 13, 92.
Ocklockony River, Fla.: Bowles escapes to, 179.
Ogeechee River, Ga.: Prevost goes to, 72; troops on, 78.
Ogilvie, Charles (refugee): mission, 113, 114; signer of memorial, 206.
O'Halloran, John: on *Eliza*, 143; cited, 143.
Ohoopee River, Ga.: Amer. on, 59.
Old Town, Ga.: on Satilla River, 47.
O'Neill, Arturo (Span. gov. of W. Fla.): drives Bowles from St. Marks, 179.

Ontario, Bureau of Archives: *Report*, cited, 53 n., 58 n., 75 n., 80 n., 111 n., 128 n., 158 n.
Orangeburgh, S. C.: Moore routed near, 127.
Oranges: exported, 68, 69; juice, exported, 68, 69.
Orde, John: gov. of Dominica, 170; detains transports, 207; distributes provisions, 208.
Orders: in council for land, 12; restricting shipments for W. Indies, 206.
Osborne, Capt. George: affidavit of, 64.
Ossabaw, Ga.: soldiers at, 145.
Otter, the: sent with force to outpost on St. Marys, 38; at bar of St. Augustine, 44; lost in gale, 60.
Owen, William: provost marshal general, 4; resigns and leaves E. Fla., 13, 16.

PALTSITS, VICTOR H.: thanked, ix.
Parr, John (gov. of Nova Scotia): cited, 158.
Passes: for embarkation, 168.
Payne, Robert: attends conference, 45; affidavit, 64.
Payne's Corner, St. Augustine: tide rises above, 154.
Peace: made with Creeks, 13, 14; Brit.-Amer., 132, 157.
Penman, James: Tonyn characterizes, 17; joins in address of loyalty, 34; receives protested bills of Tonyn, 62; volunteer in 60th Regiment, 63; affidavit, 64; assists Fuser, 79, 80; becomes resident of S. C., 210; cited, 37, 102.
Pensacola, Fla.: Stuart at, 40; Robinson at, 52.
Periodicals and Newspapers: cited, 224-226. Names — *Acadiensis*, 158 n., 224; *East Florida Gazette*, x, 133, 134, 135, 189; Fla. St. Hist. Soc., *Quar.*, 8 n., 19 n., 119 n., 225; *Gazette of the State of Georgia*, 26, 153 n., 225; *Gentleman's Magazine*, 205 n., 225; *Jamaica Mercury*, 205; *London Chronicle*, 131 n., 225; *Miss. Vall. Hist. Rev.*, 4 n.; *Nassau Guardian*, 185 n., 187 n., 193 n., 196 n., 225; *Penn. Mag. of Hist. and Biog.*, 29 n., 226; *Rivington's Gazette*, 88 n., 226; *Royal Gazette*, 128 n., 226; *St. Croix Courier* (N.B.), 154 n., *South Carolina and Amer. Gen. Gazette*, 134; *South Carolina Gazette*, 75 n.,

135, 226; *South Carolina Hist. and Geneal. Mag.*, 52 n., 201 n., 205 n., 226.
Petitions: to throne, 65; to Tonyn and council, 88; by Hume and others, 152; from people at Mosquito Inlet, 156; from Bahamas, 193; from W. Indies, 206. *See also* Memorials.
Philadelphia, Pa.: Kirkland escapes from, 50; Tattnall imprisoned in, 125; emigrants to Jamaica from, 201; Clarke in, 203.
Philips, George: bandit, 164.
Phillips, Capt. James: refugee, 31, 38.
Phillips, Col. John (refugee): in Camden District, 61 n.
Phillips, Robert (refugee): in E. Fla. Rangers, 38, 61 n.
Pickens, Col. (*or* Gen.) Andrew: repulsed, 74; Browne capitulates to, 86.
Picolata Creek, Fla.: location, 42-43; provisions carried by way of, 42-43.
Picolata Fort: *See* Forts.
Pilots: act to control, 93, 94.
Pimento: exported, 69.
Pinkroot: exported, 69.
Pitt, William: cited, 3.
Plantations: Indian communal, 10; acquired by refugees, 62; of Hume, 80, 81; spread beyond St. Augustine, 140; on Long Island, 196; tools for, needed, 109, 124, 138, 192.
Plays: for benefit of refugees, 133, 134.
Police: board, at Charleston, 113.
Ponce de Leon Inlet: *See* Mosquito Inlet.
Port Royal Island, S. C.: Prevost on, 78.
Port Royal Parish, New Providence: refugees in, 202.
Porto Rico: exchange of, rumored, 143.
Portsmouth, Eng.: Tonyn writes from, 176.
Potatoes: Indians cultivate, 107.
Powder (gun): placed in church, 122.
Powell, George Middleton: attends gathering, 34.
Powell, James Edward: appointed lt. gov. of Bahamas, 182; goes to Eng., 183; instructions to, 190; cited, 191.
Presents: given to Indians, 12.
Prevost, Col. (*or* Brig. Gen.) Augustine: arrives with troops, 38; is asked for troops, 43, 44;
his advance into Ga. feared, 45; promoted and command extended, 47; informed of proposed invasion, 50; reports loss of *Hinchenbrook*, 56; prepares to resist Howe, 57; takes post on St. Johns River, 58; goes to the Cowford, 59; asks Clinton for assistance, 60, 79; in expeditions, 71, 76-78; operates in Ga., 74, 75; returns to Savannah, 78; in anti-Tonyn faction, 80; cited, 51.
Prevost, Capt. (*or* Maj. *or* Lt. Col.) James Mark: at Graham's Redoubt, 47; drills S. C. Royalists, 52; resists R. Howe's advance, 57; takes post at Alligator Creek bridge, 58; retires to Six-Mile Creek, 59; ordered to approach St. Marys, 60; in expedition to Sunbury, 72; operates in Ga., 75; appointed lt. gov., 75; in anti-Tonyn faction, 80.
Priests: at New Smyrna, 6; in E. Fla., 173.
Prince's Fort, S. C.: occupied by Innes, 84.
Prisoners: French, in state house, 56; expenses for care of, 67; paroled by Amer. at Augusta, 85; taken at Augusta, 86.
Privateers: invasion will prevent depredations by, 42; depredations by, 60, 76.
Privy Council: *See* Councils.
Proclamations: against Bryan, 4; prohibiting and renewing trade with Creeks, 13, 14; inviting loyalists to E. Fla., 24, 48; forbidding correspondence, 33; ordering loyalists to enlist, 40; of cessation of hostilities, 110, 138, 141; relative to departure of loyalists, 143; by Zespedes, 161, 162, 164, 166; by Maxwell, 189.
Property: of land through cession, 8; confiscated, 56; awards for loss of, 111, 126; sequestered, 122, 123; memorial on, 137, 138; compensation of losses of, 169; Lothian suffers loss of, 204.
Provincial Forces: *See* Troops: Provincial regiments and forces.
Provisions: for possible siege of St. Augustine, 44; act prohibiting exportation, 93, 94; brought with refugees, 107, 109; sent from Charleston, 114; at St. Augustine and St. Johns Bluff, 116; in E. Fla., 119, 120, 126; consumed at Indian congress, 120; last beyond expectations,

121; becoming exhausted, 205; for refugees, emigrants, and loyalists, 143, 150, 153, 154, 158, 159, 190, 192, 203, 207 208; Maxwell asked to provide, 172; evacuation dependent on, 188; consigned to McArthur, 184; sent to New Providence, 187; needed, 190; restriction of shipments of, 206. *See also* the various articles of food.

Public Record Office (London): thanked, x.

QUARTER HOUSE: location, 87; S. C. Royalists at, 87, 88.

Queen's Royal Rangers: *See* Troops: Provincial regiments and forces.

Quit-rents: retard settlement of E. Fla., 95.

RAEBURN'S CREEK, N. C.: Fanning former settler on, 156.

Ramsay, David: cited, 74 n., 75 n., 81 n., 115 n., 220 n.

Ramsour's Mill, N. C.: N. C. loyalists defeated at, 55.

Rangers: *See* Troops, 13; Prevost wants to enroll mounted, 47; troop formed, 53.

Rawdon, Lord ———: at Camden, S. C., 84.

Raymond, William Odber: cited, 154 n., 220.

Refugees: from various localities, 54, 55, 87, 103, 106, 108, 109, 149, 152, 156, 157, 186, 200, 201, 207; go to, and in, various places, 49, 50, 87, 103, 106, 108, 109, 114, 130, 143, 149, 159, 186, 197, 200-208; feared lest U.S. encourage to return, 140; return to U.S., 209, 210; increase pop., 49, 50; numbers, 108, 109, 124, 129, 130, 157; members of committee of, 124; petition that E. Fla. be held for, 103; acquire possessions in E. Fla., 140; have antipathy to Span. gov't., 142; influx brings progress, 194, 195; increase in public expense due to, 62; petition land, 88; land granted to, 62, 95, 190; provisions supplied to, 121, 150, 153, 154, 187; need tools, 109, 124, 138; aid for, 133, 175; situation in E. Fla., 157. *See also* Emigrants; *and* Loyalists.

Resolutions: of house of commons, 18; of states against return of loyalists, 143. *See also* Acts.

Rice: exported, 68; Indians cultivate, 107.

Richards, Rev. John: in New Providence, 197.

Riots: in E. Fla., 132.

Ritchie, Capt. William: relations with W. Cunningham, 127.

Roads: Span., 8; from Cowford to St. Marys, 19; needed, 19.

Robertson, James (refugee): official in Ga., 75; sketch, 62 n.

Robertson, James A.: thanked, ix.

Robertson, Rev. Thomas: missionary, Eleuthera, 198.

Robinson, Col. Joseph (refugee): at Pensacola, 52; in Jamaica, 204.

Robinson, Mrs. Joseph (refugee): in Jamaica, 204.

Robinson, Robert, and family (refugees): in E. Fla., 61 n.

Rolfes, Frederick: provost marshal general, 34.

Rolfes Sawmill: name, 46; Baker at, 46.

Rollins, Carl Purington: thanked, viii; directs printing of this volume, 260.

Rollstown: location, 11; Seminoles near, 11.

Romans, Bernard: draws map, 19; cited, 19; map, reproduced, facing p. 43.

Rose, Rev. Daniel Warner: sent to Long Island, 199.

Rose, Dr. Hugh (refugee): practices his profession, 117.

Ross, Maj. ———: has care of refugees, 168.

Ross, Thomas: member of commons house, 91.

Rousseau, Jean Jacques: works read in Long Island, 198.

Royal American (*or* 60th) Regiment: sent to St. Augustine, 80.

Royal Artillery: strength, 30; at St. Augustine, evacuation, 152, 155.

Royal Bahama Gazette (*The*): Wells establishes, 189.

Royal Foresters: *See* Troops: Provincial regiments and forces.

Royal Gazette (*The*): former name, 205; size, 205.

Royal North Carolina Regiment (*or* Volunteers): *See* Troops: Provincial regiments and forces.

Royal Society (London): awards medals to Wells, 135.
Rum: exported, 68, 69.
Rumford, Count: *See* Thompson, Col. Benjamin.
Rutherford, Gen. Griffith: defeats Brit., 55.
Rutledge, John (gov. of S. C.): invites d'Estaing to besiege Savannah, 78.

SABINE, LORENZO: cited, 25 n., 39 n., 56 n., 74 n., 136 n., 147 n., 174 n., 179 n., 189 n., 205 n., 221.
St. Andrew's Parish, Jamaica: refugees in, 202; Wildman's estimates in, 204.
St. Augustine, Fla.: conditions described, 157, 158; stone wall along bay, 19; state house, 19, 56, 91, 133, 134; additions to, 140; has surplus pop., 119; house built near, 126; Span. buy houses in, 168.

Churches, 3, 5, 19; convent, 19; protestant ministers, 6, 119; priest executed, 6; schoolmaster, 22; newspaper published at, 134; books printed in, 135; courthouse, 91.

Barracks, 18, 19; garrisons and troops in, 22, 30, 41, 57, 116, 144, 145, 178 (Span.); proposed as post for Brit. army, 23; troops disbanded in, 153, 154; cargo of gunpowder lost at, 21, 22; Howe's expedition alarms, 58; Fuser assumes command in, 74; McArthur commands, 183; mil. conditions, 79; communications with N. Y. interrupted, 88; supplied to withstand siege, 99; officers in, under Leslie's orders, 101; attack on, planned from Ga., 165; defense galleys in harbor, 121; naval hospital removed from, 186.

Indians in, 9, 30, 120, 121, 148; superintendent in, 151; Indians expected in, 153; Indians dependent on, 80; reported to have massacred people near, 157.

Effect of news of Declaration of Independence on, 35; plan in, to stop revolution, 24; center of loyalism, 39; loyalists and refugees in, 25-28, 38, 50, 51, 52, 54, 62, 75, 80, 105, 109, 128, 133, 134, 144, 148, 151, 158, 173, 175, 183, 210; benefit for refugees in, 133, 134; refugees awarded in, 144.

Inhabitants to New Smyrna in, 36, 37, 173; foreigners in, 173; Span. in, 179.

Evacuation delayed, 108; effects of evacuation on, 177; ships in harbor of, 129, 143, 152, 183; attempts to recover slaves from, 123, 144; horses and cattle stolen from, 140, 167.

St. Augustine Grenadiers: make excursion to Hutson's Ferry, 75; return from Stono ferry, 77.
St. Augustine Historical Society: thanked, x.
St. Catherine's Parish, Jamaica: refugees in, 202.
St. Elizabeth's Parish, Jamaica: refugees in, 202.
St. George's Parish, Jamaica: refugees in, 202.
St. John (ship): Stuart takes refuge on, 25; aids Wright's Fort, 26; at New Providence, 30; guards passes of St. Marys, 40; sent to St. Johns River, 43, 44.
St. Johns Bluff, Fla.: name, 117; location, 117; founded, 117, 118; early promise, 118; a shipping center, 177; address posted at, 93; fit place for refugees, 105; refugees and loyalists at, 109, 117; provisions at, 116; victualing ships at, 161; horses stolen near, 167; effects of evacuation on, 177. *See also* Hesters Bluff.
St. Johns River, Fla.: easy to enter, 116; pass on, 165; shipping center for, 177; troops on, 30, 52; proclamation regarding, 40; men able to bear arms along, 33; outpost driven south of, 38; defended, 46; Browne on, 109; Cassels rents tract on, 126; W. Cunningham buys property on, 129; refugees and loyalists settle along, 109, 117, 140; ships on, 121, 129; plantations threatened, 164; Bowles at, 178.
St. Johns Road: horses stolen on, 166.
St. Johns Town: *See* St. Johns Bluff.
St. Lawrence (ship): arrives with recruits and ammunition, 30; request regarding, refused, 32.
St. Lucia Island: slaves to be sent to, 116.
St. Marks (near Apalachee Bay, Fla.): Indian town, 8; Span. trade at, 11; captured by Bowles, 179.
St. Marks Parish: rector at, 3, 5, 6; salary assigned for, 7; schoolmaster for, 22.
St. Marks River, Fla.: Bowles at, 179.

Index

St. Marys Bay, Nova Scotia: soldiers receive lands at, 154.

St. Marys beach, Fla.: negroes stolen from, 167; dismembered houses taken to, 177; sales and thefts at, 177.

St. Marys Harbor, Fla.: roadstead for vessels, 60: *See also* Amelia Harbor.

St. Marys River, Fla.: easy of entrance, 116; store on, 9; road to, 19; plantations on, 26, 32, 127; Indian alarms on, 12; raids feared, 38, 45; petition for protection, 43, 44; raids on, 37; Elbert expedition to, 46; insurgents go to, 54; settlements devastated, 95; banditti on, 164; men capable of bearing arms on, 33; troops sent to, and on, 39, 40, 57; fort on, 42; Prevost sells plunder at, 73; refugees and loyalists on, 155, 156, 159, 169, 170, 189, 190, 191; sailings from, 155, 156, 159, 170, 176, 189, 191, 207, 209; transportation of property from, 172; moveable property at, 175; cost of transportation to, 175; Span. ship at, 178; ships return to, 203; Tonyn on ship in harbor of, 207, 209; memorial presented at, 190.

St. Matthews Parish, New Providence: mission, 200.

St. Nicholas Pass: on St. Johns River, 165.

St. Peter's Church: at St. Augustine, 3, 5.

St. Sebastians Creek, Fla.: prohibition regarding, 40.

St. Thomas-in-the-Vale Parish, Jamaica: refugees in, 202.

St. Vincent Island: Graham petitions for land in, 110; Walker asks about land grants in, 187.

Salt: exported, 68, 69; on Exuma Island, 199.

Santee River, S. C.: Marion defeated on, 88.

Sapello River, Ga.: settlements on, deserted, 44.

Sarsaparilla: exported, 69.

Satilla River, Ga.: detachment at, 47; Amer. expedition crosses, 57.

Savannah, Ga.: Tonyn's proclamation in, 24, 108; Lee at, 42; Elbert's expedition from, 45-47; Campbell's expedition to, 52, 71, 73, 74; prepares for siege, 78; sends reinforcements to Charleston, 83; Leslie in command at, 101; evacuation, 102, 105-108; refugees and loyalists go to Jamaica from, 201, 204; provisions from, 109; Indians from, 111; number of emigrants from, 115; Seymour at, 118; W. Cunningham flees to, 128; Deveaux leaves, 145; letter received in, cited, 153. *See also* Georgia.

Savannah River, Ga.: Brit. and loyalists on, 75.

Savary, Alfred William (ed.): cited, 53 n., 56 n., 146 n., 221.

Sawpit Bluff, Fla.: name, 46; Elbert at, 46.

Schenck, David: cited, 56 n., 86 n., 221.

Schobert George (refugee): in E. Fla., 61 n.

Schoepf, Johann David: leaves for New Providence, 157, 158, 188; finds it unsafe to go far from St. Augustine, 167; cited, 119, 193 n. (*see also* Morrison, Alfred J.).

Schoolmasters: at St. Augustine, 22; in Harbor Island, 196, 198; John Cruden serves as, 199; better pay in Bahamas for, 199, 200.

Schools: at St. Augustine, 8; subjects taught in, 22.

Scophol, Col. ——— (refugee): his men, 54.

Scopholites: name, 54; at St. Marys, 54; on Trout Creek, 57.

Scotland: Kennedy retires to, 7, 8; Johnston considers going to, 156; Johnston goes to, 204.

Screven, Gen. James: mil. operations, 58, 72; wounded, 59.

Seminole Indians: towns and villages, 8-12; promise aid, 40; Kirkland deputy to, 50; told services not needed, 57; dependent on St. Augustine, 80; to be employed for defense of E. Fla., 89; Brit. attitude toward, 135-136. *See also* Creeks.

Seneca Indians: send chiefs to St. Augustine, 120.

Sermon for . . . gospel in foreign parts: cited, 8 n., 200 n., 221.

Seymour, Rev. James (refugee): activities, 118, 119.

Shaddock trees: planted, 80.

Shattuck, George Burbank (ed.): cited, 190 n., 194 n., 222.

Shallop: *See* Ships.

Shawnees (Indians): send chiefs to St. Augustine, 120.
Sheerwater (ship): captured, 179.
Shelby, Col. Isaac: in attack on Musgrove's mills, 85.
Sheldon, S. C.: Lincoln and continentals at, 78; church burned, 145.
Shipping: needed for removal of loyalists, 102; at Tybee Island, 106.
Ships and Vessels: Indian goods carried on, 11; gunpowder on, lost, 21, 22; commit depredations, 37; granted letters of marque, 43; bring prizes, 56; captured, 56, 76, 146, 179; men recruited for, 57; officers, 102; requested and sent, 105; used for defense, 108; wrecked, lost, or disabled, 129, 143, 176, 189, 190; Leaver manages, 155; conveyance on, asked, 156; various persons on, 170, 175, 176, 207, 209; colonists serve on, 173; heavily laden, 177.

At, leave, or bound for: E. Fla., 4, 30, 114, 129, 175, 176, 203; St. Johns River, 44; Savannah, 101; Eng., 145, 148, 152, 154, 176, 209; Jamaica, 148, 154, 163; Bahamas, 148, 159, 168, 176, 186, 187, 189; St. Marys, 156, 170; Halifax, 158; Nova Scotia, 157, 158; Dominica, 207.

Carry: refugees and loyalists, 4, 27, 28, 101, 105, 107, 113, 114, 129, 131, 148, 152, 157, 158, 167, 168, 170, 172, 174, 175, 176, 183, 186, 187, 189, 191, 203, 207; provisions and other cargo, 101, 107, 159, 170, 177; troops, 105; slaves, 107, 116, 191, 193, 203, 207.

Types: transports, 4, 101, 105, 107, 113, 114, 116, 129, 131, 145, 148, 152, 154, 155, 156, 157, 158, 159, 167, 170, 172, 174, 175, 176, 177, 183, 184, 186, 187, 189, 191, 203, 207; canoes, 11; sloops, 11, 21, 22, 27, 30, 44, 56; warships, 27, 28, 102, 129, 144; victualing, 43, 144, 152, 184; shallop, 38; fleets, 114, 129, 131; African slave, 191, 193.

Names: *Amity's Production*, 170; *Ann*, 176, 209; *Argo*, 158; *Bellisarius*, 129, 144; *Commerce*, 22; *Cyrus*, 175, 176, 207; *Daphne*, 56; *David*, 189, 190; *Eliza*, 143, *Elizabeth*, 207; *Galatea*, 56; *Hinchenbrook*, 56; *Jason*, 76; *Narcissus*, 144; *Perseus*, 56, 102; *Polly*, 176; *Rattlesnake*, 129; *Raven*, 44; *Rebecca*, 43, 56; *Savage*, 30; *Sheerwater*, 179; *Tamar*, 27; *Tuncastle*, 44; *Two Sisters*, 170, 176, 209.
Shirts: Indians trade for, 11.
Shortt, Adam; and Arthur G. Doughty: cited, 4 n., 222.
Siebert, Wilbur H.: cited, 81 n., 107 n., 150 n., 153 n., 184 n., 190 n., 192 n., 193 n., 201 n., 202 n., 205 n., 222.
Silk: exported, 68.
Sing, Christian (refugee): in E. Fla., 61 n.
Six-Mile Creek: Prevost at, 59; plantations on, 81.
Slater, William: conducts public sales, 147.
Slaves: taken to Jamaica, 107, 201; taken to E. Fla., 110, 126; at Charleston, 115; in Bahamas, 165, 188, 190, 191, 198, 199, 200; in Dominica, 208; wish to return to U.S., 210. Tonyn would arm, 33; stolen, 122, 123, 141, 167; Tonyn retains, 141; to be restored to owners, 163, 164; Tonyn tries to sell, 171; offered for sale, 188; occupations, 201; sickness among, 208. Liquor not to be sold to, 132; new code for, 191. See also Negroes.
Sloops: *See* Ships.
Smith, Capt. ———: at Alligator Creek Bridge, 58, 59.
Smyth, John Ferdinand Dalziel: cited, 29 n., 222.
Society for Propagation of the Gospel: nominates missionaries for E. Fla., 3, 5, 8, 118, 119; maintains missionaries in Bahamas, 196-200; withdraws support from Bahamas, 200.
South Carolina: congress, 25; commons house, 95; laws against loyalists, 61; citizens of, on committee, 94, 95. Ship from, invades E. Fla., 21, 22; loyalists in, 25, 27, 188, 189, 201; refugees and loyalists from, 50, 51, 54, 153, 188, 189, 201, 205; evacuation, 101, 102. Armament for, 30; frontiers protected, 84. Negroes sent to, 110; deportation of slaves from, feared, 115; citizens of, try to prevent

Index 253

plundering of slaves, 122; not returned to owners in, 123; negroes sold in, 126; negroes of, stolen from citizens of, 141, 144; negroes of, go to Jamaica, 201. Agent for sequestered and captured property in, 123, 169; *Statutes*, cited, 61 n., 222-223.

South Carolina Royalists: *See* Troops: Provincial regiments and forces.

South Carolinians: form settlements in E. Fla., 129; in E. Fla. benefit by relaxation of banishment law, 210.

Spain: Eng. signs treaty with, 147; Bowles tries to recover E. Fla. from, 178.

Spalding, James: his home, 9.

Spalding & Co. (*or* Spalding & Kelsall): trade among Indians, 9.

Spaniards: bishop for, 5; Seminoles imbibe civilization of, 10; from Cuba, 11. Leave E. Fla., 19; invasions by, expected, 81, 88, 89; E. Fla. a frontier against, 102; preparation for transfer of E. Fla. to, 157; few whites transfer their allegiance to, 101; refugees and loyalists unwilling to become, 142, 190; Minorcans wish to remain with, 158; few in E. Fla., 171, 173; settlers not admitted from other Span. dominions, 171; administration in E. Fla. niggardly, 175. Expedition of, to Pensacola, 81; surrender of W. Fla. to, 94; conquest of Bahamas by, 126, 182; loyalists in, consider joining, 187. Attitude of Indian chiefs toward, 44; soldiers protect Indian trading posts, 178; charged with theft, 167, 177, 178; oppose migration of negroes, 168; Tonyn fails to sell negroes to, 208; forbid sale of certain lands, 171; refuse to purchase certain articles from Brit., 172; attitude toward Brit. subjects, 174; force refugees to withdraw from New Smyrna, 178; number of Brit. subjects with, 208, 209.

Spanish Main: refugees go to islands of, 101, 204, 208.

Springer, Benjamin (refugee): collects stock and provisions, 76.

Squires, Capt. ———: commands ship, 44.

Stanhope, Capt. ———: brings word of Lee's expedition, 44.

Stark, James Henry: cited, 150 n., 185 n., 186 n., 223.

State House: completed at St. Augustine, 19; as prison for French force, 56; members of commons house meet at, 91; plays for benefit of refugees given in, 133, 134.

States General (United Provinces): prohibit exportation, 18.

Stedman, Charles: cited, 74 n., 75 n., 77 n., 78 n., 223.

Stetson, John Batterson, Jr.: book dedicated to, v; student of Amer. history, ix.

Stokes, Anthony (chief justice of Ga.): refugee, 106; goes to New York, 107; cited, 106.

Stono, S. C.: post at, evacuated, 77.

Stono Ferry, S. C.: protected, 77.

Stono Inlet, S. C.: forces transferred across, 77.

Stono River, S. C.: Deveaux at, 145.

Stormont, Nova Scotia: S. C. Royalists receive lands at, 154.

Stuart, Capt. Alexander (refugee): activities against banditti, 153, 167.

Stuart, Henry: sent among Cherokees and Creeks, 27.

Stuart, Col. John: superintendent of Indian affairs, 13, 14, 38; refugee and member of council, 24; retires to St. Augustine, 25; schemes of, 29; to keep Indians at St. Augustine, 30; authorized to employ Indians, 39; at Pensacola, 40; to protect Cherokees, 47; dispatches from Howe to, 50; death of, 76.

Sugar: Indians trade for, 11; exported, 68, 69; plantations in Jamaica, 201; production large in Jamaica, 207.

Sumter, Col. Thomas: attacks post at Hanging Rock, 84.

Sunbury, Ga.: Moultrie's expedition to, 43; Elbert's fleet returns to, 47; Fuser's detachment at, 71; capture of Fort Morris at, 73.

Suolanocha, Fla.: Indian town, 8.

Sydney, Lord ———: Tonyn reports Span. penalties to, 166, 170; *id.*, suggests extension of evacuation period to, 172, 173; McArthur writes to, 187; Hamilton recommended to, for governorship of Bahamas, 192; letters by and to, cited, 173, 174, 175, 176, 187, 191.

TAIT, ———: agent to Creek nation, 40.
Talahasochte: Indian town, 8; McLatchie in, 10-11.
Tar: exported, 67, 68, 150.
Tarleton, Col. [Sir] Banastre: repulsed at Stono Creek, 83; cited, 84 n., 86 n., 223.
Tattnall, Col. Josiah: member of committee of refugees, 124; in Bahamas, 182; goes to St. Augustine and back to Bahamas, 183; sketch, 125, 126.
Taylor, Peter: Penman, clerk for, 17.
Theaters: for benefit of refugees, 133, 134.
Thomas, Col. ———: joins Schopholites, 54.
Thomas's Swamp, Fla.: Baker routed at, 46.
Thompson, Col. Benjamin (loyalist): at Charleston, 87; operations of, 88. *See also* Rumford, Count.
Tims, James: customs officer at St. Marys, 32.
Tobacco: Indians trade for, 11; exported, 69.
Tonyn, Patrick (gov. of E. Fla.): administration studied, ix; assumes gov't., 3; meets and considers with council, 4-5, 13, 22, 31, 36, 88, 89, 92, 96, 98; asks legislation, 92-93, 94, 98; reports surrender of W. Fla., 94; assembly interrogates, 95-96; asks for grant of money, 96; relation with assembly, 98; dissolves it, 98-99; communicates letter to, 103; ecclesiastical measures, 5, 7; appointments by, 6, 147, 153, 155; protests and complaints by 7-8, 30, 81, 88, 135, 165, 166, 168; relations, etc., with Indians, 9, 33, 35, 40, 47, 51, 57, 135-136, 139, 143, 144, 178; Wright asks his coöperation, 12; orders salary for messenger, 13; takes action against Bryan, 14.

Relations with Drayton, 15, 31, 34, 35, 43, 45, 62, 63, 64, 66, 68; with Gordon, 15-17; with Stuart, 25, 167; with Mulcaster, 30-31; with Turnbull, 33-34, 35, 36, 37, 63, 64, 65-66; with Fuser, 79, 80; with Seymour, 119; with Zespedes, 161-162, 164-166, 168, 171, 174, 175; with Fatio, 162.

Reports first hostile act against E. Fla., 21; sends troops to Dunmore, 22; commissions recruiting officers, 26, 38; proposes volunteer company, 33; suggests arming slaves, 33; ordered to defend E. Fla., 39; receives information of designs of Georgians, 39; orders militia to organize, 40; will call out militia, 94; urged to call out militia, 121, 148; sends Browne to scout in Ga., 51; authorizes formation of horse, 153; allows troops to serve under Prevost, 53; his action regarding status of troops, 77; has mil. authority, 79; expects attack by Span., 81, 99; mil. orders to, 101; authorized to arm inhabitants, 115; asks galley for defense, 124; fears disaster if troops removed, 152.

Issues proclamations, 24, 48, 110; gives letters to Kirkland, 28; sends him to Va., 29; his orders to Furlong, 33; committee calls on, 45-46; sells cattle, 45; breaks up large estates, 50; makes landgrants, 62, 95, 99, 141, 173; refuses grants, 62; advised to make, 141; Browne sends message to, 59; borrows money, 62; sends Forbes to Havana, 81; orders oath administered, 91.

Notified of evacuation, 102; ordered to prepare for, 123; delayed beyond expectations, 170, 172, 174; unaware when St. Augustine will be evacuated, 189.

Asked to treat with Leslie, 103; Georgians recommended to, 105; estimates their number, 108, 131; criticises them, 108; Carleton asks information of, 114.

Estimates pop. of E. Fla., 115, 131; his estimates on number of refugees and emigrants, 124, 129, 174, 189, 207, 208, 209.

Reports on St. Johns Bluff, 115-116.

Warned about slaves, 122; attitude toward restoration of slaves, 123-124; retains slaves, 141; agrees to sell slaves, 171; fails to sell slaves in E. Fla., 208; sends them to Dominica, 207-208.

Hears of surrender, 131; sends commissioner to Charleston, 135; orders relative to cession, 138; his advice to people of E. Fla., 140; fears

Index

lest U.S. desire loyalists to return, 140; permits loyalists to go to U.S., 141.

Tries to keep ships, 144; asks Digby's aid, 150; transports promised to, 154; in charge of transports, 154; publishes notice about transports, 172, 190; asks aid of transports, 176.

Cession ends his gov't., 155; Leaver takes orders from, 155; informed of appropriation of lands to refugees, 159; recommends loyalists to Maxwell, 159; gives survey of conditions, 161; complaints made of Fatio to, 162; asks Howard for proclamation, 162; discredits statements, 165; demands trial of banditti, 165-166; claims he has benefited Brit. in E. Fla., 168; asked to order investigation, 170; sends various things to Bahamas, 172; charges violation of treaty, 173; charges Span. with theft, 177, 178; receives information regarding land for emigrants, 186; Maxwell promises flour to, 190; ready to sail, 207; leaves E. Fla., 4, 140, 176, 209; period of his gov't., 4; sketch, 3; promoted, 99; criticised, 30-31, 45, 79, 123-124; letters to and by, cited, 18, 22-23, 28-29, 30, 35, 39, 43, 45-46, 49, 99-100, 102, 103, 104-105, 108, 109, 114-115, 117, 122, 124, 131, 132, 138, 141, 148, 150, 152, 154, 156, 159, 164, 166, 168, 170, 172-173, 174, 175, 177, 189-190, 191; instructions by and to, cited, 33, 35, 40, 49, 57, 123, 154-155, 171; addresses and petitions to, cited, 48-49, 50, 65, 93, 97, 109, 156, 167; speeches by, cited, 92-93, 98, 103, 104; messages to legislature by, cited, 94, 109, 131.

Tortoise-shell: exported, 68.

Tortola, ———; Cruden in, 122.

Townshend, Thomas (Secretary of State): memorial of merchants and others to, 137, 138; directs Tonyn to give notice of cession, 138; letter from Tonyn to, cited, 139.

Townships: size, 4.

Traders Hill, Fla.: a place name, 9.

Transports: *See* Ships.

Treaties: made with Indians, 13; preliminary, 3d article of, 138; Brit.-Amer., 8th article of, 138; with Spain restoring Bahamas to Eng., 147; interpreted in favor of debtors, 162; its provisions to be fulfilled by Span. gov't., 166; Tonyn's letters on violations of, cited, 166, 173.

Trees: canoes made from, 11; planted, 80.

Troops: Clark leads during Indian disturbance, 13; at St. Augustine, 41, 101, 108, 116, 122, 154, 161 (Span.); at Savannah, 71, 72, 106; at Charleston, 105, 203; at mouth of Matanza River, 121; in Jamaica, 203; consideration regarding removal, 101, 105, 108, 122, 138, 151, 152; mutinous, 144; disbanded, 154; disposition, 57; burn Fort Tonyn, 59; prepare to invade Ga., 66; coöperate in expedition, 71, 72; on board transports, 107; force of horse authorized, 153; light horse in Brit. pay, 165; they are ineffectual, 167; under Wm. Young, 165, 168; Campbell enlists black, 203; Hessian, 203; land promised to, 209.

Various Brit. regiments, etc.: 6th Dragoons: Tonyn captain of, 3. 14th Regiment: detachment of, 18; soldiers of, 21; entire regiment asked for by Dunmore, 22; full strength, 30; Furlong asks to leave with remainder of, 32. 16th Regiment: three companies to come from Pensacola, 22; they arrive, 32; detachment in expedition to Savannah, 73. 37th Regiment: three companies arrive, 155; detachment goes with McArthur to New Providence, 187. 60th (Royal American) Regiment: part arrives, 38; volunteers in, 63, 64; in expedition to Sunbury, 71, 72; two battalions to go to Charleston, 144. 63d Regiment: goes to Jamaica, 203. 64th Regiment: goes to Jamaica, 203. 71st Regiment: goes to Jamaica, 203. 84th Regiment: detachment of, goes to Jamaica, 203. 104th Regiment: Tonyn lt. col. of, 3; in expedition to Savannah, 73; detachment on Ogeechee River, 78; sent to St. Augustine, 80. Royal Artillery: number at St. Augustine, 30; to remain until final evacuation of E. Fla., 152, 155. Scotch Regiment: its surgeon, 134.

Provincial regiments and forces: in expedition to Savannah, 71; to be sent to E. Fla., 113, 114; sail from Charleston, 124; in E. Fla.,

132; Carleton asks intentions, 138, 141; rumors among, 142; leave E. Fla., 153, 186. Various provincial organizations — Carolina King's Rangers: at Savannah, 78; attempt escape, 86; ordered to E. Fla., 105; promised lands, 154; apply for transportation, 184. East Florida Rangers: at Fort Tonyn, 50; make sallies into Ga., 51; strength, 53; rumored threats of desertion, 57; at Fort McIntosh, 58; detachment near Augusta, 59; retreat, 60; their surgeon, 64; in various expeditions, 72, 74; carry off livestock and provisions, 76; status, 77; sail for Charleston, 107; go to St. Augustine, 114. New Jersey Volunteers: in expedition to Savannah, 73. Queen's Royal Rangers: Connolly commands, 28. Royal Foresters: Deveaux organizes, 146. Royal North Carolina Regiment (or Volunteers): organized, 55; various operations, 74, 77, 78, 83, 84, 86, 87, 114; after the war, 142, 153; major in, 144. South Carolina Royalists: Prevost organizes, 52; officers, 53, 204; Penman advances money for, 79; in Thompson's force, 88; mil. operations, 57, 58, 60, 72, 77, 83, 84; 85; their evacuation, etc., 113, 114, 142, 153, 154. *See also* Forts and Fortifications; Garrisons; Militia; *and* Soldiers.

Trout Creek, Fla.: Scopholites on, 57.

Turks Island, Bahamas: occupied, 184; pop., 197.

Turnbull, Andrew, Jr.: 36, 45; becomes resident in S. C., 210.

Turnbull, Dr. Andrew: arrives with colonists for New Smyrna, 6; involved in Bryan's lease, 14; conduct, 34; departs for Eng., 35; reinstated in council, 36, 37; files charges against Tonyn, 62, 63; founds colony of New Smyrna, 173; Minorcans in colony, 209; removes to S. C., 210.

Turner's Station, S. C.: W. Cunningham captures, 128.

Turpentine: exported, 67, 68, 150; trees boxed for, 81.

Tuscaroras Indians: send chiefs to St. Augustine, 120.

Tybee Island, Ga.: Brit. fleet arrives at, 71; loyalists at, 106; Graham at, 107.

Tyger River, Ga.: Col. Innes on north fork of, 84.

Tyrell, Elizabeth: sells proprietary rights, 193.

Tyrell, Mary: sells proprietary rights, 193.

UNITED STATES: gov't. takes measures against Bowles, 179.

VAN TYNE, Claude Halstead: cited, 61 n., 224.

Vinegar: exported, 69.

Virginia: armament destined to, 30; troops, 43; loyalists and slaves go to Jamaica from, 201.

Virginians: help defeat Cherokees, 47, 48.

Voltaire, François Marie Arouet de: works read in Long Island, 198.

WALKER, William: cited, 186.

Wambaw, S. C.: plantation at, 126.

Ward, Lt. ———: killed, 46.

Washington, Col. William: repulses detachment, 83.

Watlings Island, Bahamas: pop., 197.

Watson, Brook: suggestion regarding provisions, 184.

Wayne, Gen. Anthony: operations, 106, 145.

Wells, John (refugee): prints books, 135; goes to Bahamas, 135; establishes *Royal Bahama Gazette*, 189.

Wells, Louisa Susannah (refugee): marries Aikman, 205; cited, 136 n., 205 n., 224.

Wells, Robert (refugee): bookseller and printer of newspaper in Charleston, 134, 205.

Wells, Dr. William Charles (refugee): issues *East Florida Gazette*, 134, 189; in trouble in Charleston, 135; sketch, 134.

Welsh, Maj. Nicholas: enlists loyalists in N. C., 55; Tonyn explains policy to, 109.

Western District, New Providence: whites and blacks from E. Fla. in, 188.

West Florida: missionaries for, 5; rumored Span. expedition against, 89; surrenders to Span., 94; loyalists in Bahamas go to, 187.

West Indies: supplies and lumber for, 24; Mathews sends provisions to, 184; Amer. products shipped to, 206; cotton crop in, affected by winds, 207; negroes shipped to, 78, 128; d'Estaing returns to, 79; place for refugees, 108, 140, 154, 158, 159, 186; refugees and loyalists consider going and go to, 142, 157, 158, 159, 170, 171, 192, 193, 203, 208; French capture some, 203; soldiers serve in, 204; ships at, 157, 170, 171, 203.

West Virginia, Dept. of Arch. and Hist.: *Report*, cited, 29 n.

Weymouth, Lord Viscount ———: sells proprietary rights, 193.

Whaley, William (bandit): captured, 164.

Wheeler, Capt. ———: with Deveaux's expedition, 146.

Whig Association: colonists advised not to join, 127.

White, Col. ———: Browne escapes from, 58; encounters force from E. Fla., 72.

White, George: cited, 179 n., 224.

Whitehall, England: letter on purchase of land in Bahamas from, 154.

White House (trading house): name, 85; Indians driven into, 85.

White King (Indian chief): gives banquet, 11; attends council, 11.

Wildman, James: member of Jamaica council, 205.

William and Mary (ship): in Bahamas, 176.

William (ship): Lord Dunmore refugee on, 27, 28.

Williams, Col. ———: in attack on Musgrove's mills, 85.

Williams, John Lee: cited, 179 n.

Williamsburg, Va.: detachments of troops sent to, 30.

Williamson, Thomas: founds town, 117; unable to sell lots, 177; ships house to Jamaica, 177.

Williamson's Stockade, S. C.: troops at, 127.

Wilmington, N. C.: Craig at, 87; merchants of, 169; Cobham from, 186.

Wilson, Lt. John: goes to St. Augustine, 114; plans defensive measures, 121; ships plundered negroes, 122; sent to New Providence, 149;

sent to view Bahamas, 150; makes survey of Bahamas, 184; repairs Fort Nassau, 195; reports, cited, 151, 185.

Windward Islands: preferred by people with negroes, 150; black troops raised in, 203.

Wine: Madeira, exported, 68, 69; claret, exported, 69; licenses for sale, 133.

Winn, Capt. Richard: surrenders Fort Barrington, 44.

Winniett, John: estimates of refugees and negroes, 116, 117, 130.

Wodehouse, Sir John: sells proprietary rights, 193.

Wood's Tavern, Fla.: meeting at, 34.

Wright, Alexander: signs memorial, 206.

Wright, Charles (refugee): constructs road, 19; brother of Sir James, 42; maintains fort, 42; signs address and petition, 48.

Wright, Sir James: makes peace with Creeks, 13; opposes Whig party, 15; gov't. of Ga. wrested from, 23; to resume governorship of Ga., 75; protests surrender of Ga., 107; sails for Charleston, 107; aided by Tattnall, 125; crops destroyed, 145; captured, 182; has slaves in Jamaica, 202; letters to and by, cited, 14, 102, 105.

Wright, Jermyn (refugee): brother of Sir James, 42; owns plantations on St. Marys River, 37; has fort on St. Marys, 38, 42, 47; fort attacked, 26; affidavit, 64.

Wylly, ———: mission of, 135.

Wylly, Alexander (refugee): signs address, 48.

Wylly, Capt. William: plans to go to Eng., 144.

YEATS, David: appointments, 35; clerk of council, 169; looks for stolen negroes, 178.

Yellow Fever: in Jamaica, 204.

Yonge, Henry, Jr. (refugee): signs address, 48; withdraws negroes from mil. works, 79; introduces act, 93.

Yonge, Julien C.: thanked, ix.

York, Capt. John: mil. activities, 52, 58.

Young, Capt. Thomas: signs petition, 156.

Young, Col. William (refugee): opposes banditti, 153, 164, 165; protects E. Fla., 165, 166; his troop, 168; letter cited, 164.

ZESPEDES (Céspedes), Vicente Manuel (Span. gov. of E. Fla.): régime studied, ix; assumes gov't., 3, 4, 161; supplants Tonyn, 161; early acts of administration, 161-166; posts troops, 161; appoints justices of peace, 162; encloses memorial of bandits, 164-165; encourages banditry, 164-165, 166, 167; Tonyn protests to, 165-166; permission for marriages asked from, 171; extension of evacuation period petitioned from, 171; extends period, 175; his dispute with Tonyn, 209; attitude of Brit. toward, 162; resents Hume's criticism, 163-164; his attitude toward negroes, 163, 164; his classification of them, 163-164; attitude toward Indians, 178; proclamations, cited, 161, 163-164; letters to and by, cited, 168, 174, 175.

www.ingramcontent.com/pod-product-compliance
Lightning Source LLC
Chambersburg PA
CBHW020644300426
44112CB00007B/228